SEXUAL

AWARENESS

BARRY McCARTHY & EMILY McCARTHY

SEXUAL

YOUR GUIDE TO HEALTHY COUPLE SEXUALITY

AWARENESS

FIFTH EDITION

Routledge
Taylor & Francis Group
New York London

Routledge
Taylor & Francis Group
711 Third Avenue
New York, NY 10017

Routledge
Taylor & Francis Group
27 Church Road
Hove, East Sussex BN3 2FA

© 2012 by Taylor & Francis Group, LLC
Routledge is an imprint of Taylor & Francis Group, an Informa business

Printed in the United States of America on acid-free paper
Version Date: 20120213

International Standard Book Number: 978-0-415-89643-6 (Paperback)

**Visit the Taylor & Francis Web site at
http://www.taylorandfrancis.com**

**and the Routledge Web site at
http://www.routledgementalhealth.com**

CONTENTS

INTRODUCTION

Sexuality is a positive, integral aspect of your personality that impacts your intimate relationship. Furthermore, sexuality enhances satisfaction and stability in all areas of a relationship, including nonsexual areas. However, like any other aspect of our personalities, sexuality requires attention if it is to reach its potential to enrich your life.

This book is a step toward valuing sexuality as a positive and satisfying part of life for the individual, couple, and culture. It is designed to help people—especially married and serious couples—enhance sexual awareness, communication, feelings, and function. We focus on changing core sexual attitudes, behaviors, and feelings rather than on performance or the necessity to prove you are sexually liberated. Our goal is to increase sexual awareness and acceptance, which lead to the new mantra for healthy couple sexuality: enhanced desire, pleasure, eroticism, and satisfaction. We do not advocate esoteric sex performance techniques. You do not have to prove anything to yourself or to anyone else.

This is our fifth revision of *Sexual Awareness*, which was first published in 1975 and has sold more than 400,000 books worldwide. We believe that now more than ever there exists a core need to address basic components of sexual awareness, desire, comfort, and function. This book focuses on enhancing sexual attitudes and communication that lead to desire, pleasure, eroticism, and satisfaction, *but it is not do-it-yourself sex therapy.* The psychosexual skill exercises we present are designed to give both the individual and couple an opportunity to learn healthy sexual scenarios and techniques. There is no requirement that all the exercises must be tried or that you must become proficient in a particular technique. Our hope is that the pro-sexual attitudes conveyed, the psychosexual skill exercises described, and the feelings discussed will enhance your acceptance, comfort, and sexual pleasure.

For individuals and couples experiencing sexual dissatisfaction or dysfunction, this book is not a substitute for therapy. It is an aid in expanding sexual understanding. Couples and sex therapists can use these psychosexual skill exercises as an adjunct to treatment. Chapters 11 to 18 discuss the most common sexual problems and dysfunctions. This helps you realize that you are not alone in experiencing sexual difficulties and that these problems are resolvable. Appendix A presents guidelines for choosing an appropriate couple or sex therapist.

This book is aimed also at educational audiences: college students and advanced students in the fields of psychology, medicine, marriage therapy, counseling, social work, health education, and the ministry. If students develop an awareness and comfort with sensuality and sexuality, their lives and the lives of clients with whom they work will be much improved. Education is the best means to prevent or remedy the harm that comes from sex myths, self-defeating attitudes, and negative experiences.

SCIENTIFIC INFORMATION OFFERS
POSITIVE GUIDELINES

We have more information about human sexuality than any culture in the history of the world. Yet there is no evidence that people are functioning better sexually or enjoying their sex lives more—contrary to the myth perpetuated in the media that everyone is liberated and having an abundance of great sex. We have gone from a sexually repressed and inhibited culture to a sex-saturated, performance-oriented, ambivalent, and confused sexual culture. Sexual intercourse is a core element of sexuality, but it is not the only—or even the most important—one.

Sexual Awareness provides up-to-date scientific information about sexuality and sexual function. The more information you have, the better you can choose how to integrate sexuality into your life. Sexuality is your responsibility, not the responsibility of the culture, religion, schools, parents, or friends—although they can and do influence your sexual values and decisions. Sexuality is neither value-free nor governed by rules set in concrete. We provide guidelines for sexual awareness and decision making that clearly state our values:

1. Sexuality is a good, healthy part of life, not bad or evil.
2. Sexuality is a positive, integral part of each individual's personality.

3. You are responsible for choosing how to express your sexuality. Sexuality can enhance your life and intimate relationship. It need not be a cause of anxiety, guilt, or problems.
4. A healthy sexual relationship is based on respect, trust, and intimacy.
5. An intimate relationship is the most secure and satisfying way to express sexuality.

SOURCES FOR OUR MODEL OF SEXUALITY

The approach we utilize comes from two main sources: sex researchers (especially those engaged in social learning approaches) and sex therapists. Masters and Johnson were pioneers in the sex research and therapy fields. Their contributions have increased our knowledge of sexual behavior tremendously, both in the physiology of human sexual response and in the treatment of sexual dysfunction. They dispelled myths that had caused damage to millions of men and women.

The social learning approach consists of strategies and techniques to help people learn new attitudes, skills, and emotional responses. Its premise is that the best way to learn or relearn healthy sexuality is through a gradual step-by-step method (assure your comfort with one type of experience before moving on to the next) and through the utilization of supportive and constructive feedback to facilitate the learning process. The optimal condition for sexual awareness is commitment, which fosters the ability of partners to become intimate and erotic allies, a sexual team.

WHO WE ARE

Emily and Barry McCarthy have spent more than 2 years revising this manuscript—and 46 years building a marital bond based on respect, trust, and intimacy, and a couple sexual style that values intimacy, pleasuring, and eroticism. In reviewing research, conducting marital and sex therapy, teaching human sexuality, conducting sexual enhancement workshops, and thinking about our marriage, our belief in the validity of these concepts has grown.

It is crucial to set aside couple time and value your relationship. Intimacy and nondemand pleasuring are the bedrock of sexual desire. The key to sexual arousal is erotic scenarios and techniques, with each partner's arousal building on the other's. It is vital to reduce performance anxiety and replace unrealistic expectations with a pleasure-oriented, flexible, broad-based view of couple sexuality. This book offers strategies and techniques to help you develop this view based on your couple sexual style.

This is the 10th book we have coauthored. Barry is a practicing PhD clinical psychologist and a certified marital and sex therapist. Emily has a degree in speech communication. We believe in the guidelines we offer to you—theoretically, clinically, and personally. We have found this book a pleasure to write and hope you find it worthwhile and valuable in enhancing your sexual awareness and satisfaction.

THE AUDIENCE FOR THIS BOOK

People without regular partners are encouraged to read this book to increase understanding and change attitudes. However, a good relationship is essential to reap the most benefit from the psychosexual skill exercises themselves. It is better simply to read the material than attempt to do the exercises with someone with whom you are not comfortable, to whom you are not attracted, or whom you do not trust will be supportive of your sexual growth.

The recommended process is to read, talk, and then engage in the exercises. The exercises were written mainly (but not exclusively) with the married or serious couple in mind—especially those who relate well but experience sexual anxiety, inhibition, dissatisfaction, or dysfunction. These exercises have been used successfully by new couples who are committed to improving sexual communication and satisfaction. We have been particularly gratified to find that the exercises have been used successfully by couples 40 years of age and older, who report that they have helped resensitize their relationship and reawaken sensual and erotic feelings. Chapter 11 deals with sexual expression with aging (over 60) and is particularly important because sexuality in later years is such a neglected area. You can function sexually into your 60s, 70s, and 80s. Sexual function becomes more variable and flexible, but sexual satisfaction can remain high. The idea that sex belongs to the young is one of the cruelest sex myths.

In addition, the exercises we present have been used by gay and lesbian couples. Although focused on heterosexual couples, these exercises are applicable to gays and lesbians with relatively few modifications. Of course, the exercises also can be used by sexually well-functioning couples, since we can all benefit from enhancing sexual awareness.

In most chapters there is a case study. These are composite cases of clients Barry has seen in his practice, with names and details altered to protect confidentiality. The purpose of case studies is to make it clear that "normal" people have sexual difficulties; to illustrate the variety of psychological, relational, and situational causes of sexual problems; and to offer reassurance that people can change and their sexual relationships can improve. Problems and solutions sound easy in a two-page summary, but in fact changing your sexual pattern takes time and commitment. Developing healthy couple sexuality is seldom a smooth, miraculous process.

COMFORT AND PLEASURE

We do not present specific exercises for sexual intercourse until Chapter 9. Couples put too much emphasis on intercourse, which they equate with sex. This belief interferes with full expression of your sexuality. If partners are comfortable with their relationship and each other and with feelings of sensuality and their ability to give and receive pleasure-oriented touch, then intercourse and orgasm are a natural continuation of the pleasure/eroticism process, not a pass–fail sex test. Throughout the book there is consistent emphasis on slow, gentle, loving touching. When these elements are present during pleasuring, intercourse, and afterplay, couples experience intensified enjoyment and satisfaction. An intimate relationship, nondemand pleasuring, erotic scenarios and techniques, and positive realistic sexual expectations are the core ingredients in sexual satisfaction.

PROCEDURE FOR PSYCHOSEXUAL EXERCISES

We suggest the following procedure to facilitate using the exercises. Begin by deciding what you want to learn about yourself and your partner. Be aware that the best way to learn sexually is to understand your individual sexual desires and responses first, and then give feedback and guide your partner. Among the best ways to process feedback are

1. Be caring and constructive
2. Give positive feedback before negative; the best learning ratio is five positive to one negative
3. Be specific, especially about requests for change
4. When giving feedback, request the change you would like and avoid making negative comments about your partner as a person or lover
5. Support your partner in making the changes you request; emotional and sexual change is based on a positive influence process—not threats, demands, or coercion

Agree on how much time to spend on the exercises during the week. At least once a week is the minimum needed. Twice a week would be better, and three times a week is ideal. Seven times a week is overkill.

The psychosexual skill exercises presented in this book should be regarded as guidelines rather than rigid rules. If you view the exercises as required homework or something you are forced to do, you will experience little enjoyment or benefit. Use these exercises to help you explore, learn, accept, and increase comfort with sensual and sexual feelings. The exercises are meant to provide choices and alternatives so you can discover what you, individually and as a couple, find pleasurable. The focus is to enhance sensual and sexual function, so try different pleasuring techniques, share and communicate, take sexual risks, and vary your approach to touching and sexuality. For example, we emphasize the importance of slow, tender, gentle, rhythmic, flowing touching. However, if that is the only style of touching you use, it would become boring. At times, each partner might like rapid, intense, erotic touching. We suggest showering or bathing together, but you can also enjoy sex while sweaty, as sensations can be enhanced by natural body essences. Variety, experimentation, and unpredictability are major ingredients in enhancing your eroticism and sexuality.

Each chapter includes four sets of exercises, intended to gradually increase comfort and skill. Feel free to move at your own comfortable pace; sensual and sexual feelings cannot be forced. Pushing too fast is a common problem. It is crucial that neither partner feels pressure to perform. The core sexual awareness exercises consist of nongenital pleasuring (Chapter 2) and genital pleasuring (Chapter 3). Pleasuring enables you to increase awareness of sensual and sexual feelings, to learn to be comfortable both giving and receiving pleasure, to initiate and respond to sexual experiences, to process feedback, and to appreciate slow, gentle caresses. Pleasure-oriented sexuality produces feelings of comfort, awareness, and intimacy—without which the exercises will lack value and can, in fact, be counterproductive.

It is our hope that this book and these exercises will make you aware of and comfortable with a view of sexuality in which the pleasures of touching, eroticism, intercourse, and afterplay flow in a natural, comfortable manner. Orgasm is the natural culmination of sexual arousal, not the ultimate goal you have to achieve. We advocate an attitude toward sexuality that encompasses your whole body, not just your genitals, and considers sensual, playful, and erotic touch as valuable as intercourse. This can occur only when you communicate sexual feelings and preferences in a sensitive, open manner.

There are chapters you might read but decide not to engage in the exercises presented in them. Although you can benefit from just reading, we encourage you to experience the exercises so you are comfortable with developing your unique couple sexual style. Psychological and sexual functioning is enhanced when your attitudes, feelings, and behavior are congruent and reinforce one another. Reading the exercises helps modify attitudes. Doing the exercises (and thereby increasing comfort and skill) changes behavior. Being aware of reactions and giving and receiving feedback change feelings. In these many and different ways we hope that you will grow in sexual awareness, comfort, pleasure, eroticism, and satisfaction as you proceed through the following pages.

Barry and Emily McCarthy

1

ENHANCING SEXUAL AWARENESS
Getting Started

A new sexual myth has appeared on the sexual scene—that people are sexually knowledgeable and comfortable and are having the best sex in history. The scientific facts are that 50% of married couples and 65% of unmarried people report sexual dysfunction or dissatisfaction. Young couples have as many, if not more, sexual difficulties than couples in their parents' generation. The media is rife with sexual material; people joke more openly and frequently about sex than ever before. Sexual experiences begin at a younger age. However, the sad fact is that sexual awareness, comfort, and satisfaction have not increased. The promises of the sexual revolution have not come true.

YOUR SEXUAL KNOWLEDGE

Part of the problem with the current state of intimate relationships stems from our lack of knowledge about what a healthy sexual relationship really is. We base our knowledge mostly on what we see and hear about on the Internet, on television, or at the movies. But how much do you really know about sexuality and sexual function? Are you willing to take a test? Do not worry about performance anxiety; it will not be graded.

True–False Test

1. Sex is purely natural, not a function of learning or communication.
2. Foreplay is for the woman; intercourse is for the man.
3. Once a couple establishes a good sexual relationship, they do not need to set aside time for intimacy, pleasure, or experimentation.
4. If you love each other and communicate, everything will be fine sexually.
5. Sex and love are two sides of the same coin.
6. Technique is more important than intimacy in achieving sexual satisfaction.
7. Sex is more satisfying in a new relationship than in an intimate, secure relationship.
8. In a healthy relationship, each sexual experience is mutually satisfying.
9. Interest in sex decreases over the years and is lost by age 60.
10. It is the man's role to initiate sex.
11. If one or both partners become aroused, intercourse must follow or there will be frustration and feelings of failure.
12. Men and women are very different sexually; men initiate sex with a focus on intercourse, while women focus on intimacy and affection.
13. Having G-spot orgasms and multiple orgasms proves you are a sexually liberated woman.
14. Since men have fewer spontaneous erections after age 40, they are unable to have intercourse without Viagra.
15. When you lose sexual desire, the best remedy is to seek a new partner.
16. The most common female sexual problem is pain during intercourse.
17. The most common male sexual problem is lack of variety.
18. There is a significant relationship between the size of the man's penis and the woman's ability to reach orgasm during intercourse.
19. Oral–genital sex is an exciting but perverse sexual behavior.
20. Simultaneous orgasms provide the most erotic pleasure.
21. Married people do not masturbate.
22. Using sexual fantasies during intercourse indicates dissatisfaction with your partner.
23. The woman has two kinds of orgasms—clitoral and vaginal.
24. The man-on-top position is the most satisfying position for intercourse.
25. Viagra cures almost all erectile dysfunction.
26. Couples in this generation are doing much better sexually than those in the previous generation.

Add the number of true answers you checked, and discover the number of sex myths you believe. This was a sex-myth test, and all the answers are false. Do not be surprised if you didn't realize this; the average number of true answers is nine. Sexual myths are rampant in our culture, and they die hard.

We can all benefit from greater understanding of human sexuality. Knowledge is power. Old myths based on repressive sexual attitudes have given way to new performance-oriented myths. These sex myths need to be replaced by positive, realistic, psychological, biological, and relational scientific information and expectations.

UNDERSTANDING AND ACCEPTING YOUR SEXUALITY

Healthy sexuality begins with understanding and accepting yourself, your body, and its sensual and sexual potential. In adolescence there are two powerful negative teachings about sex. The first is that sex is basically bad (exciting, but bad) and becomes good only in the context of marriage. The second is that sex refers exclusively to intercourse.

We believe that sex is a good thing in life and that sexuality is an integral part of being a person. Sexuality, however, is much more than intercourse. Sexuality includes everything from an affectionate glance to a gentle caress, from passionate intercourse to loving afterplay. The psychologically healthy question is how to express sexuality so that it enhances your self-esteem and increases satisfaction with your intimate relationship. Healthy sexuality involves each partner valuing his or her "sexual voice" (autonomy) and becoming an "intimate team" that integrates intimacy, pleasuring, and eroticism.

WHEN MEDICAL FACTORS PLAY A ROLE

In instances where there is a question of physical or medical causes of sexual dysfunction, the ideal referral is to a physician with a subspecialty in sexual medicine. Although the majority of sexual problems are not caused primarily by medical problems—exceptions being alcohol or drug abuse, uncontrolled diabetes, medication side effects, and chronic illness—it is worthwhile to assess medical factors. Anything that impairs your physical health can negatively impact your sexuality. People typically begin with their internist or family practice physician. Or women might consult a gynecologist and men a urologist. Many physicians are not comfortable dealing with sexual issues and try to quickly dispose of the problem by giving a prescription or making a joke. That is not what you want or need.

There is a growing trend to "medicalize" sexual problems. This was highlighted by the introduction of Viagra to treat erectile dysfunction in 1998. Our position is that Viagra, testosterone replacement, and other medical interventions can be valuable resources in treating sexual dysfunction. However, medical interventions alone are seldom the right answer for the complex psychological, relational, and sexual comfort and skill issues at the core of couple sexuality. In the coming years there will be more pro-sexual medications, hormone treatments, creams, and patches that can be valuable supplemental resources, but they must be integrated into your couple style of intimacy, pleasuring, and eroticism.

SAFER SEX ISSUES

When we wrote the first edition of this book in 1975, the world had not heard of HIV/AIDS. How does this frightening reality (sex can cause death) affect sexual awareness?

Sexual comfort requires sexual health and safe sex. The safest sex involves couples who are committed and who have tested negative for HIV and sexually transmitted infections (STIs). This allows the full range of sexual experience to unfold and provides freedom from fear of contracting HIV or other STIs. Is that too idealistic? A new tradition among committed couples is to be tested for HIV and other STIs and to have an agreement of monogamy. The backup is an agreement to inform the partner if one engages in any risky sexual activity with another person. If so, they will use a condom until they are retested. This involves trust in yourself and your partner, which is a solid base for comfortable, healthy sexuality.

When Barry first began teaching a college sexuality course in 1970, the main STIs were gonorrhea and syphilis. In the 1970s herpes began to spread and became the most feared STI because it has no cure. Herpes was and remains a serious STI that affects over 40 million Americans, but currently the most frequently contracted STIs are chlamydia and human papillomavirus (HPV, or genital warts). However, STIs have been forgotten (which is not wise) in the furor over HIV/AIDS, which has dominated sexuality fears since the 1980s and will do so for the foreseeable future.

STIs and AIDS are not irrational fears. In their lifetime, approximately two of five people will contract an STI. This needs to be dealt with as a health problem, not a moral judgment. The atmosphere of fear and stigma, viewing AIDS as God's revenge, nature's way of halting sexuality, or punishment for sexual excess is counterproductive as well as untrue.

HIV (human immunodeficiency virus) is spread primarily through the mediums of blood, semen, and vaginal secretions. HIV is considerably easier to transmit sexually by men (whether by heterosexual or homosexual contact) because semen is a more powerful medium for the virus than vaginal secretions. Vaginal and anal intercourse is more dangerous for the woman than the man. In other words, the transmission is most often from male to female or from male to male. Female-to-male transmission does occur but is less likely. The exception is childbirth: The woman can transmit HIV to her baby.

One of the scariest aspects of the epidemic is that the carriers of HIV are healthy people who have no symptoms and are often unaware they are HIV-positive. Once infected, they stay infectious even though not outwardly ill. People with HIV eventually do become ill with AIDS, but usually not for several years (the average is between 8 to 12 years).

So how can the person not in a monogamous relationship practice safer sex? The more aware, knowledgeable, and responsible they are about sexuality, the more they can protect their health against HIV and other STIs. Unfortunately, like other STIs, HIV has a "sexist" bias. For example, with gonorrhea, 90% of men are symptomatic, while only 25% of women are. The woman is more vulnerable and, therefore, dependent on the man to be honest and share the sensitive information that he is infected and she needs to be tested and treated. In the matter of HIV, the woman needs to be assertive about asking her partner whether he is "at risk" because of sex with men, IV drug use, or sex with prostitutes (the highest risk groups for HIV infection). However, be aware it is sexual behavior, not types of people, that spreads HIV.

The best method is for both partners to be tested for HIV and other STIs and have an agreement not to be sexual with others. This means they trust that their partner will be honest if there is an incident. The second-best preventive is to avoid activities involving exchange of semen and vaginal secretions. The highest-risk activity is anal intercourse, followed by vaginal intercourse. Oral sex is less risky, especially if the man does not ejaculate into the woman's mouth. Some couples use condoms during fellatio or a dental dam during cunnilingus. Another preventive is to use condoms during intercourse, which is highly recommended for nonmonogamous couples.

The most realistic criterion for judging sexual behavior is whether it is harmful to them or their relationship. This includes vulnerability to HIV, other STIs, unwanted pregnancy, physical pain, or psychological coercion. This is not to promote hysteria or paranoia but to make both partners aware that now more than ever it is crucial to establish a respectful, trusting, and communicative relationship. Guidelines for healthy sexual behavior—awareness, knowledge, caring, and being responsible—will serve them well in dealing with STIs and HIV/AIDS.

AVOID A PERFORMANCE ORIENTATION

The exercises included in the book should be done at a pace that is comfortable for you and put no pressure on either partner. We suggest you devote at least 2 weeks to the initial nondemand pleasuring exercises, refraining from intercourse during that time. So much sexual activity is goal-oriented and intercourse-oriented that sensual and sexual awareness is inhibited by the rush to intercourse and orgasm. Staying away from intercourse for 2 weeks is a worthwhile investment that can help you attain a solid, satisfying sensual and sexual relationship for years to come. In fact, we recommend that once a month, or every 3 months, you spend time in nongenital and genital pleasuring that does not culminate in intercourse. This reinforces awareness that not all touching is goal-directed. Intercourse is not the only means of sexual expression, nor does sex equal intercourse. Develop a variable, flexible, sensual, and sexual repertoire and enjoy non-goal-oriented experiences.

During the weeks you are involved with nongenital and genital exercises, we suggest you individually engage in the self-exploration/masturbation exercises (Chapter 4). Most men and women are neither as aware of nor as comfortable with their own body and sexual response as they could be. Accepting your body's responsivity and knowing your orgasm triggers are the basis for sharing. Masturbation exercises can provide an orgasmic outlet during the period of nondemand pleasuring, but, even more important, it enhances your sexual awareness.

A good guideline for self-exploration exercises and all other exercises is not to do anything that causes you pain or is against your values. Do not proceed to the next step until you are comfortable with the preceding step. Remember, psychosexual skill exercises are learning experiences.

COMMUNICATION IS KEY

It is not easy to express your most intimate feelings, but honest and ongoing communication is essential to sexual satisfaction. Typically, after the first romantic conversations, a curtain falls between lovers. For some, the reduction in communication is slight. However, when it comes to serious sexual communication, for most couples the curtain is heavy and dark. Alienation and secrets are of special concern since sexuality is an intimate sharing experience. Supportive communication can lower this curtain and dispel the feeling of personal isolation.

Sexuality has many functions in your relationship. It is a means of sharing pleasure, of reinforcing and deepening intimacy, and of reducing tension to help you cope with the hassles inherent in a relationship and everyday life. An additional function is procreation—a planned, wanted child.

Nearly everybody at some time in life finds it difficult to verbally express love, caring, or even concern. Touching and nonverbal requests serve to bridge gaps and allow you to connect. Both verbal and nonverbal communication are vital. No matter what else you do with this book, we urge you to find or make ways to communicate your interest, caring, and desire for intimacy. Tell your partner what you appreciate and value about them. An intimate relationship is one of life's major satisfactions.

REMAIN FLEXIBLE AS YOU WORK
THROUGH THE EXERCISES

Be as flexible as you wish in utilizing the exercises. We suggest you first read through a chapter by yourself. The exercises should be attempted only after you and your partner have read and discussed them. What have you experienced and what do you want to experience? Talk about feelings of intimacy and caring as well as erotic scenarios and techniques. It takes effort to break through the natural hesitation you feel, but the personal and relational benefits can be immeasurable. Some couples go through each exercise step by step, while others combine two or more exercises or improvise as you go along. Decide what procedure is most comfortable for you.

We advise against doing an exercise with the book open. This is not a cookbook. Sexuality requires two involved participants. For the exercises to be a positive learning and sharing experience, the most important ingredient is verbal and nonverbal feedback. It is crucial to work as an intimate team and not get thrown off track by feelings of rejection, embarrassment, disappointment, or frustration. The psychosexual skill exercises are flexible guidelines to enhance sexual attitudes, feelings, and function.

Be sure to tell your partner what you like and dislike. For example, people may want to talk about sexual odors (turn-ons and turn-offs) but have trouble bringing up that subject. Our culture has many sensitivities about hygiene, so sexual partners deprive themselves of pleasurable experiences (or expose themselves to unpleasant experiences) for fear of mentioning this sensitive, yet important, topic. Talk about what is important to you—fantasies, sounds, settings, smells, positions, temperature, amount of light. Remember that sexual requests are integral to a positive influence process. Breaking free of cultural restrictions helps your sexual relationship become open and satisfying.

Sexual demands, on the other hand, subvert intimacy and desire. Under the guise of open communication and being sexually free, some individuals pressure your partner to perform for you and threaten to end the relationship because of poor sexual performance. This is antithetical to the concepts of intimacy, pleasuring, and trust, which form the basis of healthy couple sexuality. Feel free to make sexual requests, but avoid making demands.

EXPRESS WHAT YOU FEEL

How best can you express your feelings? Each individual and each couple develop their own style of expression. Here are some suggestions and guidelines for expressing your feelings to your partner:

- "I desire you." It can be validating to admit desire and energizing to feel desirable. The expression of desire reinforces your partner's sense of personal and sexual worth and promotes intimate communication. You can "desire" your partner in affectionate, sensual, playful, erotic, and sexual ways.
- "You make me feel good." This is almost a definition of a good lover. It is important to tell your partner that they please you. Feeling good is not limited to sexual expression. It includes respect, trust, and emotional intimacy.
- "I care about you." Expression of interest and concern is always welcome, but it is especially important in times of stress and trouble. It is a fact of human behavior that *expressing* care increases the amount of genuine care and intimacy. Caring and sharing increase sexual desire.

PLANNING PSYCHOSEXUAL SKILL EXERCISES

After you complete the nongenital and genital pleasuring exercises, share what you have learned individually and as a couple. Then discuss what you want to try next. You might decide to focus on exercises to enhance desire, exercises dealing with a specific sexual problem, or exercises that integrate pleasuring, eroticism, and intercourse. Proceed according to your needs rather than adhere rigidly to the order of the book. For each subsequent exercise, we suggest following the approach of reading a chapter individually, discussing it as a couple, and choosing whether to proceed.

Discuss how you will integrate intercourse with the exercises. We recommend that not every exercise end in intercourse. One possibility is to have intercourse at times other than when you are doing the exercises. Another is to complete an exercise and then transition to intercourse if both partners are interested. Utilize the exercises so you get the most learning and enjoyment from each without putting pressure on yourself or your partner. Sexuality is about sharing pleasure, not proving anything or performing for your partner.

DISPELLING THE MYTHS

Now let us examine the self-defeating myths contained in the true–false test you took at the beginning of this chapter and replace them with accurate information and attitudes that increase your awareness and lead to enhanced sexual desire and function.

1. Sex Is Both Natural and Learned

You are a sexual person from the day you are born until the day you die. For both women and men, sexual arousal occurs as a natural physiological function during the sleep cycle. The potential for sexual response is natural for all people. Attitudes, behavior, and feelings develop as part of a complex process of sexual socialization and experiences. Sexual learning occurs throughout life, and negative learning and experiences can be overcome.

2. Pleasuring and Intercourse Are Mutual Activities

Artificial, rigid roles for men and women inhibit sexual satisfaction. The foreplay/pleasuring period can be involving and enjoyable for the man as well as for the woman. Rather than the man "doing" the woman so she is aroused enough for intercourse, both can enjoy the give-and-get pleasuring experience. Intercourse, too, is a mutual activity that can be as enjoyable and arousing for the woman as for the man. The best aphrodisiac is an involved, aroused partner. The "give-and-get" guideline means that giving your partner pleasure enhances your pleasure.

3. A Satisfying Sexual Relationship Needs Time and Nurturing

You cannot take your sexual relationship for granted. Establishing a satisfying sexual relationship requires continual communication, caring, and sharing. It also takes time. Setting aside couple time (not all of which involves sexual activity) is the chief guideline for maintaining an intimate relationship. Sex can become routine and stagnant, especially when done late at night with little variety, communication, or experimentation. If you value sexuality, invest time, emotion, and energy in nurturing your intimate, erotic relationship.

4. Love and Communication Are Not Enough

There is a romantic myth that if you are in love and communicate, sex always works well. If the man is a premature ejaculator or the woman experiences pain during intercourse, all the love and communication in the world will not solve the problem. Increasing sexual comfort and learning specific psychosexual skills are necessary. There are loving couples who communicate feelings and work together in parenting yet are unable to transfer this caring and sharing to sexual function. Communication is necessary but not sufficient. To overcome sexual problems, you need to learn and practice sexual communication and psychosexual skills.

5. Sex and Love Are Not the Same

The most human and satisfying relationships integrate intimacy and eroticism. Sex and love, however, are not identical. This myth has done immeasurable harm. When we speak of love, we do not mean the romantic high that comes intensely, but fleetingly, early in a relationship. Love evolves into a mature intimacy whereby you respect, trust, and care about each other. You experience a secure, safe, and warm bond. Sex is not limited to the initial excitement that comes with knowing you are attracted to and excited by your partner. Sexual function involves not only experiencing desire, arousal, and orgasm but also feeling emotionally satisfied and bonded. You can be sexually functional with people you do not even like and can love someone but still have a chronic sexual dysfunction. Sex and love are different. The healthiest relationship integrates a loving intimacy with eroticism, resulting in sexual vitality and satisfaction.

6. Technique Versus Intimacy

Many people dislike sex books because they emphasize technique (many read like sophisticated, erotic cookbooks) rather than emotional intimacy. Our aim is to integrate sexual comfort and skills with emotional expression and the trust and caring of an intimate relationship. To attain full sexual awareness, the challenge for you as a couple is to integrate intimacy and eroticism.

7. Casual Sex Versus Intimate Sex

Although an intimate sexual relationship is a valued goal, many people have experienced casual sexual relationships, especially in their teenage and young adult years. The excitement and illicitness of new sex is difficult to replicate in a serious or marital relationship. An intimate relationship involves caring, trust, and security—including freedom from coercion or fears of STIs and HIV—that cannot exist in casual sexual encounters.

8. Variability in Sexual Relationships

Unrealistic expectations place a heavy burden on your sexual relationship. No matter how great the intimacy or how inventive the erotic scenario, not every sexual encounter can be "dynamite." In fact, couples with a healthy sexual relationship report that only 35 to 45% of their sexual encounters involve equal desire, arousal, orgasm, and satisfaction. In 5 to 15% of sexual encounters the experience is mediocre—the unsatisfying or dysfunctional kind where in the middle you say, "I hope you're enjoying this," and your partner responds, "No, I'm doing this for you." Couples who can laugh or shrug this off and try again the next day or so when they are more receptive and responsive will maintain satisfying sex. We are not sexual machines that perform perfectly on demand. If all sex were like a five-course steak-and-lobster dinner with the finest wine, it would become routine and dull. Variability and flexibility are normal aspects of sexual expression. The expectation that both partners will be equally desirous, orgasmic, and satisfied every time is unrealistic and self-defeating.

9. People Are Sexual Even in Later Years

Some of the cruelest myths involve sex and aging. If you are in good health and have an interested partner and a positive attitude toward sexuality, you can enjoy sex into your 60s, 70s, and 80s. Physiological changes that occur with aging are gradual rather than dramatic and alter sexual function rather than stop it. The more you understand and accept normal bodily changes, the easier it is to integrate these into your sexual relationship. The major advantage of sex after 60 is that you spend more time in sensual and sexual pleasuring since subjective and objective arousal takes longer. Emotional intimacy, nondemand pleasuring, and eroticism reach their greatest fruition as a couple ages.

10. Both Partners Have a Say

Sexual myths and bad habits develop during the dating period. One of the most harmful myths is that it is the man's role to initiate and that there is something wrong with the woman who wants and initiates sex. Sex is a shared pleasure; each person has the right to initiate and the right to say no. Men have more trouble learning to say no than women have learning to make clear, direct sexual initiations and requests. He feels that to be a "real man," he should be able to have sex at any time and in any place. Being comfortable saying no when one does not want intercourse allows the woman to be freer in her initiations and encourages both partners to enjoy a range of sensual, playful, and erotic activities.

11. It's Okay Just to Touch

You can be comfortable touching whether you are clothed or nude, inside or outside the bedroom. If you understand that not all touching has to proceed to intercourse, you are less inhibited by the fear that if your partner becomes aroused and you do not desire intercourse, frustration and an argument will follow. Pleasure and arousal are valuable in themselves, not just as a prelude to intercourse. Touching is a way to connect, to show affection, to express sensuality, to be playful, or to share eroticism. People who avoid touch unless you want intercourse cheat yourselves and your relationship. Touching is integral to your intimate relationship. Couples who touch in a variety of situations have more frequent intercourse because you share connection and pleasure. Pleasure may be enjoyed for itself or as a bridge to intercourse.

12. Men and Women Are More Alike Sexually Than Different

The traditional double standard was that men are interested in sex and that women are interested in affection and merely submit to sex. Sex researchers, however, find that the same physiological processes underlie male and female sexuality. There are many more sexual similarities than differences. Women have the potential to be multiorgasmic, so based just on the criterion of orgasm you could argue that women are more sexual. These arguments fuel competitiveness and misunderstanding. An empowering concept is that men, women, and couples value intimacy, pleasuring, and eroticism.

13. The Tyranny of Female Orgasm

Women now experience the same performance pressure that has so plagued men—the pressure to prove you are liberated by having multiple orgasms or identifying your G-spot and having the "perfect" orgasm. Such thinking is scientifically wrong and psychologically self-defeating. Female orgasm (like male orgasm) is the natural culmination of sexual involvement, arousal, erotic flow, and letting go. Women have different patterns and preferences for being orgasmic. No two people are exactly the same sexually. Arbitrarily judging an orgasm as "right," "mature," or "liberated" is self-negating. A healthy attitude emphasizes experiencing and sharing sexual pleasure, not regarding sex as an individual performance or feeling the need to prove something to yourself or your partner.

14. Spontaneous Erections and Intercourse

For males under 25, spontaneous erections are the rule. As a man ages, the frequency and intensity of spontaneous erections gradually decline, most noticeably in his 40s and 50s. Instead of erection being easy, automatic, and autonomous, arousal is a result of partner stimulation and the give and take of pleasuring. Arousal and erection become a function of intimate, interactive sexuality. For the man over 50, it takes longer to get an erection and requires direct penile stimulation. The good news is that sexuality becomes increasingly more involved, shared, and cooperative as partners age. Couples can continue to enjoy erection and intercourse into their 80s. Lack of spontaneous erection does not mean lack of sexual desire or the inability to enjoy pleasure, eroticism, and intercourse.

15. Regaining Sexual Desire

Inhibited sexual desire is the most common sexual dysfunction. There are a number of factors that can inhibit desire, including anger, depression, abuse of alcohol or drugs, disappointment or frustration with the partner, chronic illness, side effects of medications, an arousal or orgasm dysfunction, and lack of couple time. Sexual problems devitalize your intimate relationship. Couples, especially those in a committed relationship, can resolve sexual difficulties. Confronting inhibitions and blocks in sexual communication and being open and receptive facilitates a revitalized sexual desire.

16. Common Female Sexual Problems

Although a significant number of women experience painful intercourse on occasion (caused by fatigue, low arousal, anger, lack of lubrication, anxiety, and poor sexual technique), this is usually not a chronic problem. Spending time on pleasuring, the woman guiding penile intromission, using a lubricant, or switching intercourse positions usually alleviates the pain. In complex cases, a team approach involving a gynecologist, a couple therapist, and a female physical therapist is of great value. The most common female sexual problems are inhibited sexual desire, lack of subjective arousal, orgasmic dysfunction, and dissatisfaction with couple intimacy.

17. Common Male Sexual Problems

Men tend to brag about and exaggerate their sexual exploits and joke about never having enough sex. In reality, about 50% of men experience sexual dysfunction or dissatisfaction, which they are loath to admit even to their partner. Men are sexual people, not sexual machines. The most common male sexual problems are premature ejaculation, erectile dysfunction, inhibited sexual desire, and ejaculatory inhibition (difficulty reaching orgasm).

18. The Myth of Penis Size

Many men—indeed, 75% of men—worry that their penis is smaller than average. Statistically, that is absurd, but it is even more misdirected from a psychosexual perspective. There is a wide range of penis sizes in the flaccid state. This evens out when your penis becomes erect. Since larger penises grow in circumference but less so in length and smaller penises grow in both length and circumference, in the erect state there are minimal size differences. The difference that exists does not matter since the vagina is an adaptable organ that adjusts to the penis inserted. The major nerve endings are in the outer third of the vagina, so larger does not mean better. Men spend their lives worrying about penis size and feeling self-conscious about something that is a myth and has nothing to do with male or female sexual function and satisfaction.

19. Oral–Genital Sexuality

A major change in sexual behavior is the growing popularity of oral–genital sex, both fellatio and cunnilingus. Couples who utilize oral–genital pleasuring techniques report higher levels of satisfaction. Fellatio and cunnilingus do not replace intercourse; they are complementary sexual activities. Variety, experimentation, unpredictability, and communication enhance sexual satisfaction. Oral–genital sex is a special turn-on that facilitates eroticism and satisfaction.

20. Simultaneous Orgasm: A Performance Myth

Orgasm is a 3- to 10-second experience for men and women. Sex manuals herald simultaneous orgasm as the ultimate sexual experience. Trying to reach this rigid performance goal has frustrated untold thousands of couples. Orchestrating sexual arousal so that both people reach their emotional and physical climax at exactly the same time is more a task for engineers than lovers. Some couples enjoy reaching orgasm at the same time, although few report it to be the overwhelming experience promised by the media. Some report simultaneous orgasm as pleasant but are disappointed by the lack of intensity. We suggest a pleasure-oriented approach to sexuality: Accept and enjoy orgasm in whatever sequence you experience it.

21. Married People Masturbate

Masturbation is a normal, healthy sexual behavior at age 15, 35, or 65, whether you are single, divorced, cohabitating, or married. The majority of married men and women masturbate on occasion. There are many reasons to masturbate: when you are physically separated from your partner, when you want to enjoy your sexual responsiveness and fantasies, when you feel sexual but your partner does not. Masturbation also can serve negative purposes, such as avoiding partner sex, indulging in an obsessive fantasy, or compulsively using Internet porn. Any sexual behavior can be misused. Masturbation is not a regressive, unhealthy behavior. It is a normal, positive sexual expression for both women and men that can be enjoyed throughout life.

22. The Positive Functions of Erotic Fantasies

Both men and women utilize sexual fantasies. Erotic fantasies elicit sexual desire and serve as a bridge to arousal. Fantasies are the most common form of multiple stimulation. A majority of both men and women enjoy erotic fantasies at least occasionally during partner sex. Fantasies seldom involve the partner. What makes fantasies erotic is that they are illicit and socially unacceptable. Does that mean that the sex you fantasize about is the sex you really want? Not at all. People fantasize about being sexually humiliated or raped; this can make for an arousing fantasy but would be a traumatic sexual experience. Fantasies are in a different dimension from sexual behavior. You can utilize erotic fantasies to intensify your involvement and pleasure during partner sex.

23. The Clitoral Versus Vaginal Orgasm Myth

Physiologically, an orgasm is an orgasm whether it occurs during masturbation, cunnilingus, intercourse, vibrator stimulation, or manual stimulation. Depending on your attitudes, expectations, preferences, and experiences, her psychological satisfaction will vary. The old view of "mature versus immature" orgasms or "more feminine versus less feminine" orgasmic response is not true. The clitoral area has the most sexual nerve endings, and the clitoris is indirectly stimulated by a number of arousal techniques, including intercourse. The woman's (and her partner's) acceptance of your pattern of orgasm is the most psychologically enhancing way to deal with myths and demands concerning female orgasm. The typical woman is orgasmic during 70% of couple sexual experiences. Less than 15% of women are orgasmic during all partner sexual encounters.

24. Intercourse Variations

Man-on-top intercourse is the most commonly used position in our culture because it is the easiest for the man to guide intromission and prevent his penis from slipping out of a woman's vagina. It is a fine intercourse position and has advantages for both men and women. However, there is nothing "natural," "superior," or "the right way" about it. In some cultures, man-on-top is rarely used. Most couples enjoy experimenting with intercourse positions such as woman on top, side by side, rear entry, standing, and kneeling. Couples develop their unique style of being sexual, which includes preferred variations of intercourse positions.

25. Integrating Viagra Into Your Couple Sexual Style

The trend of medicalizing male sexuality (as well as female sexuality) with Viagra-type drugs and testosterone enhancement is misguided and ultimately self-defeating. Viagra can be a helpful resource, and in the coming years a new generation of prosexual drugs, creams, and patches will be introduced. However, unless the medical interventions are integrated into couple intimacy, pleasuring, and eroticism, they will not help either the individual or the couple. Medical interventions work best as a supplemental resource to enhance your couple sexual style than as a stand-alone intervention.

26. Making Sexuality a Positive, Integral Part of Your Relationship

The myth that couples are doing much better sexually than couples in their parents' generation is one myth we wish were true. Sexuality is discussed more openly, there is greater scientific knowledge, and people are having intercourse at an earlier age. There also is an increase in sexual experimentation, STIs, and extramarital affairs. But has there been an increase in sexual awareness, pleasure, and satisfaction? Has the increase in sexual quantity led to an increase in sexual quality and satisfaction? It has for some people, but not for the majority. The number of "casualties" of the sexual revolution through sexual trauma, STIs, and failed relationships continues to grow. Our goal is to empower you by increasing sexual awareness, enhancing sexual intimacy, and making sexuality a positive, integral part of your life and relationship.

ON TO THE NEXT PHASE

The following chapters present information, guidelines, case studies, and psychosexual skill exercises to increase your awareness, comfort, pleasure, eroticism, and satisfaction. Freeing yourself from self-defeating attitudes and myths is an important step toward adopting sexual attitudes, behavior, and feelings that promote and enhance your sexuality and intimate relationship.

2

REAWAKENING YOUR SENSUALITY
Nongenital Pleasuring

Many couples find that their sex life has become routine, mechanical, and unsatisfying. Sex is narrowly focused on intercourse with the goal of orgasm. You think back to your first sexual experiences and remember with fondness feelings of anticipation, seductive touching, unpredictability, excitement, playfulness, and spontaneity and wonder how you lost those feelings. What has happened is that intercourse and orgasm have overshadowed the joys of pleasurable touching, sensual feelings, and broad-based sexuality. Playfulness and unpredictability have given way to a pattern in which all touching leads to intercourse. Fun and spontaneity have disappeared, replaced by a rigid goal orientation that pressures the couple to make each sex experience mutual and perfect.

The focus of this chapter is to reorient you toward sensual, pleasurable feelings. The emphasis will be on discovering, in a relaxed, non-goal-oriented manner, the sensual pleasure you feel from touching and being touched—holding, stroking, and caressing that feels both comfortable and sensuous. Couples develop assumptions (often based on misperceptions), fall into ruts, and feel awkward asking for a different type of touch.

The psychosexual skill exercises presented here are designed to increase comfort with touching, discovering, and sharing, with as little performance demand or goal orientation as possible. These exercises are meant as suggestions and flexible guidelines rather than rigid rules. Their purpose is to engage you in a process of exploring and experiencing. The focus is to facilitate feeling comfortable as a sensual and sexual couple, without the need to prove anything to yourself or your partner. They are about intimate feelings and shared sensuality, not individual sexual performance. When you accept yourself as a sensual being, you will be better able to focus on your partner and appreciate their feelings, preferences, and sensitivities. The essence of couple sexuality is giving and receiving pleasure-oriented touching.

Time and privacy are crucial. It is important not to be distracted by factors such as the phone ringing, people coming over, or children walking in. Plan a time when you will not be disturbed—when the children are asleep, with a babysitter, or at friend's house. Lock the bedroom door. If you do not have a lock, make the investment and buy one; it will pay sexual dividends. Take the phone off the hook or put the answering machine on.

Each exercise can take from 15 to 90 minutes, depending on your feelings and preferences. You are encouraged to proceed in a gradual, step-by-step fashion, so you become comfortable with one experience before moving on to the next. It is important to feel comfortable and receptive so you can explore, discover, and enjoy sensual feelings.

Begin the psychosexual skill exercise by bathing or showering together. We recommend this for two reasons: first, it serves to relax you and induce comfortable feelings about your body; second, caring for your body and cleanliness are important in enhancing sensual feelings.

At this point we want to discuss the subject of "no." Suppose one person suggests a sensual or sexual activity and the other is not interested. The partner who is denied may feel rejected and avoid contact if their invitation is met with a no. Rather than simply saying no, propose an alternative you are receptive to. This principle applies to all sexual activity and cannot be overemphasized. Refrain from just saying no; suggest sensual or sexual alternatives or another time to be together. You might say, "No, I don't want to have sex now, but I would like to have my back rubbed or to hold hands and talk." Or: "I don't want a massage, but I would like to lie down with you and cuddle." This keeps you open for intimate connection. It allows you to say that although one activity does not appeal, something else does. It affirms an interest in sensual contact and in maintaining an intimate dialogue.

Intimate communication lies at the heart of a satisfying sexual experience. Intimacy is reinforced if you initiate an activity with caring and consideration and your partner responds by expressing their feelings clearly and openly. This exchange also emphasizes your intimate relationship as a positive process.

People find appearance important. Individuals fall into the trap of not being aware of their appearance, especially at home with their partner. You fail to fix your hair, do not wear fresh clothing, neglect to brush your teeth or maintain a healthy weight. Lack of care can detract from sexual attractiveness. For some, the trap is always dressing formally, being so fastidious that you lose your natural attractiveness. A different trap is the requisite that you appear perfect and beautiful, which is likely to result in avoidance of touching and sensuality. Individuals vary in what they find attractive and sensual, so it is important to be aware of your desires and feelings and learn your partner's preferences. Remember, the essence of sexuality is two comfortable, involved people giving and receiving pleasure-oriented touching.

JOAN AND ANDY

Joan and Andy consulted Barry after 7 years of marriage. It was Joan's first marriage and Andy's second. They were part of the "liberation movement" and thought of themselves as sexually free and sophisticated. Their sexual relationship was excellent while they lived together before marriage and for the first 10 months after they married. But it had become increasingly unsatisfying and had fallen off precipitously in the ensuing 3 years. Andy and Joan had been in couple therapy and in a couples group. They had explored a number of relationship issues, including financial problems, dealing with in-laws, power struggles, adolescent stepchildren, and avoidance of intimacy. Some issues were successfully dealt with; others remained problematic.

Joan and Andy continued to search for the nonsexual causes of their sexual problem. They could not imagine how two such sexually sophisticated and liberated people could be sexually dysfunctional. They were taken aback when Barry confronted their pattern of minimal touching, which would lead either to "dynamite" sexual intercourse or to a bitter, frustrating argument. When given the prescription for nongenital pleasuring exercises, they were resistant. Andy and Joan saw nongenital touch as an exercise for people who were sexually anxious and inhibited, not for them. While it is true that psychosexual skill exercises are designed to increase comfort with nudity, touching, and initiating for couples who are anxious and inhibited, they provide sensual experiences most couples (including you) can benefit from. If you ignore nondemand sensuous experiences, it is hard to have a satisfying sexual relationship. Sensuality is the basis of sexual response and a crucial ingredient in maintaining a satisfying intimate relationship.

Andy and Joan found the exercises of great benefit. They reawakened forgotten pleasurable feelings of being caressed and touched for its own sake. Joan and Andy rediscovered a playful, comfortable way of being with each other. A second, and unexpected, effect was to elicit specific problems in their manner of sexual expression. Under the thin guise of liberation, there were serious difficulties in sharing feelings, acknowledging intimacy, and being open to the needs and requests of their partner. They learned that by not retreating into anger, they could continue to share sensuality and feel safe and trusting, thereby increasing intimacy.

As you prepare to engage in the following psychosexual skill exercises, be aware of what you want to learn and experience through non-goal-oriented, nondemand pleasuring. Give yourself permission to explore, feel, and share.

EXERCISES FOR NONGENITAL PLEASURING

First Exercise: Exploration

Before beginning, sit and talk for 10 or 15 minutes over a cup of coffee or glass of wine. Contrary to popular mythology, alcohol is a central nervous system depressant that interferes with arousal (although it can temporarily facilitate desire and reduce self-consciousness), so limit yourself to one drink.

Recall a particular experience when you felt close and intimate. Express this feeling. Put your hands palms down on the table. Ask your partner to do the same, and allow your hands to be caressed. Much can be communicated by affectionate touch.

If you shower or bathe as a prelude to pleasuring, experiment with different types of spray or temperature; try a new bath oil or soap. This can increase awareness of sensual stimuli. Start by soaping your partner's back, caressing it as you do so. Trace the muscles and contours; gently rub and massage. Ask your partner to face you. Soap the front of the neck and chest, but go around the breasts. Touch the hollows of the neck and the soft area below the ribs and navel. Move downward to the hips, bypassing the genital area. Wash your own genitals. Soap your partner's legs while telling them how it feels. Let your partner soap you. Be aware of what feels particularly sensuous.

When you have finished, dry each other. Take your time; being slow and tender is important. Stand still for a moment and take a good look at your partner as if they were a person you had never seen before. Notice one or two things you find particularly attractive. Walk toward each other, hands extended, and hold your partner's hands. Slide your partner's arms around your waist; enjoy the closeness. Share your feelings as you spark a new warmth, closeness, and intimacy.

Proceed to your bedroom, feeling natural being nude. If you do not feel comfortable walking through the house nude, put on a robe or towel, but take it off when you reach the bedroom. Pleasuring is best done in the nude. Later you can vary the amount of clothing, which can be tantalizing. But first learn to be comfortable with your own and your partner's nudity. Be sure your bedroom is at a comfortable temperature with a moderate amount of light. If you prefer, partially darken the room, but be sure you can see your partner's body. If you like, put on your favorite music or burn a candle with a pleasant fragrance.

Designate one partner as the pleasure giver and the other as the pleasure recipient. Typically, you will switch roles during the exercise, though some prefer to do one session as the giver and the next as receiver. Be sure each partner has an opportunity to do both at some time since a mutually satisfying relationship is facilitated by being comfortable receiving and giving. It is interesting that many people (especially men) find it harder to receive than to give. Neither role connotes dominance or submission, femininity or masculinity.

As recipient you have three tasks. The first is to be passive and receive pleasure. The second is to keep your eyes closed throughout the exercise so you are able to concentrate on feelings and sensations. The third is to be aware of what parts of your body and what types of touch are sensuous.

Let the man begin as giver. View your partner in a new way and feel comfortable giving her a wide variety of sensual touch. Rather than trying to second-guess her, touch for yourself, engaging in stimulation you enjoy giving. The recipient should lie on her stomach, feeling as receptive, relaxed, and comfortable as possible. You can look at and touch your partner from the top of her head to the bottoms of her feet. This exercise focuses on the back of her body. Throughout this exercise, the emphasis is on communication by touch rather than words; refrain from talking or joking. Talking can distract from the focus on sensations and feelings.

Begin by massaging her shoulders. Gently massage, being careful not to squeeze the upper neck muscles. Rub tenderly with your entire hand, moving slowly down her back and sides; avoid sudden movements. Be aware of what is appealing that you might not have noticed before— freckles, a tiny scar, muscle indentation. When you reach her waist, place your thumbs together, spread your fingers, and press and knead as you caress her side and lower back. Move to the head, and either give a scalp massage or gently run your fingers through her hair. Return to the back, but this time press vigorously and give her a back rub. Next, run your fingers over your partner's back in a playful, unorganized manner. You could trace special features of her back with your fingertips.

The task of the giver is to provide the recipient with a variety of experiences to increase her awareness of sensual feelings. The giver can enjoy trying various types of touching and experience her body in a new way. The emphasis is on exploring rather than working to arouse your partner or prove yourself as a lover. Feel comfortable; enjoy the experience. These exercises are guidelines, not hard and fast rules. Feel free to be creative, playful, and innovative.

Hold your partner's feet and caress them. Notice the length of the toes, the texture of the nails. Place your palm so it covers the arch, and curl your fingers over the top of her foot. Notice the heel as you rub the palm of your hand against it. Outline the division between the top and bottom of her foot with your fingertips. Holding one foot, caress the top with your fingers and trace the valleys between the toes. Gently massage her foot up to the ankle. Moving up the same leg, hold the ankle in one hand while exploring it with your other hand. Gently and slowly move up the calf, caressing and massaging to help your partner relax even more. Pay attention to rubbing the soft area behind the knee. Examine and explore her thigh; look for little places you have not touched before. Move to the buttocks and massage both simultaneously. Some people feel negative about this area because of the association with defecation. The buttocks and anal area can be a sensuous part the body, an erogenous zone with a multitude of nerve endings. Touch in a manner that is sensuous and enjoyable.

When you have provided a nondemanding sensuous exploration, switch giver and recipient roles and repeat the pleasuring experience. There can be large differences in the time spent, ranging between 15 and 90 minutes for each person. The giver explores and touches in her own way. This is not a "tit-for-tat" task. The focus is on comfort, exploring, enjoying, touching, and learning. The key concepts are *slow, tender, rhythmic, caring.*

After this exercise, discuss the experience and share feelings over a drink or cup of coffee. Because talking tends to isolate you from bodily feelings, it is best to do the exercise in silence. Afterward, we encourage sharing and processing feelings and reactions in a direct, open manner. We suggest doing this clothed over the kitchen table or on a walk. Processing a sexual experience while nude in bed is too vulnerable, especially when dealing with sensitive or difficult feedback. First share positive feelings; then talk about what was problematic. Try to maintain a five to one positive–negative ratio. Rather than seeing the negative as blame or a put-down, view it as constructive feedback with requests and suggestions of what to try next time.

Second Exercise: Guiding

Begin by taking a bath or shower. Allow this experience to be more relaxed, comfortable, and sensuous than the first time. Dry your partner, commenting and sharing as you do. The woman begins as giver so she can become comfortable with initiating intimacy, while the man learns to become comfortable with being passive and accepting pleasure.

In this exercise he keeps his eyes open and guides her hands to sensuous, pleasurable areas of his back. He is free to use touch or words to guide and make requests. The receiver can find at least two areas on his back that are particularly sensuous. Let your partner know so that she can be fully aware of your preferences. The giver can use additional types of sensual stimulation. This includes kissing the back of his neck, running your tongue from the top to the bottom of his spinal cord, blowing in his ear and flicking your tongue in and out, and covering his legs with gentle "love bites." Different people like different things. One partner cannot really know what the other likes without feedback. This is not a test; there are no right or wrong responses. Explore and enjoy.

When the giver feels ready, you can help him turn over on his back. He keeps his eyes closed, relaxes, and assumes a passive, receptive attitude. The technical term for this is *self-entrancement* arousal. Men are not used to the passive role, but it is important to experience being passive and receptive to learn his body's responsiveness to sensations and feelings evoked by his partner's caresses. Visually examine the front of his body and notice what parts are particularly attractive.

Cover his hand with yours. Notice differences in size and texture. Gently massage the fingers; then run your fingertips along the palm. Slide your fingers down his hand and look for things you have not noticed before. Trace the knuckles and small lines on his fingers. Gently kiss the soft inner palm of each hand. Caress your partner's forearms, one at a time. Notice the softness of the skin on the inner side of his arm. Trace the elbow with your fingers. Placing your thumb in the bend, grasp his forearm and slide your hand down to the wrist. Caress both arms in their entirety.

Gently explore his face. Notice the signs of relaxation and comfort; be aware of the difference between these expressions and the tension you observe in other situations. To enhance feelings of relaxation and sensuality, gently massage his forehead. Move from his cheeks to his chin, and with your fingertips outline favorite facial features. Tenderly kiss your partner's closed eyes. In fact, you might want to kiss all the parts of his head and face.

You can massage around his nipples and see if he is responsive to your touch. Many men find this sensual but inhibit their natural response because they think men are not supposed to feel good there. When you are exploring his chest, use smooth, tender strokes and cover his sides as well. Move up to his armpit and run your hands over it, noticing the feel of his hair on your hands. How does it feel to touch your partner's navel? Run your hands sideways around his stomach. Be aware of how his stomach muscles react to your touch. Avoid the genital area, but do use sensual touch to explore his inner thighs.

It may happen that he feels sexually aroused. He might get an erection, and you may vaginally lubricate. Accept this as a natural, healthy sexual response. If it does not happen, that is fine too; the purpose is to explore, learn, and enjoy sensuality. Nongenital pleasuring is a comfortable experience without pressure for sexual arousal. Whether you or your partner feel subjectively or objectively aroused or not, keep your focus on sensuality; do not feel a need or demand to respond sexually.

Explore the front of his legs and feet. In ending this exercise, visually reexamine the front of your partner's body and caress the two or three areas you find most attractive. Remember, there are no right or wrong areas. Perceptions of attractiveness vary; you might especially like his eyes, neck, chest, inner thighs. Touch what is appealing to you.

Switch giver and recipient roles, and repeat the touching sequence. He refrains from touching or caressing her breasts. Each person does touching and pleasuring differently, which is as it should be since you are learning to be comfortable with your personal style of giving and receiving pleasure. Afterward, spend time discussing differences between your style and your partner's. How can you utilize these differences to create a more satisfying sensual and sexual relationship?

Third Exercise: Mutuality

Sit across from each other, separated by a table. Make sure it is narrow enough so you can easily reach your partner's hands and face.

Put your hands palms down on the table. Ask your partner to do the same and caress his hands. Cover your partner's hands with yours. Grasp gently and lift them from the table. Slide your hands underneath so they support your partner's hands. Releasing one hand, cover the other so it is enclosed within yours. Lift the hand to your face and rub the back on your cheeks, one then the other. Make eye contact as you do this. Repeat with your eyes closed.

Pick up both hands and place them on your face so they enclose it from your cheeks to your chin. Close your eyes and slowly move your face from side to side. Holding his wrists, bend your neck forward, inclining your face toward your chest, and move his hands to the sides of your neck. Then raise your face, bring the hands together under your chin, and separate them so they slide up your face; stop when the fingertips reach your eyes. Gently kiss the soft inner palm of each hand. Make eye contact and communicate how you feel about the closeness.

Placing hands back on the table, imagine you will never be allowed to touch again. How would you approach these hands if that were true? Touch, squeeze, kiss them as if it is the last time you'll be able to do this. Share feelings about this experience and verbalize your intimacy and caring.

You can go directly to the pleasuring exercises, or if you prefer start with a shower or bath. The focus is on guiding and teaching your partner what feels sensuous on the front of your body. Allow this to be a mutual give-and-take experience. Technically, this is called *partner-interaction* arousal (in contrast to self-entrancement arousal).

Move away from the structured roles of giver and recipient. Keep your eyes open so you can communicate feelings through eye contact. Most of the communication will be nonverbal. Guide your partner's hand with yours to show what kind of touch and where on your body the feelings are particularly sensual and pleasurable. To enhance this experience, we suggest using a lotion while massaging. Experiment with several varieties, such as wild lemon lotion, aloe vera, abalone lotion, and baby oil. Make sure they are water-based and hypoallergenic so they do not cause a skin reaction. It can be fun to go shopping together and choose one or two lotions you would like to try. It is important to have the lotion readily available so you do not have to stop caressing to get it. If possible, heat the lotion. Cold lotion poured on bare skin can shock anyone out of a sensuous mood. If the lotion is not heated, leave one hand on your partner's body and pour the lotion onto the back of that hand. When it is warm, rub it on your partner's body.

Be aware of your partner's breathing. Find the rhythm of the breathing and follow it with the caressing motions of your hands. Be especially aware of the response to kissing or running your tongue over your partner's body. Mutually explore and share.

In ending this experience, lie with his chest against your back, bodies touching, with his arms gently around your waist (the "spoon" position). Talk and share feelings. Then lie quietly until sleep overtakes you.

Fourth Exercise: Sharing

Begin by discussing what degree of cleanliness is comfortable for you. Allow yourselves increasing amounts of mutuality, spontaneity, and playfulness. Both people can initiate touching and caressing, which will transfer into a mutually satisfying pleasuring pattern. Let the touching remain nongenital. We suggest using a different lotion so awareness of various smells, sensations, and sensual feelings is enhanced.

Try not to miss an opportunity to share honestly. Express feelings and make requests. Communicate your thoughts in new and different words. Express your desire for each other. Your body is learning to give and receive tenderness, warmth, and pleasure; your words can convey these new feelings. Let your partner know how special a person she or he truly is.

Try a different position. The woman can lie on her stomach with the man lying on his side, facing her and touching her entire body, upper leg bent at the knee so his leg rests across her legs. Slowly and gently caress her back from the neck to the waist. Gently move your leg up and down her legs, feeling her skin with the inside of your thigh and calf while exploring and touching with the instep of your foot. Talk while touching. Tell her how you are feeling emotionally and physically. Ask her what she likes and how you can please her.

Switch to a different position, perhaps kneeling and facing each other or lying across from each other. Exchange gentle, tender, mutual caresses. Enjoy simultaneously giving and receiving pleasure. Allow this to be a mutual sensuous, sharing experience, which is valuable in itself or at a later time as part of pleasuring leading to erotic touch and intercourse.

CLOSING THOUGHTS

Be aware of and accepting of your body's natural responses to nongenital touch and the pleasures of sensuality. Couples fall into a trap where the only touching they do is genital, leading to intercourse. We hope you have learned to appreciate feelings of sensuality and nongenital touch and are increasingly aware of what kinds of nongenital pleasuring are most enjoyable and what parts of your body are responsive. Share this awareness with your partner verbally and nonverbally, communicating in a direct, comfortable manner.

With a basic foundation of acceptance of touch and an emphasis on slow, tender, warm, intimate sharing, you are on your way to developing a strong, resilient couple sexual style.

3

WHOLE-BODY TOUCH
Genital Pleasuring

Through the nongenital exercises suggested in Chapter 2, you have become comfortable with your natural bodily feelings and with sharing sensuality. You've also relearned the enjoyment of nondemand touching without worrying about the pressures of goal-oriented sexual performance. Now that the base of slow, gentle, caring, rhythmic touching has been established, you can build upon it by adding genital touch.

The exercises in this chapter are aimed at allowing you to experience a natural, integrated approach to being a sensual and sexual couple. During these exercises, do not fall into the trap of having all touch become genitally oriented, with the goal of arousal and orgasm. Rather, genital pleasuring should be preceded by and integrated with nongenital touch. They complement each other.

Continue to explore and enjoy giving and receiving pleasure. The goal of sexual intercourse is not appropriate at this point because it raises performance anxiety and distracts from the pleasuring experience. The emphasis remains on nondemand pleasuring, integrating nongenital touching with genital touching and sensual feeling with sexual feelings.

RUTH AND KYLE

Ruth and Kyle were an affectionate couple who felt good about their marriage. People thought of them as a "golden couple." Women friends would gossip, saying they wished their husbands were as affectionate and caring as Kyle. Ruth and Kyle, however, had an embarrassing secret: They had a nonsexual marriage. Like one in five married couples they had intercourse less than 10 times a year. They were a couple who did well with affection, communication, and emotional intimacy but not with erotic and sexual encounters.

Barry assured Ruth and Kyle they had an excellent prognosis for overcoming the problem. Committed partners who are able to communicate feelings and have a solid intimate relationship make the ideal sex therapy candidates. Sexual intercourse was a major chronic problem. Ruth was poorly lubricated, and Kyle initiated quickly and awkwardly. He ejaculated rapidly, which was fine with Ruth since she did not derive pleasure from intercourse.

They had skipped a major step in the sexual process—the pleasure and arousal that comes from nongenital and genital touching. Sexual stimulation was a perfunctory touch on the breasts and vagina, two or three caresses, one or two hand strokes of the penis, and then on to intercourse.

A prohibition on intercourse and orgasm was imposed in order to give them the space and freedom to explore a variety of nongenital and genital pleasuring scenarios and techniques. The first week of exercises brought a dramatic change as Ruth and Kyle engaged in nongenital touching and discovered the joys of shared sensuality. They particularly enjoyed showering together and engaging in nongenital body massage. They felt more open and comfortable with nudity than they had in the past 8 years.

The second week involved genital touch and exploration and a continued prohibition on orgasm. The ban was lifted the third week, with the guideline that they could allow erotic flow to naturally culminate in orgasm if they wished but not feel a demand or pressure to do so. Some couples enjoy being orgasmic with manual, oral, rubbing, or vibrator stimulation; others do not. Kyle and Ruth had never tried it. The process was a real eye-opener; they discovered they enjoyed genital stimulation as a natural extension of nongenital pleasuring. Although shy at the beginning, they had a breakthrough and both enjoyed being orgasmic. In fact, rather than a "quickie intercourse," Ruth preferred manually pleasuring Kyle to orgasm. Kyle found oral stimulation of Ruth was great for her arousal and lubrication. With this base of genital pleasuring, they were able to develop comfort, pleasure, arousal, erotic flow, and satisfaction with intercourse. While most couples do not progress as rapidly as Ruth and Kyle did, they illustrate that comfort with genital pleasuring is a crucial ingredient in your couple sexual style.

PREPARING FOR GENITAL PLEASURING

The following psychosexual skill exercises are suggestions and guidelines designed to help in the exploring and discovering process. These are not rigid tests you must pass to prove your sexuality, and you aren't expected to follow them in minute detail. Focus on being aware of genital feelings and acceptance of a broad-based, flexible approach to sexuality. This attitude is facilitated by an open, honest exchange, which allows full acceptance of yourselves as sexual individuals and a sexual couple.

Each exercise is intended to take 30 to 90 minutes; however, this is flexible. You may want to separate parts of an exercise and do these independently. Some couples choose to devote more time to a specific exercise, not switch roles during the exercise, repeat part of an exercise—such as genital touching with clothes on—or place value on integrating nongenital and genital touch. Nondemand genital pleasuring is an integral step in accepting yourselves as a healthy sexual couple. So plan a relaxed time during which you will not be disturbed or feel hurried.

EXERCISES FOR GENITAL PLEASURING

First Exercise: Breast Stimulation

Before beginning, sit and talk about the highlights of your nongenital touching experiences and then discuss what you need in order to feel receptive and comfortable with genital touch. Remind your partner what you value about touching and how important it is to continue this pleasure-oriented sharing process.

Hold hands as you go to take a shower or bath. Soap and caress as before, with one addition: wash your partner's entire body. When you reach the genital areas, name each part aloud: *penis, mons, scrotum, vagina*. You might use your favorite slang words, such as *dick, jinnie, junior*, or *clit*. Feeling comfortable with sexual language—whether it be slang, proper terms, or your private sexual vocabulary—facilitates communication. If arousal occurs during the bath or shower, view it as a healthy, natural process. Do not feel pressure to do anything other than simply accept your natural sexual response.

Dry each other, including your genitals, in the natural progression of drying from top to bottom. Do not save the genitals for last. Include them as an integral part of your partner's body.

Be sure the bedroom milieu is conducive to feeling sensuous and receptive. Are you comfortable with the lighting? Some people like it bright; others prefer a darker room. Do not make it so dark that you cannot see your partner's nude body. If music facilitates a sensuous mood, then by all means put on your favorite music.

He initiates first. Begin with a favorite position from the nongenital exercises that gives you access to your partner's body and breasts. With your right hand, gently caress her breasts as an extension of caressing her chest and sides. She can close her eyes to increase awareness of the rhythm and type of breast touch she finds particularly sensuous. She need not pressure herself into feeling sexually aroused, nor should you try to arouse her. The role of the receiver is to be passive and allow herself to be receptive to and accepting of pleasure. The idea of being "selfish" and accepting sensual and sexual stimulation is difficult for some women—especially those who always worry about pleasing their partner and ignore their own needs and desires. It is important to be selfish in the sense of accepting pleasure. This facilitates developing a vital sexual relationship. When the woman is open to receiving pleasure, she can give more to her partner. This is the reciprocal function of the "give-and-get" guideline.

Think of her breasts as an integral part of her to discover and investigate. He can view her breasts anew and feel comfortable in exploring a variety of touches and caresses. She is aware and comfortable with her sensations and feelings.

Focus on breast stimulation. With the palm of your hand, start at the waist and move up to her neck with one long motion. Be careful not to press hard; breasts can be sensitive and you might inadvertently cause discomfort. She is free to tell you if it hurts or if there is discomfort and to request that you move to a different area or use another type of touch. Sometimes the difference between pleasurable and irritating touch is less than an inch or a small variation in pressure. Trace the nipple with your fingertips and see if it becomes erect. Notice the different sensations of an erect, as opposed to non-erect, nipple. As you caress her breasts, be aware of and respond to warm, sensuous feelings.

Place your hand on your partner's opposite side so that you nearly surround her with your arm and, in a slow, continuous movement, draw your hand over the soft skin underneath her armpit, across the upper side of both breasts and slowly back again. As you pass over a breast, if the nipple is soft, gently caress it until it is erect. If erect, stop stimulation and see if it becomes soft.

Lift your elbow for support, and kiss and caress her breasts and chest. Feel the texture changes with your tongue. Make certain that manual and oral stimulation is gentle and nondemanding. Harder, focused, erotic stimulation is inviting if she is aroused but is counterproductive (or irritating) if she is not. For both woman and men, direct genital stimulation at low levels of arousal increases self-consciousness, which reduces arousal. Genital touching facilitates arousal when your partner is receptive and feels pleasure.

Throughout this exercise, the emphasis is on nonverbal communication since talking can get in the way of bodily sensations. As the giver, be sensitive to signs of tension or anxiety. If you feel her become tense, back off, but do not avoid body contact; that is, keep the connection but alter the touching. If you feel that kissing her breasts makes her tense or she tells you it does, move your kisses to her face, arm, or stomach until she is comfortable. Do not move away or cease contact. Neither of you has made a mistake. It takes time and experience to attain a high level of comfort and learn what is pleasurable. Intermix nongenital touch with breast stimulation. Stay with the feelings, enjoying the sense of exploration and discovery. Your openness and nondemanding approach help your partner feel comfortable and receptive to pleasuring.

After you have given her a variety of experiences—including touching the areola with just the palm of your hands—gently bring her breasts as close together as they will go, and explore the difference in separate versus simultaneous breast stimulation.

Partners can then change roles. Having the woman focus on his breast in a sensual and sexual way is a new experience for most men. Explore the difference in feeling between an erect and nonerect nipple and note how, or if, your partner enjoys having his nipples touched and kissed. Some men find this pleasurable, while others do not. There are no right or wrong responses. You both are engaged in a process of discovering how your bodies react to touch. She can express warmth by touching and kissing attractive parts of his body, including his chest and breasts. End the pleasuring on a caring note.

Afterward, sit and discuss each partner's feelings about breast touching, both manual and oral. Some couples find breast stimulation is not their "thing." That also is acceptable. Determine how you would like breast stimulation to fit into your sexual sharing.

Second Exercise: Genital Exploration

Begin with a bath or shower. This time, while soaping your partner's genitals describe verbally and in detail such things as skin appearance, sensations, and attractiveness. What do you find particularly fascinating about your partner's genitals? Use proper, slang, or your private sex names for genitals, depending on which you find most comfortable.

The woman begins as giver while he keeps his eyes closed. During the exercise, we suggest a minimum of verbal interaction. Focus on sensations and feelings. He lies on his back, his eyes closed, his body relaxed and passive (technically *self-entrancement* arousal). Find a comfortable position, perhaps kneeling near his stomach or sitting or lying beside him.

Visually explore his body. Allow your eyes to range over his entire body, not just the genitals. Spend time massaging and caressing your favorite nongenital body parts. As you do this, observe his genitals. Be aware of your feelings about his erect penis, as opposed to when it is flaccid. A commonly believed myth is that when the man has an erection you must do something—either have intercourse or bring him to orgasm. An erection might indicate sexual excitement, or it might not. Men sometimes become erect during a sports event or while wrestling with their children. Do not assume his erection is a demand for you to do something. It is interesting that men also believe the myth that an erection must mean sexual arousal and thus attempt intercourse even when they do not feel like sex. This time refrain from doing anything with his erection except enjoy it without feeling any demand.

While massaging around his stomach, lower your hand and touch his penis and scrotum. As you explore his genitals, be aware of each part you touch—*penis, glans, shaft, frenulum, scrotum, testes*. Touch and verbalize each genital area until you feel comfortable. Touch the way you want, using a variety of playing, rubbing, and caressing. If either of you feel anxious, do not remove your hand; simply massage a body part with which you feel comfortable. Take a few long, deep breaths and allow yourself to relax. If you still feel anxious, hold your partner until the anxiety dissipates. Stay close; you are not in a sexual race. Proceed at your own pace and comfort level.

As you explore his testes, notice which is larger and what the shapes remind you of. Remember, these are sensitive body parts. Move slowly and gently. Notice how his testes move inside the scrotum. If your partner is circumcised, trace the glans of the penis with your fingertips. If he is uncircumcised, gently move the foreskin back and explore the glans. Enjoy nondemand massage and caresses around his inner thighs, perineum, and scrotum. If he becomes erect, keep your hand on his penis and stroke it. Notice the pulse as blood collects in his penis and enjoy the feeling as he becomes more aroused. Place your hands in a cuplike curve and hold the scrotum. Notice how his scrotum changes as arousal intensifies. After his penis has been erect for a while, either move to nongenital touching or discontinue stimulation until his erection subsides. An erection naturally waxes and wanes, as does your arousal and lubrication. Note the differences in his penis and scrotum in the nonerect state.

He is aware of feelings as his erection subsides. A man traditionally becomes anxious or panicked with the waning of an erection because he is used to proceeding to intercourse and orgasm on his first erection. His erection waning is nothing to be anxious about or threatened by. An erection decreases and is regained if he allows it to happen without reacting with anxiety or feeling pressure to achieve another erection. During a prolonged pleasuring period (30 minutes or more), it is not unusual for his erection to wax and wane two to five times. This is a natural physiological process. He is unaware of this because the stereotyped pattern is to have an orgasm on his first erection.

Run your fingers through his pubic hair. Notice the texture, thickness, and length. With your fingertips trace a line down to his anus. Then, flattening your hand, caress the inside of one leg while you continue to hold and gently squeeze his penis. Try to coordinate the rhythm of his breathing with your stroking of his penis. Gently pull and squeeze at the same time. Place your other hand on his lower abdomen and caress with a circular movement.

The role of the giver is to provide a variety of stimulation so the receiver can discover what is pleasurable. At this point, use manual touch. Oral stimulation can occur in subsequent psychosexual skill exercises. When you feel comfortable with genital touch and have given your partner a pleasurable experience, switch roles.

The woman lies on her back and lets herself relax. The man finds a comfortable position, whether sitting, kneeling, or lying. It is important that he can see and touch her, especially her genitals. Begin by touching your favorite nongenital areas and then let her guide your hands over her breasts by placing her hand over yours (the hand-over-hand technique). Let her teach you the type of breast touch that is most pleasurable. She can tell you what pleases her by touch and gesture, or she can use verbal guidance if she prefers.

It is especially important to keep your communication process comfortable and clear. Learning to embrace your sexuality is based on positive influences, not on demands or intimidation. Repeat gestures or words so your partner understands and appreciates them. Remember, sexual learning is a gradual process.

You might enjoy kissing, sucking, licking, tongue gliding, or biting on the areola, nipple, or entire breast. She can guide by moving your head, touching your forehead, or using a mutually understood gesture. Be careful as you kiss or suck because breasts can be sensitive; hard sucking is enjoyable only when she is moderately aroused. Sensitivity and awareness enhance the experience for both the giver and receiver.

Massage around the stomach, and then explore her genitals. Gently run your fingers through her pubic hair and caress the mons. Be aware of the texture of her pubic hair and its appearance. Place the heels of both hands below her vulva on the soft inner part of her legs. With both hands cupped over her pubic hair, move your hands rhythmically in small circles.

Spread the labia majora with your fingers. Be comfortable with the sight and feel of her genitals. Identify her clitoris and clitoral shaft, and look carefully at the labia minora. Notice how the labia surround the vaginal introitus (opening). Spread the vaginal opening with two fingers and notice the color and texture of the interior. Gently insert one finger into her vagina and notice the sensations of containment. Feel the warmth and dampness. Touch the mons and perineum. As you explore, verbalize the names (using proper, slang, or your personal language).

Move slowly and gently. Be open to tender touch and exploration. Her clitoris can be especially sensitive, so rather than stimulating it directly run your fingers around the clitoral shaft. When she becomes aroused, her clitoris becomes enlarged and withdraws under the clitoral hood. This is her body's way of protecting itself from discomfort. Hard, direct clitoral stimulation causes pain for most women. Massage around the labia and clitoral shaft, thereby indirectly stimulating her clitoris.

Allow touching and exploring to be sensuous, tender, and caring. If she becomes aroused, lubricated, and responsive, remember to respond with her rather than feel the need to do something. Genital response and arousal are natural and normal so accept and enjoy these reactions. Intermix nongenital touching; do not focus solely on her genitals. When you are feeling comfortable with genital touch and have provided her with a variety of experiences, end the exercise in a warm, close manner.

Hold your partner, sharing feelings of tenderness and caring. Get dressed and go downstairs to talk, or if you prefer go for a walk and talk. Share feelings; talk openly and frankly about genital exploration and touch as well as the positive things you have learned and what you want to try next time.

Third Exercise: Guiding

During this exercise, keep your eyes open and use eye contact to facilitate communication. Use your favorite lotion to enhance feelings of sensuality, remembering to warm it or pour it on your hand so it is warm before you rub it on your partner's skin. Use the hand-over-hand technique to guide and teach your partner the places and types of touch that give pleasure and increase responsiveness.

Couples typically do not discuss how they like having their clothes taken off. Traditionally, the man undresses himself and then hastily undresses his partner. Begin with both partners dressed, and let the woman undress the man. She can start by looking at him fully clothed and then mentally undressing him. Maintain good eye contact and keep verbal interaction at a minimum so you can focus on the experience.

Begin undressing by playing in a teasing manner with the middle buttons on his shirt. Unbutton the shirt slowly; while doing so, put your hand on his crotch and notice his reaction. After you have taken his shirt off, you could unbuckle his belt and pants, turn him around, and lower his pants. Take off his shoes and socks and let him step out of his pants. Turn him around again so he is facing you, look at him, and give him a big hug. Then take off his underpants. How do you feel about undressing him in a seductive, sensuous way? How does he feel? How does it feel to hug and kiss with you clothed and him nude?

Now he can undress her. First, do it visually. Then kiss and hold her. Start in the middle of her back and run your finger up and down the zipper or buttons. Unzip or unbutton a little at a time; then stop and run your fingers up and down her back. Take one shoulder of her blouse or dress off, stroking her arm. As you touch her back, check where the hooks on the bra are. Undo one strap at a time but do not take the bra off; just let it hang. Turn her around and take her shoes off. Next take off her skirt or roll her slacks down slowly. Face each other. Notice how she looks with her panties and loosely hanging bra. As you take off her bra and panties, say the warm, sexy things you are feeling. When she is nude, take her in your arms and start the genital pleasuring.

In subsequent undressing experiences, vary these techniques according to your personal style—sometimes sensuous, sometimes playful. Undressing can be seductive and fun rather than routine.

Decide who will begin. Whoever has more discomfort in giving can start as the giver. Attend to your partner's feelings and guidance. Remember the "give-and-get" guideline for sexual satisfaction. Try a different pleasuring position. The giver sits on the bed, with back support from the wall, headboard, or pillows. Spread your legs far enough apart so your partner can sit between them.

The recipient might need back support, too. Arrange pillows so the receiver is in a semireclining position. There is no set way to place the pillows; fix them so both people are comfortable. The recipient's legs will be over the giver's. Be sure the giver has full access to the receiver's entire body.

As giver, begin by caressing genitals, using your favorite lotion. Go over the genitals as if your goal were to cover them completely with lotion. Do this slowly, tenderly, and rhythmically. Follow your partner's guidance. The receiver is free to guide the giver's hands to areas of the genitals that feel particularly pleasurable and arousing.

Those who masturbate or who have done self-exploration exercises are in a particularly good position to understand and share their natural bodily responses. Help your partner by making open, clear requests. Be present emotionally and sexually. Share your pleasure.

When you begin feeling aroused, switch to nongenital touching. Typically, touching goes quickly from nongenital to focused genital stimulation. How does it feel to reverse that process? Allow nongenital touch to be slow, tender, and rhythmic. Be responsive to your partner's guidance and feelings. Make nongenital touching as involving as genital touch. Guide your partner back to genital stimulation or your favorite combination of nongenital and genital touch. If you want, you can proceed to orgasm, but do not feel pressure to do so.

Switch roles and repeat the sequence. Afterward, lie in bed and share feelings. Discuss how you feel about giving as opposed to receiving. Do you like taking turns or doing mutual pleasuring? How do you feel about combining nongenital and genital touching? Be frank, direct, clear, and supportive. Most important is to share how you feel about yourselves as a sexual couple. Sexuality enhances and reinforces intimate feelings.

If you have difficulty talking about the experience, cannot express feelings of pleasure, or cannot express dislike of specific activities, consider the following verbal exercise. This is more comfortably done when you are clothed—over the kitchen table, in the living room, or on a walk. If there has been a negative experience or you are giving difficult feedback, get up, get dressed, and talk outside the bedroom. Lying nude in bed leaves you too vulnerable to deal with difficult feelings and issues. It is potentially explosive to share negative feelings in bed after a difficult sexual experience. The usual outcome is much heat, little light, and bruised feelings.

Choose an exercise you can comfortably talk about. There are no laws or rules dictating what exercises must be done in which order. Discuss blocks and inhibitions that interfere with sexual communication. Be aware that a difficult experience or miscommunication is not a personal rejection or due to malevolent intent. You are an intimate team trying to develop a respectful, trusting relationship and a comfortable, functional couple sexual style. If you have a good feeling you want to express but cannot, ask your partner about her or his feelings. Find a common ground where you can help each other express feelings and preferences. Do not become bogged down with self-questioning thoughts such as, Am I really attractive? Can we be sexual? Do I deserve love? These can precipitate a self-defeating, destructive cycle. Focus on specific issues and feelings that build sexual comfort and confidence.

Fourth Exercise: Erotic Massage

The focus of this exercise is to integrate genital and nongenital touch: oral and manual stimulation, eye contact, hand guiding, and verbal feedback. During the first half of this exercise, engage in mutual touching with as much spontaneity and sharing as possible. Allow the exercise to be unstructured, with mutual giving and receiving (*partner-interaction* arousal).

The second part of the exercise focuses on erotic massage. Return to giver–receiver roles (self-entrancement arousal), and let the man be the giver first. Erotic massage integrates genital and nongenital touching. It is both sensual and sexual, involving caresses that are slow, tender, caring, rhythmic, and flowing.

She lies on her stomach; her eyes can be open or closed, whichever feels more comfortable. Begin by massaging the back of her neck with both hands. Be sure her neck muscles are relaxed. Gently move your hands to about 3 inches above the tailbone, and massage her upper and lower back in smooth, rhythmic motions.

Move your hands to the backs of her thighs and caress her buttocks. Bring your hands together at the small of the back; using the same motion, move to the thighs. She is receptive to feelings of sensuality, pleasure, and eroticism.

Help your partner turn over. Gently place both hands on her thighs. With a smooth, sweeping movement, move your hands up her thighs and over her vulva, and then bring them together at her stomach. Spread your hands in an outward movement toward her breasts. Bring her breasts together. Then move to the thighs. Be sure to touch her genitals fully. Intermix manual and oral genital stimulation, so the pleasurable process feels more integrative. Give your partner several different sexual caresses. Be aware of feeling pleasure at your partner's enjoyment and responsiveness. You can proceed to orgasm if you wish. Continue caressing until your partner requests you stop or she transitions to orgasm.

Change roles and let the woman repeat the same series of exercises. She can use her personal style of integrating pleasuring with an erotic massage.

There is an additional experience that can be particularly pleasurable. Typically, a woman will not use her breasts actively; instead, she is passive while he stimulates her breasts. Active breast stimulation can be enjoyable to the woman as well as her partner. After hand massage of the man's thighs, genitals, stomach, and chest, you can put lotion on your breasts and repeat the same movements using your breasts.

Notice the feelings in your breasts; some women find breast responsiveness heightened during this experience. When you have done this long enough to determine whether it feels pleasurable and erotic, have your partner lie comfortably on his side, put your hand on his chest, with your front to his back, and follow the rhythm of his breathing. This can engender a warm, close, intimate feeling. Allow yourselves to breathe together and drift off to sleep.

CLOSING THOUGHTS

You can feel comfortable giving and receiving sensual and sexual stimulation in a non-goal-oriented atmosphere. Develop a healthy attitude about yourself as a sexual person and yourselves as a sexual couple. Accept your sexuality and special style of giving and receiving pleasure. Nongenital and genital pleasuring provide a solid foundation for sexual communication, desire, pleasure, eroticism, and satisfaction.

4

SELF-EXPLORATION AND MASTURBATION

You are a sexual person from the day you are born to the day you die. Acceptance and enjoyment of sexuality varies depending on the individual, life experiences, cultural norms, values, and your relationship. For some, sexual feelings develop naturally and at a young age; for others, sexual feelings and the acceptance of sexuality are delayed and a challenge. Many people develop positive sexual self-esteem and have a satisfying sexual life; others do not.

The purpose of this chapter and the following psychosexual skill exercises is to increase your knowledge of and comfort with your body and its natural, healthy sexual response. One way to remove blocks to naturally occurring sensual and sexual response is through a systematic, anxiety-reducing self-exploration of your body and its capacity for pleasure. Becoming comfortable with your body and understanding how it responds help build the sexual self-esteem that allows you to experience sexuality in all its guises.

ORGASM

A major difference between men and women is how they learn about orgasm. Boys explore and touch their genitals earlier and more frequently than girls do. Typically, males have their first orgasm between ages 10 and 16, either through a nocturnal emission (wet dream) or self-stimulation (masturbation). They have a range of psychological reactions. Some are very pleased and see it as a passage into manhood; others are guilty and anxious; still others feel excitement mixed with confusion or shame. Learning that your body can react to touch with pleasure, arousal, and orgasm is a positive for both men and women.

Women tend to experience their first orgasm later than men, some through self-stimulation and others by partner stimulation. Less than 10% have their first orgasm during intercourse. Eight percent of adult women are nonorgasmic; in other words, they have not learned to experience the feeling of increasing excitement and responsivity followed by a moment of release (orgasm, climax) accompanied by a great deal of pleasure. It is more common that a woman can be orgasmic with self- or vibrator stimulation but has difficulty being orgasmic during partner sex.

Both women and men have the potential to be orgasmic during masturbation and partner sex. Physiologically and psychologically, orgasmic response is similar for men and women. Orgasm lasts from 3 to 10 seconds and consists of rhythmic muscle contractions followed by the release of tension and vascular congestion in your pelvic area. A man typically experiences a single orgasm, which is accompanied by ejaculation. Women have the potential to experience multiple orgasms; about one in five women have a multiple orgasm response.

The media overdramatizes the need and centrality of orgasm. Orgasmic experiences differ depending on the person, situation, and relationship. Orgasm has been described by some as a "pop" that replaces built-up tension by a feeling of warmth and calm. Others have compared orgasms to waves—sometimes a gentle ripple, at other times a roaring cascade—in which the person might lose consciousness for a second or two. Still others view orgasm as an "insignificant spasm."

Orgasm is a natural culmination of sexual responsivity, arousal, and erotic flow. An orgasm cannot be willed or forced. The more you concentrate and strive for it, the less likely you are to experience and enjoy orgasm. A healthy way to think about the process of arousal and orgasm is as a delightful heightening of pleasurable feelings—beginning with sensual touching , then moving to sexual pleasure that progresses to arousal and increased erotic flow—naturally culminating in intense sensations (orgasm), followed by afterplay. You can learn to be comfortable with your body and its sensual and sexual responsivity, including being orgasmic.

GAIL AND JACK

Gail and Jack were experiencing sexual dysfunction. In reviewing their sexual histories, it was apparent that attitudes and experiences with masturbation were a contributing factor.

Jack's problem was premature ejaculation. He had begun masturbating at 13. Jack found masturbation and ejaculation very enjoyable but was troubled by thoughts that he should not be doing this. He was afraid of being caught by his parents or discovered by his brother or sister. Jack vaguely remembered his father deriding a neighborhood boy for "playing with himself" and vividly recalled the priest warning against the sin of "self-abuse." Jack developed a pattern of fast, intense, totally penis-and-orgasm-focused masturbation. He ejaculated as quickly as he could and cleaned up immediately so he would escape discovery. For Jack, masturbation and orgasm were intense but not an integrated part of his life. As soon as he ejaculated, he wanted to forget about sex. This pattern extended to premature ejaculation during partner sex.

Gail wanted a sensuous, slow, tender lover, whereas Jack was genitally oriented, fast both in touching and intercourse, and abrupt in his movements. Gail misinterpreted this to mean he did not care about her sexual feelings and preferences. In fact, although Jack valued their intimate relationship, he was mindlessly repeating the pattern he had learned during masturbation.

Slow, gentle body exploration was a central ingredient in treatment. If Jack could appreciate sensuality himself, it would be easier to share this with Gail. During psychosexual skill masturbation exercises, Jack identified the point of ejaculatory inevitability and practiced extending ejaculatory control. As his comfort, skill, and confidence improved, he transferred those learnings to sex with Gail.

Gail's experience with self-exploration and masturbation was quite different. She learned "good girls" were not to touch themselves "down there." Gail was not knowledgeable about her genitals and was confused about the role of her clitoris. When she bathed and the stream of water ran over her vulva, there were positive sensations that caused ambivalent feelings. Gail felt similar ambivalence about her vagina. Her learning about menstruation was negative. She dreaded her monthly period. Boyfriends tried to touch and enter her vagina with their fingers or penis, and she was used to saying no. Gail's first intercourse was a disappointment. She was minimally lubricated, intromission was painful, and she felt cheated by the man not caring about her physical or psychological feelings. Sex with Jack added to her disappointment since his stimulation was rough, ejaculation was rapid, and sex ended with his orgasm. She felt Jack did not care about her emotional feelings or sexual needs.

For Gail, developing comfort with her genitals and being responsible for learning her arousal and orgasm pattern were challenging. Jack's support, especially taking care of the children when she engaged in self-exploration and self-stimulation exercises, was of great value. Gail experienced initial discomfort, fearing she was "selfish." This was countered by realizing that if she could become aware of her arousal and orgasm pattern, it would facilitate her sexual self-esteem and improve her and Jack's sexual relationship. Gail discovered that touching her labia, stimulating her clitoral area, and using erotic fantasies allowed her to be orgasmic. As her comfort and confidence increased, she became an involved, active partner. Gail and Jack learned to share desire, pleasure, eroticism, and satisfaction.

SELF-EXPLORATION GUIDELINES

Each person is different, so consider the following exercises as guidelines rather than rigid rules. You are a unique person; only you can know what is comfortable, pleasurable, and erotic for you. A first step in increasing sexual satisfaction is to increase comfort with and knowledge of your body. Set aside a time when you will not be interrupted. This is your time; do not answer the door and take the phone off the hook or put on the answering machine. If you have small children, use their afternoon nap time or put your spouse in charge of the house and children.

Remember these three guidelines:

1. The focus is on comfort, exploration, and learning rather than the accomplishment of an orgasmic performance goal. Self-exploration is not a test with right or wrong answers.
2. Be flexible about time. Ideally, one exercise is done during each session, which can be from 15 to 45 minutes. At first there might be embarrassment and hesitancy, which could cause you to stop prematurely. Try to have the first session last for at least 10 minutes and allow these psychosexual skill exercises to become progressively longer.
3. Set up your surroundings to facilitate comfort and sensuality. Do you want the lights off or on? Do you enjoy music? Do you like using lotions or powders? Make this a special time to learn about your body and its potential for sexual pleasure and responsivity.

We have designed separate sets of exercises for men and women, although the concepts of self-exploration are very similar.

EXERCISES FOR WOMEN

First Exercise: Body Exploration

You can become aware of and comfortable with your body. Make sure you have uninterrupted time and privacy. Draw a bath (or take a shower) and add your favorite bath oil. Stretch out in the tub and soap your body. Enjoy the sensations of touching your calves, thighs, and arms. Spend time on your toes and feet, massaging them until they feel relaxed. Feel the softness behind your knees and the inside of your upper arms. Cross your arms so opposite hands grasp your waist. Slide your hands across your body and down the sides to rest on your thighs. Sitting up, place your palms and knees together. Slide your hands through your thighs and caress your legs. Be aware of and responsive to your whole body. Dry yourself in a slow, comfortable manner, almost caressing yourself dry.

Go into the bedroom without clothes on and lie on your bed. You may want to darken your bedroom, turn up the heat, light a candle, put music on. Do what is best for you. Use pillows to support yourself in the most comfortable position you can find.

Close your eyes and concentrate on relaxing. Be aware of any tension. The easiest way to discover and reduce tension is to tighten each muscle group (arms, legs, back, chest, face) in turn and then relax. To facilitate relaxation, repeat to yourself expressions like "relax and feel my body" or "relax more and more, deeper and deeper." Use slow, deep, regular breathing to enhance relaxation. Each time you inhale, think the word *relax*; each time you exhale, think the word *calm*.

When you are feeling relaxed and comfortable, gently clasp your thighs, curl up slowly, and roll to one side. Notice the feelings of movement. Touch your feet, legs, thighs, stomach, chest, lower back, neck, face, arms, and fingers. Try different types of touch—light stroking, patting, heavy massaging, rubbing, scratching. Be aware of the sensations resulting from each type of touch on different parts of your body.

Take time for visual exploration. If possible, use a full-length mirror. An interesting technique is to take a piece of cardboard or paper and hold it first in front of one eye and then the other. Which parts of your body look different? Find at least one part that is different from its other side. Look at your whole body (front, side, and back views) and be aware of at least two nongenital areas you find particularly attractive.

View your genitals with a small hand mirror as you lie on the bed or lie facing a full-length mirror with pillows propped under your buttocks. Identify the parts of your vulva. Be comfortable with the sight and feel of your genitals. Do not be concerned about sexual arousal.

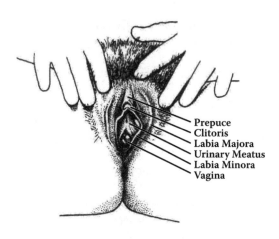

Figure 4.1 The genital anatomy of the female.

Separate the labia majora with your fingers; look carefully at the labia minora and find your clitoris under its hood. Notice how the labia minora surround the vaginal opening. Spread the vaginal introitus with two fingers and notice the color and texture of the interior. Insert a finger into your vagina and watch with the mirror. Be aware of the warmth, softness, and dampness. Touch your mons, the perineum (the area between the vagina and anus), and around the urethra.

Close your eyes. Touch these areas again, imagining how they look in the mirror. Develop comfortable, positive feelings about your body and genitals, including the following:

Mons: A raised area created by a layer of fat over the pubic bone. The mons becomes covered with hair at puberty. Some women shave pubic hair, while others prefer the natural look.

Labia majora: The literal translation is "greater lips."

Labia minora: These folds of sensitive tissue become engorged as blood flows into them when you become sexually aroused.

Prepuce: This hood-like fold of tissue is formed by the joining of the labia minora. The prepuce covers your clitoris.

Clitoris: This is the most sensitive and responsive part of your genitals. Your clitoris becomes enlarged and erect when stimulated. It is the organ with the most nerve endings and has no other function than sexual pleasure.

Urinary meatus: This is the outlet for urine from the bladder.

Vagina: This organ is about 4 or 5 inches long. Its walls normally touch each other, but during intercourse they stretch considerably and, of course, they stretch greatly during childbirth. Your vagina receives lubrication from mucus secretions when you are aroused. A thin elastic membrane, the hymen, partially covers the opening of the vagina. Your hymen can be broken or stretched in a number of ways. The outer third of your vagina is the most sensitive, although sensitivity varies from woman to woman. The pelvic muscles, including the most sensitive muscle (the pubocoygeal), are especially important. The anterior wall of the vagina, when stimulated while highly aroused, is particularly erotic for many women.

Second Exercise: Sexual Exploration

Begin by taking a long, relaxing bath. Get used to the feeling of caressing your body and notice things you may not have been aware of. Exactly where is that mole? How does it feel to gently pat your shoulders? How does your body feel after you stop stroking?

The bath serves two functions: to help you relax and to clean your body. Using a mild hypoallergenic soap, gently cleanse your genitals. Separate the labia with your fingers and clean to remove secretions.

Two sensitive subjects need to be mentioned. First, whether to keep or cut genital hair is your preference. Some women shave; others do not. Make your decision to suit your comfort and taste (although be aware of your partner's feelings), not to follow some ideal promoted by the depilatory and razor industries or because it's the "in thing to do." Second, everybody has odors. We suggest you cleanse odor-causing substances, but in doing so we are not advocating you give up your humanity to the soap manufacturers. Genital cleanliness is a sign of consideration for your partner, but some women (and men) find sanitization is sexually unappealing.

Gently wash your clitoral area. Take extra time to dry your body. Some women prefer a soft towel to caress their bodies; others choose a stiff terrycloth for a stimulating massage while drying.

Engage in the types of touching that you enjoy. Allow yourself to be inventive. Feel comfortable with genital touch. Start with your breasts. When you slowly move one hand to the opposite side of your body, then over your chest, your areola will rise. Notice the difference in feeling when your areola is hard and when soft. Touch your breasts, be aware which is more responsive. What is the most enjoyable form of breast stimulation—touching concurrently, touching the areola with just the palm of your hand, rubbing downward on the breast and then pulling up? Women vary in breast responsivity. Some very much enjoy having their breasts caressed; others do not. What are you receptive and responsive to?

Curl up on your side. Slide your hands up the inside of your legs until they reach your genitals. Run your fingers through your pubic hair. Feel the soft skin covering the area between your vagina and anus: this is the perineum. How do you feel about your labia majora? Separate the lips, and with your fingertips touch and outline the labia minora. Find your clitoris, and placing a finger above it, slide back the clitoral hood.

This is a small movement, and at first you may have a hard time identifying your clitoris. Do you enjoy indirect clitoral stimulation?

What type of touch and pressure feels best? Trace the outer edge of the vaginal opening with your fingertip. Notice that it becomes damp, moist, and warm. This normal body secretion is clean and germ-free. It is natural, positive, and necessary. Vaginal secretions reflect healthy responsiveness. You might want to take a drop on your fingertip, put it on your tongue, and taste it.

Become aware of the pelvic floor muscles. These muscles affect intravaginal sensations and can be strengthened by doing physical exercises. The easiest way to locate the pelvic muscles is to stop your flow while urinating. The muscles you use are the pelvic muscles.

Practice exercising your pelvic muscles. Tighten them, hold for 3 seconds, and release. Repeat this exercise 10 times in succession; it will only take a minute. Some women use these exercises to increase vaginal awareness and sensitivity. Other women tense and contract the pelvic muscles during intercourse to heighten sensations and feelings.

If at any time you feel anxious or uncomfortable, do not stop completely or remove your hands. Move back a step until you again feel comfortable and keep your focus on relaxation and pleasure. There is no rush; proceed at the pace that works best for you. Gradually you become more comfortable and enjoy your natural body response.

Third Exercise: Enhancing Sexual Pleasure and Arousal

As awareness and comfort increase, you may skip some steps. Continue exploring and learning, with a focus on enhancing feelings of pleasure and responsiveness. You have a right to feel sexual and to bask in feelings of pleasure, arousal, and erotic flow.

Enjoy the freedom of owning every feeling you have. You might try using imagery, fantasy, and pictoral, written, Internet, or video material to facilitate arousal. What kinds of fantasies are turn-ons for you? Erotic fantasies enhance desire and arousal. You might visualize yourself running free and naked on a beach. Imagine your partner saying you are the best lover in history. Fantasize having sex for 3 hours, being stimulated by two lovers simultaneously, having sex with forbidden partners in exotic places—anything that turns you on. Give free rein to your fantasies. Utilize fantasies or erotic material to enhance desire, arousal, and erotic flow.

Most women find clitoral stimulation particularly arousing. However, clitoral stimulation at low levels of arousal is likely to make you self-conscious rather than aroused. Start with nongenital touching, and as receptivity and responsivity increase move your hand to your clitoris and let your fingers move across it slowly, back and forth. This can produce intensely erotic feelings. As your arousal increases, your clitoris becomes engorged and withdraws under the clitoral hood. This is your body's way of protecting you from discomfort. Massage around the clitoral shaft, which indirectly stimulates your clitoris. Enjoy feelings of pleasure, arousal, and eroticism. If at any time you become anxious or uneasy, relax; move back a step, focus on the sense of comfort, and then return to stimulation. Enjoy the comfort, pleasure, arousal, erotic flow process.

While massaging your vagina, take the secretions and spread them throughout your vulva. Spread your vaginal opening with two fingers and notice the texture of the interior. Feel the warmth and dampness. Insert a finger into your vagina and be aware of your feelings. Move your finger inside the vagina and study the sensations. Be aware of special places and feelings. When aroused, some women find anterior wall stimulation highly arousing: others prefer clitoral stimulation. What is your responsivity and arousal pattern?

Focus attention on your clitoral area. Massage the clitoral shaft while caressing a breast with your other hand. Or you can combine clitoral and vaginal stimulation while focusing on erotic fantasies. Do what gives you the most erotic feelings. As arousal builds, go with the erotic flow, which naturally culminates in orgasm. If arousal does not result in orgasm, that is fine. Remember, you are learning to increase awareness, responsivity, and eroticism.

Fourth Exercise: Building and Reinforcing Erotic Flow

Experience your body as an integrated sensual and sexual whole. There is no artificial barrier between touching your genitals and the rest of your body. You can facilitate the pleasuring/eroticism process by repeating sentences like "relax and enjoy my body" or "find what feels good" or "let go and feel it all."

Give yourself permission to enjoy erotic feelings. Some days certain scenarios and techniques feel particularly good; other days they do not. Discover the areas and touches that are a turn-on; be conscious of the pattern and rhythm to which you are most responsive. Experiment with different types of stroking (circular, upward, patting, quick touch, slow build-up, rhythmic, teasing). Try variations in pressure to discover what is most stimulating. Stroke your clitoris with one hand while touching your breast or inner thigh with the other. Try massaging your clitoral shaft with one hand and engaging in intravaginal or anal stimulation with the other.

You might entertain explicit sexual fantasies or read erotic material; do whatever enhances your sexual responsiveness. You might imagine making love with the sexiest man you ever saw. Imagine being sexual in a variety of exotic situations. Think about a favorite passage from an erotic poem or watch an erotic video on the Internet. Fantasizing is not only normal; it is also a healthy bridge to sexual desire and erotic flow.

You can experiment with a vibrator to enhance arousal. Try an electric two-speed handheld vibrator with rubber attachments. Play with the vibrator on nongenital areas to become accustomed to the sensations. Then spread your knees, begin at the thighs, and move the vibrator slowly until it is resting against your labia. Spread the labia with your fingers and gently place the vibrator close to your clitoris. Experiment with placement until you find sensitive parts of your clitoral area and allow the vibrator to provide stimulation. As arousal builds, move your pelvis in rhythm with erotic sensations. If you experience the physical and emotional release of orgasm, accept it as the natural culmination of your body's receptivity and responsivity.

Experiencing orgasm signals that you have made a major leap in acceptance of yourself as a sexual person. You can share these learnings with your partner.

CLOSING THOUGHTS: WOMEN

The psychosexual skill exercises presented in this chapter are designed to help you experience your body in sensual and sexual ways and to increase awareness of natural, healthy responses. You may or may not be orgasmic. If you are experiencing orgasm, congratulations. You have taken a major step. If not, do not be discouraged. You have taken the crucial first step in learning about sensual and sexual responsiveness: you have become aware and accepting of your body. In time, practice, discovery, and reinforcement of the feelings and stimulation that you find sexually arousing will carry you to orgasm. If you keep enjoying and exploring, the sexual arousal and erotic flow that you experience will culminate *naturally* in orgasm—whether you are by yourself or engaged in partner sex.

EXERCISES FOR MEN

First Exercise: Body Exploration

Begin with a bath or shower. Soap your body in a leisurely fashion, gently massaging the larger muscle groups: arms, shoulders, neck, back, thighs, and calves. Spend time on your toes and feet. Keep massaging until your body is relaxed. Be aware of the muscle tension in each body part. Healthy muscle has natural tension that does not interfere with relaxed feelings. Anxiety and stress cause the type of muscle tension that produces uncomfortable, tight feelings. Identify psychological and physical tensions you might be feeling and relax these away.

Allow anxiety and tension to drain from your body and replace them with feelings of calm and comfort. Let go and allow yourself to relax. Be aware of physical feelings of warmth, heaviness, and comfort and psychological feelings of calm, confidence, and control.

The coarse spray of a shower provides a good massage. Soak in the warmth. Turn your face into the spray to massage and relax the muscles of your face. Bow your head and let the water run over your head, face, and neck. Let your worries, concerns, or embarrassments drain away. Be receptive to the sensations of your body. Learning to feel relaxed and comfortable takes focus; it is not something men in our culture easily accept. This is your time. Enjoy it!

When you are feeling comfortable and relaxed—not when you think you *should be* feeling that way—get out of the shower and enjoy the feeling of your wet, dripping body. Notice the cooling sensation of water evaporating from your skin. As you dry, use the towel to give yourself a rubdown.

Go to the bedroom in the nude and sprawl on your bed. Be sure the bedroom is warm. Make the room as comfortable as possible. Do what you prefer; put on your favorite music and darken the room if you wish.

Settle back on the bed; close your eyes and relax. Be aware of any tension in your body. The easiest way to identify tension is to deliberately tense muscle groups (arms, legs, back, chest, face) and then to relax and release the tension. Prolong the feelings by letting your muscles relax more and more. To facilitate and enhance feelings of relaxation, breathe deeply and regularly for 2 minutes. Each time you inhale, think the word *relax*; each time you exhale, think the word *calm*. You might repeat to yourself expressions like "relax and feel my body," "let go completely," or "relax more and more, deeper and deeper."

When you are feeling relaxed, double up in a ball and roll to one side. Notice the feelings as you move. Begin touching yourself slowly and gently, first focusing on nongenital areas. Touch your feet, legs, thighs, stomach, chest, lower back, neck, face, arms, and fingers. Experiment with and be aware of different sensations from stroking, rubbing, gentle patting, light touching, and heavy massage. Change positions and enjoy sensuous feelings.

Take time for visual exploration. Look at yourself in the mirror (a full-length mirror is preferable). Take a piece of cardboard or paper and place it in front of one eye (or simply close one eye). Examine half of your body and then switch. Find at least one body part that does not look the same on both sides. Then look at your whole body (front, side, and back views) with both eyes and be aware of at least two nongenital areas you particularly like.

Thus far we have emphasized nongenital examination and touching because men put undue emphasis on their genitals. For example, three-quarters of men worry that their penis is smaller than average. Myths about penis size and its relationship to sexual prowess abound and are blatantly false. There are significant differences in the size of flaccid penises, but in the erect state smaller penises enlarge in length and circumference while larger penises become more firm. In the aroused state there are few differences in penis size. More important, penis size does not affect sexual function since the major nerve endings are in the outer third of a woman's vagina. In addition, the woman's main source of erotic pleasure is her clitoris, which is indirectly stimulated during intercourse. With extremely rare exceptions, penises and vaginas are quite compatible.

Be comfortable with the sight and feel of your genitals rather than obsessive about erection and penile performance. Touch the glans of your penis, frenulum, coronal ridge, and underside of the penile shaft. Examine your scrotum and discover which of your testes is larger. Notice how one testis is lower than the other, and be aware of the sensitivity of the scrotal sac. Observe the placement and feeling of your genitals while standing, sitting, or lying down. Close your eyes and touch the areas again, imagining how they look. Be aware of what parts of your body feel most comfortable and relaxed. End this exercise when you feel comfortable with your whole body, including your genitals.

Second Exercise: Sexual Exploration

Enhance awareness of sensual and sexual feelings. Start with a shower or bath, which has the twofold purpose of cleansing your body and helping you relax. While showering or bathing, be aware of body hair. Which places are hairy and which are hairless? How does it feel to touch your beard? Notice particularly the hair in your armpit and pubic areas, and be sure to wash them. Body secretions and smells can be sensuous and sexual; however, body odor caused by not washing is a turn-off for

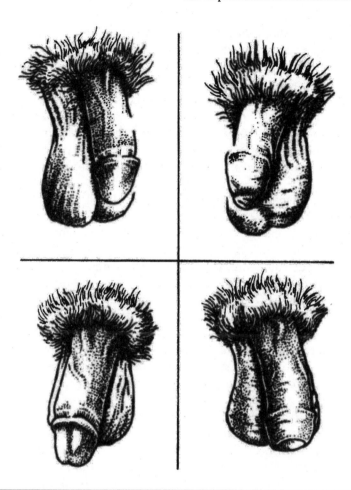

Figure 4.2 Variations in size and shape of external male genitals. Left: penises of uncircumcised males. Right: penises of uncircumcised males.

both you and your partner. Inhale the natural scent of your body. If you use deodorant, talc, cologne, or other products, choose one that has an inviting scent.

Go nude into your bedroom and make yourself comfortable. Begin sensuous touching. Explore touching your breasts. Some men find breast stimulation enjoyable and arousing; others have no particular sensations. Watch your nipples and notice differences when they are soft and hard; note how they become erect when you massage them.

Lying on the bed, place your hands on your knees and slide them upward along the inside of your thighs; note the changes in sensitivity as you approach your genitals. Notice, too, how the hair on your legs thins out until the front of your upper thighs is nearly hairless. Enjoy the feeling of running your fingers through your pubic hair. Touch and massage the soft skin that covers the area between your genitals and anus; this is the perineum, which can be quite responsive to touch.

If at any time you feel anxious or self-conscious, do not stop. Move your hand to a body area where you feel comfortable. Take your time and move at your own pace. This is meant to be an exploring and learning experience; do not pressure yourself to feel arousal. Increase awareness of and comfort with your natural body reactions so that you can share them with your partner.

Now move your hand to your genitals. What type of penile touch is most enjoyable and arousing? Be aware of how it feels to touch your penis when it is flaccid as opposed to erect. Experiment with different types of genital touching; touch your penis using two fingers around the glans, put your hand around the shaft and stroke, let one hand touch your testicles and the other massage the frenulum. Experiment with different types of stimulation. Be aware of the degree of pressure on the shaft that elicits the most pleasure. Play with different rhythms of penile stroking. Carry this to ejaculation if you desire, but do not feel pressure to do so. What kind of genital touching do you find most arousing? Continue self-stimulation until you feel comfortable with your pattern of genital receptivity and responsivity.

Third Exercise: Sexual Pleasure, Arousal, Erotic Flow, and Orgasm

As you become comfortable with your body's sensual and sexual responses, focus on specific feelings of pleasure, arousal, and eroticism. In order to guide your partner and teach her your arousal pattern, you must learn it for yourself. Make the milieu as comfortable as possible in terms of lighting, music, and atmosphere. To increase feelings of desire and arousal, do not hesitate to use written, Internet, or visual materials. Many men find arousal increases when they look at pictures from sex magazines, watch videos, look at Internet porn, or read erotic stories or sexually explicit letters. Experiment and discover what is most arousing for you. Remember, there are no right or wrong, normal or abnormal methods of enhancing your sexual response. Whatever feels sexually arousing is healthy as long as it is not compulsive and is transferable to partner sex.

Erotic fantasies can greatly increase feelings of desire and arousal. Some men fantasize about having intercourse with a movie star, many about exotic positions and situations, and others about group sex or dominant–submissive scenarios. Feel free to utilize a range of erotic fantasies. Do not worry about their content: Fantasy and behavior are different domains. There is no such thing as an abnormal fantasy as long it does not become obsessive or guilt-ridden. Secrecy, eroticism, and shame form a poisonous combination that results in fantasies becoming narrow, compulsive, and self-defeating. The role of erotic fantasies is to enhance desire and erotic flow to orgasm. Fantasies are the most common form of multiple stimulation in masturbation and partner sex. Free yourself by using a variety of erotic fantasies.

The issue of Internet porn and sex addiction is one of the most controversial in the human sexuality field. It is important to note that the great majority of men (80% or more) who occasionally use Internet porn do not abuse it, nor does it subvert their intimate relationship. Porn is all about erotic fantasy, a totally different dimension from real-life sexual desire and partner sex.

It is crucial to recognize that a minority of men (fewer than one in five) do misuse porn in a manner that subverts healthy sexuality for themselves and their intimate relationship. In that situation, the compulsive, addictive use of Internet porn must be confronted and changed because it is destructive for both individual and couple sexuality. For some the change process is relatively simple, such as asking for help from your intimate partner or a close friend and blocking specific porn sites. For other men, it is a difficult, challenging process that entails using a number of resources including a Sex Addicts Anonymous (SAA) group and a sponsor in addition to individual or couple therapy and medication. You'll find resources for choosing a therapist in Appendix B.

Begin touching with a focus on sensual feelings. A major trap men fall into is making masturbation rapid, strictly genitally oriented and orgasm driven. This can result in a pattern of goal-oriented sex performance and premature ejaculation during couple sex. Slow down and enjoy the pleasure/arousal/eroticism/orgasm process. Notice the feelings in your genitals and in your whole body as erotic flow builds. Focus on the type of stimulation that enhances arousal and allows you to be orgasmic (i.e., orgasm triggers). This might be a slow, gradually increasing movement of your hand along the shaft of the penis, rubbing the area around the frenulum and glans, one hand massaging your scrotum while the fingers of your other hand manipulate the glans. Do what is most arousing for you.

When you ejaculate, be aware of the pleasurable feeling of sexual release. Enjoy your sexual arousal and orgasm. Be aware and accepting of your semen. You might want to look at the semen, touch it, and perhaps even taste it. It is a natural, positive aspect of you. Allow yourself to bask in the healthy, natural feelings of your body and sexual responsivity as arousal naturally culminates in orgasm.

Fourth Exercise: Integration

Focus on integrating sexual scenarios and techniques. Experiment with different techniques of self-stimulation to increase awareness of the variety of sensual and sexual experiences. Do not fall into the trap of touching being completely genitally or orgasm oriented.

Enhance your mood by using music, relaxation, lighting, atmosphere. Begin with sensual whole-body touch before focusing on your genitals and penis. Experiment with a lotion to increase sensations. Feel free to use erotic fantasies and materials, but do not fall into the pattern of Internet porn controlling your sexuality.

Rather than utilizing touch as the only form of stimulation, try a different means of arousal. Turn over and rub your penis against the sheets of the bed or perhaps against a blanket or pillow between your legs. Feel the sensations on your thighs, buttocks, and chest. Be aware of your entire body as you stroke and enjoy feelings in your scrotum and penis. Focus on what you find to be the most enjoyable type and amount of genital pressure. A consistent stimulation rhythm builds erotic flow that leads to orgasm.

You might experiment with the stop–start technique of stimulation. Be aware of the point of ejaculatory inevitability, the period 1 to 3 seconds before ejaculation begins. The point of ejaculatory inevitability is the beginning of the orgasm phase. After this point is reached, orgasm is no longer a voluntary response; you will ejaculate even if your mother-in-law walks in on you. Allow yourself to experiment with and experience different types of penile stroking and massaging (circular, patting, heavy touch, light touch). Let yourself go and feel the maximum in sensuality and sexuality as you experience arousal, erotic flow, and orgasm.

CLOSING THOUGHTS: MEN

Self-exploration and masturbation exercises allow you to experience your body in sensual and sexual ways. You can be comfortable with your whole body and its natural, healthy responsiveness rather than focus your attention only on your penis and the 3 to 10 seconds of orgasm. As awareness and comfort increase, it will be easier to share with your partner. A mixture of sensual nongenital touching and genital touching enhances pleasure and arousal during partner sex. Goal-oriented sexual experiences are less satisfying than sensual, pleasurable, playful, erotic, mutually arousing experiences that naturally flow into orgasm. You have taken an important step toward understanding and accepting your sexuality.

5

NONDEMAND PLEASURING

The Key to Sexual Intimacy

One of the most widely believed and harmful myths is that all touching must end in intercourse. Sexual expression is crippled by the idea that you cannot just enjoy sensual or playful touch. Every physical intimacy is an invitation to intercourse—basically turns it into a demand for a goal-oriented sexual performance.

Spontaneity and openness increase the quality and quantity of intimacy and offer the freedom to express sensual and sexual feelings and give and receive pleasure without expectations or demands. The focus is on the enjoyment of being together, not on an arbitrary idea of what you should be doing and where you should be doing it. You can enjoy touching in a nondemanding atmosphere both inside and outside your bedroom.

Sexual pleasure is enhanced if you feel free to engage in clothes-on affectionate touching and clothes-off sexual touching. This increases warm, caring feelings. It also serves as a bridge to sexual desire, which might be crossed at that time or later. However, the bridge is blocked if touching is seen as a demand for intercourse. The key to a vital and satisfying sexual relationship lies in the value that both partners place on integrating intimacy, nondemand pleasuring, and eroticism. The essence of healthy couple sexuality is giving and receiving pleasure. Demands, intercourse pressure, and seeing sex as a performance subvert healthy couple sexuality. Sexual desire is enhanced by freedom and choice and is undermined by demands and pressure.

SHARING THOUGHTS AND FEELINGS

Much stress and confusion exist because people do not share how they feel about being together or tell one another how much they enjoy being close and affectionate, including when they want to be playful but not sexual. A sexual relationship based on the myth that satisfaction lies only in both partners achieving orgasm, or the even more harmful myth that simultaneous orgasm should be the goal, subverts couple sexuality with its narrow focus and perfectionist performance pressure. It is great to be orgasmic, or even orgasmic simultaneously, but to believe that intercourse and orgasm *must* happen during every intimate encounter is dangerous for sexual desire and satisfaction. This negates spontaneity and puts stringent demands on what should be an enjoyable, free-flowing sensual and sexual experience.

When you develop a comfortable couple style of giving and receiving pleasure and sharing intimacy in a nondemand atmosphere, you will experience enhanced sexual desire, pleasure, eroticism, and satisfaction. However, when intercourse and orgasm become the criteria for success, your sexual relationship loses. The mantra of desire, pleasure, eroticism, and satisfaction is enhanced if both partners value nondemand pleasuring. You can share fulfilling intimacy simply by being together and engaging in affectionate touch, sensual pleasure, playful sexuality, and erotic nonintercourse sexuality. This nondemand attitude and pleasure orientation turns your intimate moments into a win–win situation.

TOUCHING

Touching is integral to your intimate relationship. Touching allows both partners to express feelings of warmth and caring. Spontaneous touching in nondemand positions and situations, without expectancy that sexual intercourse *must* follow, keeps your relationship free. This open attitude promotes affection, sensuality, playfulness, and sexual desire. If you choose to proceed to intercourse, the decision is free-flowing, cued by involvement and arousal rather than by the feeling, "We've gone this far; we have to go all the way." When it's "intercourse or nothing," nothing eventually wins out.

A helpful and motivating metaphor for touching involves "five gears." First gear is clothes-on affectionate touch (holding hands, kissing, hugging). Second gear is nongenital sensual touch, which may be done clothed, semiclothed, or nude (massage, cuddling on the couch, touching while going to sleep or on awakening). Third gear is playful touch, which intermixes genital and nongenital touching, clothed or unclothed, which may take place in bed, while dancing, in the shower, or on the couch. Fourth gear is erotic touch (manual, oral, rubbing, or vibrator stimulation), which can lead to arousal and orgasm for one or both partners. Fifth gear integrates pleasurable and erotic touch that flows into intercourse.

Nondemand touching does not have to occur principally in bed or even in the bedroom. Keeping a relationship fresh and spontaneous involves a willingness to experiment with touching at various times, in various places and situations. It is inappropriate to engage in sexually arousing touching in a public place such as a street corner, but being sexual on a deserted beach, during a walk in a wooded area, or in a car parked by a lake adds spice to your relationship. More comfortable is touching in the privacy of your house—using all the rooms, including the rug in front of the fireplace, the big chair in the living room, the dining room table, or even the kitchen floor.

One variation to explore is clothing. Most sexual encounters involve nudity. This is fine. Yet why limit pleasure in that manner. The woman who appears wearing only a shirt can be quite enticing, as can the man wearing only his pants. We dress attractively when in public, so what about dressing attractively, seductively, or playfully for your partner?

Another interesting and exciting variation involves positioning. There is no right or normal position for sexual activity. We suggest pleasuring positions to facilitate exploration. We also suggest experimentation with intercourse positions, patterns of initiating sexual activity, and variations on the way you play during intercourse. In addition, we encourage experimenting with afterplay scenarios and techniques.

Nondemand pleasuring keeps spontaneity, experimentation, unpredictability, and communication alive in your relationship. The couple that enjoys affectionate exchanges such as kissing, holding hands, and hugging has a solid intimate base. This is enhanced by sensual and playful experiences such as showering together, head or back massages, whole body massages using lotion, or dancing semiclothed. These scenarios and techniques are valuable in themselves and also serve as bridges to sexual desire.

JEAN AND DAVID

Jean and David are an example of a couple who value nondemand pleasuring, have been married for 22 years, and feel satisfied with their sexual relationship now more than ever. The last of their two children is about to leave for college, and they are looking forward to "being a couple again."

Although not "feely-touchy" in public or at parties, they are warm and affectionate in private. Both are busy but consciously set aside couple time without the distractions of children, household tasks, bills, or practical decisions. Couple time involves taking walks, having a glass of wine or cup of tea while sitting on the porch, lying in bed talking and caressing, or going out for a cup of coffee and dessert. Their conversation is about ordinary things, but each knows that if there were something serious or difficult to be discussed their spouse would be receptive.

Typically, couple time involves affectionate and playful touching. Depending on moods and circumstances, about one-third of the time this proceeds to intercourse. David and Jean have learned to communicate what they want and do not want sexually. The majority of their sexual activities are mutually involving and culminate in intercourse. When Jean is not aroused and does not feel like a "quickie," she will pleasure David to orgasm. This does not feel like she's mechanically "doing" David; rather it feels as if she is "giving" to him and enjoying his arousal. When Jean is aroused and wants to be orgasmic but David is not feeling sexually desirous, he is open to giving her oral stimulation. Occasionally, they get their signals crossed and have a "blah" or negative experience. They accept that, laugh it off, and try again the next day when they are feeling more receptive and desirous. They hold to a 48-hour guideline: If they have a frustrating experience, they will do something sensual or sexual within 2 days rather than let negative thoughts and feelings fester.

EXERCISES FOR ENHANCING NONDEMAND SEXUALITY

First Exercise: Communicating Alternatives

Discuss feelings about nondemand touching. Be aware when and how you feel sexual pressure that diminishes spontaneity and playfulness. In these exercises, there is no demand involved. Your desires and choices are what count. Develop and refine a "signal system" that tells your partner whether you desire to proceed to intercourse. This communication may be verbal, such as "I really want to make love," "I'm not in the mood to screw," "Let's get it on," "Let me just hold you," or "I've enjoyed this; let it be." The communication also could be nonverbal—for example, massaging your partner's genitals and switching to an intercourse position, moving to sensuous pleasuring, using eye contact to say yes or no, or moving your partner's hands to or from your genitals. Your partner can answer with a signal that says, "Okay," or "Not tonight; let's just play." However, don't stop at saying or signaling "no." Suggest something you would like to engage in: a backrub, lying and talking, holding each other, taking a sensuous bath, giving manual or oral sex, taking a walk, cuddling, and going to sleep. Remember, pleasure-oriented touching is the key to couple intimacy, not sexual performance.

Begin this exercise nude in your bedroom. Lying on the bed, the woman positions herself behind her partner with their entire bodies touching, her chest to his back, her knees bent inside his, her arms around his body while he holds her hands. This is a nice position in which to lie together and feel close and connected. He is in a protected and passive position, allowing himself to feel cared for.

In this scenario, it is the woman's prerogative to indicate whether she wants to extend pleasuring into intercourse. You can use any signal system you want, verbal or nonverbal. The criterion of effectiveness is whether he clearly receives and understands your communication. If your signal is positive, he can say whether he also desires intercourse. Couples make a mistake in assuming that the man always wants intercourse and must accede to your initiation. This sets unrealistic expectations and pressures.

The optimal relationship is one in which both partners feel comfortable initiating intercourse and both feel they have the right to say no. If he does not desire intercourse, he can suggest an alternative way to connect. One possibility is to hold each other and talk. Another might be manually or orally stimulating you to orgasm. Another is engaging in whole-body pleasuring. If you signal you do not desire intercourse, suggest an alternative sensual or erotic experience. Possibilities include sleeping in this position, pleasuring him to orgasm manually or orally, or engaging in mutual genital stimulation that could proceed to orgasm for one or both.

If you or he becomes highly aroused, the usual pattern is to go to intercourse. This is especially true when you have just recently become a sexual couple and sexual frequency is the focus. This is fine, but it is not a realistic model for sex in a serious relationship. Nothing bad happens if arousal does not culminate in intercourse or orgasm. Sexual expression is a choice, not a demand. Many women see his erection as a demand for intercourse, so they don't engage in touching unless they want intercourse. This is a loss for you, him, and your intimate relationship.

Discuss your experience in the morning, focusing on how comfortable and clear your communication system was. If there was a problem, what would you be willing to try next time to improve the communication process and sexual experience? Be aware there are a number of affectionate, sensual, playful, and erotic alternatives (remember the five-gear metaphor). Sexuality is not intercourse or nothing.

Second Exercise: Change of Setting

Are you as comfortable initiating intercourse as having a sensual experience? Does your partner accept your request or change it to something different? If you decide not to continue to intercourse, are there feelings of pressure, grumbling, or rejection? If there are difficulties or miscommunication, feel free to repeat the first exercise or use the same roles (woman initiating, man responding) with this set of exercises. If things went well last time, let him decide whether to continue to intercourse.

Choose a place other than the bedroom. It can be the living room, den, guest bedroom, bathroom, basement—anywhere you choose. This exercise is best done in the nude so you can be comfortable with nudity outside the bedroom. Be sure you will not be disturbed by children. Being affectionate in front of children and with children is positive. However, engaging in sensual or erotic activity in front of children is not healthy for adults or for the children. Sexuality involves privacy, comfort, and personal space. Children who grow up in families surrounded by overt sexuality find that as adults they are no less uncomfortable than those from families where there was no touching or communication about sexuality. You want your children to feel comfortable, not intimidated, with their bodies and sexual issues.

The man can lie on his stomach, arms extended over his head, resting on cushions or pillows. Lying on her side, the woman covers your arms and with one hand holds your hand. Her other hand is free to caress your back. One leg is placed over yours for more contact. This position allows her to touch and caress your body. You can be passive or return the caresses. Since men tend to become active and initiating, she may have to remind you that this is a nondemand position where the pleasuring and caressing come from her. This position—as other nondemand positions—can be reversed, with you covering, holding, and caressing her.

It is the man's prerogative to decide whether to continue to intercourse. Use a verbal or nonverbal signal to communicate whether you want to continue nondemand pleasuring or proceed to intercourse. Be aware of your feelings and desires. If you signal that you want to proceed to intercourse, it is because you want to, not because you are expected to. She in turn responds by indicating what she really wants rather than doing what you want or what she thinks she "should" do. She should have no fear of your disapproval or repercussions. This is especially important because she may have come to view your erection as a demand for sex rather than as a sign of pleasure and responsivity. Couple sexual functioning improves when both partners are aware of feelings and desires and communicate them clearly and directly. If desires are different, it is easier to resolve them by suggesting an alternative sensual or erotic activity rather than by just saying no. If you communicate honestly, you will usually discover a way of proceeding that is good for both of you. Remember, your intimate relationship is based on a positive-influence process. "Intimate coercion" poisons sexual desire.

Third Exercise: Undressing and Mutual Scenarios

You are developing a growing awareness of the benefits of nondemand pleasuring. Learning to value pleasuring for its own sake enhances sexual intercourse when you decide to continue and can be an affirmation of you as an intimate couple when you choose to remain sensual, to be playful, or to engage in erotic, nonintercourse sex. To make nondemand pleasuring more like your real-life sexual relationship, it is worthwhile to experiment with the amount of clothing you wear as well as locations in which to be intimate.

Begin by disrobing your partner slowly or teasingly to a state of undress (other than nudity) that you find appealing. Undress your partner in a manner that is seductive or playful. Some women find their man most enticing when he is wearing only underwear. Others like him fully clothed on top and nude on the bottom. Do what you like. Some men like their partners best in an unbuttoned blouse and panties or nude on the bottom and wearing the man's shirt and a headband. Your personal tastes are what matter.

The man can sit propped on pillows with his legs spread. The woman can lie between his spread legs with her knees near the side of his body. Use pillows to support your lower back so you are in a comfortable position to look and touch. Rather than one partner being initiator, this position encourages both of you to give and receive pleasurable and erotic touch. Use eye contact to communicate feelings. Be receptive and responsive to pleasuring and eroticism.

The decision whether to proceed to intercourse is mutual. Follow your feelings instead of doing what you think your partner expects. You can communicate with your eyes, hands, and body—verbal communication is not required. When you rhythmically thrust your body against him, this clearly communicates your desires. Continue to work toward establishing a clear, honest, and mutually acceptable communication system. You can feel comfortable with a range of affectionate, sensual, playful, erotic alternatives. Intercourse can range from a "quickie" to prolonged, passionate lovemaking.

Fourth Exercise: Mutuality and Choice

Discuss whether you have fallen into any traps, such as having intercourse every time you engage in touching and pleasuring, not establishing a sensual way to enjoy each other, not negotiating a positive sexual scenario if one partner does not want intercourse, or finding that one partner always pushes for intercourse and the other wants an alternative. If you have fallen into a rut, discuss how to develop your flexible, variable couple sexual style. Being aware of traps allows you to monitor them so they do not interfere with developing a vital, satisfying sexual relationship. Be especially aware of the trap of inflexible male–female sex roles and pursuer–distancer relationship roles. Satisfying sexuality, particularly for serious couples, involves flexibility, variability, and sharing. There is no place for intimate coercion in couple sexuality.

Approach this exercise with the atmosphere and clothing most conducive for an inviting sexual scenario. Begin with the man lying on top of his partner. You can move slowly down her body until your head is resting on the soft area beneath her rib cage. Put your arms around her, with her hands free to caress your head and shoulders. This arrangement can be particularly arousing because it positions you so that you can easily caress her genitals. There is little eye contact, but sometimes that too can be arousing. The decision whether to continue nondemand pleasuring, move on to erotic sex, or switch to intercourse is mutual. This experience will provide an opportunity to test your signaling system because you will not have eye contact. Be aware of your needs while being in tune with your partner's receptivity so that the sexual scenario allows you both to feel your needs and desires have been understood and accepted.

CLOSING THOUGHTS

Comfort with nondemand pleasuring is integral to a successful sexual relationship. The knowledge that not all touching is goal directed and intercourse oriented enhances intimacy, spontaneity, playfulness, and sexual desire. A good guideline is that at least once every 3 months (and preferably each month) you can reserve an evening for nondemand pleasuring that does not end in intercourse.

Touch is of value both inside and outside the bedroom. Being affectionate is good for your relationship and provides a positive model for your children. Perhaps the best sex education children can have is to see their parents hugging, kissing, and caring about each other.

The message to them is that the parents feel good about themselves as a couple. Knowing that Mom and Dad love each other is reassuring for children, as is the realization that there is affection (and sexuality) after marriage.

The sexual scenarios and techniques suggested here are just a few of the many possibilities that can help you be an intimate sexual team. They can be reversed and varied. It can be fun to explore different feelings, degrees of pleasure, and ways of connecting. To deepen your intimacy, continue to explore pleasuring positions, refine your communication system, introduce erotic scenarios and techniques, enjoy both mutual and asynchronous sexual experiences, experiment with intercourse positions and scenarios, and be open to both spontaneous and planned sexual encounters.

6

DEVELOPING YOUR COUPLE SEXUAL STYLE

The majority of couples begin their relationship in a blaze of romantic love, passionate sex, and idealism. Typically, couples have very positive memories of that 6-month to 2-year relationship phase. However, healthy couples, whether married or in a serious relationship, are aware that for sexuality to continue to play a positive 15 to 20% role in their lives they need to develop a couple sexual style that integrates intimacy and eroticism and balances each person's "sexual voice" with being a sexual team.

The traditional belief was that the more intimacy and communication, the better the sex. This is a seductive approach that on the surface seems to make sense. However, it is not true for the majority of couples. Although we are in favor of good communication and genuine intimacy, this is only half the story. Intimacy alone does not ensure strong, vital sexual desire. Healthy couple sexuality requires finding a mutually comfortable level of intimacy, valuing nondemand pleasuring, adding erotic scenarios and techniques, and establishing positive, realistic sexual expectations.

COMMON COUPLE SEXUAL STYLES

Relational styles are based on how couples deal with differences and conflicts. Your couple sexual style depends on the way you balance intimacy and eroticism. No matter what you read or hear about "ideal sex," the truth is that sexually one size does not fit all.

The most common couple sexual styles are as follows:

- Complementary: mine and ours
- Traditional: conflict-minimizing

- Soul mate: best friends
- Emotionally expressive: fun and erotic

The key for you as a couple is to find a mutually comfortable balance between allowing each person's sexual voice to be heard and forming a sexual team whose integration of intimacy and eroticism facilitates sexual desire and satisfaction. Let us carefully exam the strengths and vulnerabilities of each of the major couple sexual styles.

Complementary Couple Sexual Style

This is the most commonly chosen couple sexual style. It emphasizes that each person has a positive sexual voice within a securely bonded relationship. Both partners value intimacy and eroticism. You are not clones of each other, but you do value your partner's feelings and preferences in terms of initiation, pleasure, and eroticism. A particular strength of the complementary sexual style is its "his," "her," and "our" bridges to sexual desire. This style both affirms autonomy and reinforces the crucial importance of being an intimate, erotic team.

The vulnerability of the complementary sexual style is treating your sexual relationship with "benign neglect." It is easy to allow sex to go on automatic pilot. Couple sexuality cannot rest on its laurels: Your sexual relationship needs new energy and inputs. As life changes—whether this change involves the birth of a child, parenting adolescents, or retirement—your sexual style needs to adapt so that you reestablish a sense of equity and sexual vitality.

Traditional Couple Sexual Style

The major strength of the traditional sexual style is that both partners understand and accept that their sexual relationship is organized around traditional gender roles. It is the man's role to initiate intercourse with a focus on the frequency of sexual encounters, while intimacy and affection is the woman's domain. Sex is seldom a source of conflict and requires minimum negotiation. This style emphasizes the core role of marriage, children, family, and religion and results in the most stable marital bond. In addition, same-gender friends are supportive of you and your relationship and joke about the foibles of the opposite sex. A strength (although also a problem) is that if and when the marriage becomes nonsexual, the spouses accept this as normal.

There are two major vulnerabilities for the couple that selects the traditional sexual style. The first is that as the man ages, his ability to achieve predictable, autonomous erections decreases as his vascular and neurological systems become less efficient and are particularly vulnerable to side effects of medications. The traditional man feels he should not need to turn to his partner for physical stimulation and emotional support. Thus, traditional men often stop being sexual in their 50s or 60s because they've lost confidence in erections and intercourse. They allow frustration and embarrassment to control them and eventually avoid any type of couple sex. The good news is that many men turn to their partner as an intimate sexual friend and adopt the Good Enough Sex (GES) model, which allows the traditional couple to enjoy sexuality with aging.

The second major vulnerability of the traditional sexual style is that the woman feels her needs for intimacy and affection are negated and overwhelmed by his demand for intercourse. She feels that she and her partner are not an intimate team, so she avoids sensual, playful, and erotic touch because she sees it as inevitably leading to intercourse. Traditional couples do better when they maintain affectionate connection. However, even when there is disappointment about intimacy and sexuality, traditional couples are at the least risk for divorce.

Soul Mate Couple Sexual Style

Traditionally, this was believed to be the ideal sexual style. Soul mate couples have a high degree of intimacy, communication, and mutuality. The partners are best friends and feel accepted, cared for, and loved. Being intimately connected is more highly valued than intercourse frequency. Feeling loved and accepted for who you really are and trusting that your partner "has your back" is highly validating. When this sexual style functions well, it is emotionally and sexually affirming.

Unfortunately, there are several vulnerabilities in the soul mate sexual style. The major one is that the couple feels so intimate that the partners "de-eroticize" each other. Another is that the overemphasis on mutuality causes them to have lower sexual frequency because sexual needs are not always mutual. Additionally, this is the couple style that is least resilient when dealing with conflict, like an extramarital affair. They remain stuck in the quagmire of thinking, "How could my best friend betray me?" rather than focusing on the healing and recovery process. An additional vulnerability is feeling that your partner and relationship do not live up to the high expectations inherent in the soul mate couple sexual style.

Emotionally Expressive Couple Sexual Style

This is the fun and erotic sexual style emphasized in novels and movies. Other couples envy this playful and sexually liberated couple and admire their vibrant and fun approach to sexuality. Major strengths include being a resilient couple, enjoying freedom from traditional cultural constraints, valuing erotic play, and utilizing role enactment scenarios (playing out erotic fantasies, using sex toys or erotic videos, and sexual role-playing).

The biggest vulnerability of the emotionally expressive sexual style is instability. This is the least secure couple sexual style. In essence, there is too much drama, which wears out the partners emotionally and drains intimacy. Resilience is a strength; however, after healing from a series of major fights or affairs the couple runs out of steam, and vital, passionate sex gives way to blame and bitterness. Maintaining clear boundaries and a firm commitment to being nondestructive is crucial for the emotionally expressive couple.

COMMITTING TO A SEXUAL STYLE

Each couple creates a unique balance of autonomy and coupleness and develops a special way to blend intimacy and eroticism. It is crucial to create a couple sexual style that is mutually comfortable and functional. If one partner demands the emotionally expressive style and the other prefers the traditional style, their sexual relationship will be a continual self-defeating power struggle where no one wins and your relationship loses.

Once you've emotionally committed to a couple sexual style that is the right fit for you, play to the strengths of your chosen style while being aware of the vulnerabilities so you can avoid these traps. Remember, the key concept is that you want intimacy, pleasuring, and eroticism to contribute 15 to 20% to overall relationship vitality and satisfaction.

LYNNETTE AND CONRAD

The first 10 months of Conrad and Lynnette's relationship were very exciting and special. Theirs was an idealized couple relationship, characterized by romantic love and passionate sex. Unfortunately, Lynnette and Conrad, like most couples, were not aware that the challenge for serious relationships is to create a couple sexual style that will continue to promote desire, pleasure, eroticism, and satisfaction long after the first bloom of being in love fades. They blamed decreased sexual desire and frequency on the transition to living together and then on the stress of negotiating the logistics and details of the wedding. They hoped that being married would magically reignite passionate sex—an unrealistic expectation. The essence of a stable, satisfying marriage is respect, trust, and commitment. This is a sound foundation, but in itself this does not promote healthy couple sexuality.

The time to build a strong, resilient couple sexual style is early in a marriage rather than after 10 years of confusion, demoralization, and blame–counterblame. Lynette and Conrad were confused and frustrated that their sexual relationship was more of a struggle than a pleasure and energizer. Fortunately, their best couple friends loaned them *Discovering Your Couple Sexual Style,* and after reading and discussing the suggestions it contained Lynnette and Conrad were motivated to create a sexual style to suit their situation. Rather than continue with the cycle of Conrad arguing for more frequent sex and Lynnette feeling that her needs for intimacy and playfulness were being ignored, they chose the complementary sexual style. The classic power struggle that controls so many couples is the conflict of sex frequency versus intimacy. People engaged in power struggles do not focus on achieving a "winning" relationship and instead fight against being the person who "loses."

Sexuality is a "team sport." In adopting the complementary sexual style, Conrad and Lynette felt that they were validating each person's sexual voice. Their joint challenge was to integrate intimacy and eroticism into marital sexuality so it energizes their bond and encourages both of them to desire and feel desirable. In couple sex therapy, the most chosen sexual style is complementary because it best fits the model of personal responsibility for sexuality while being part of an intimate team. However, it is not the right sexual style for all couples.

The focus of the following couple psychosexual skill exercises is to discover the right sexual style for you. Play to the strengths of your chosen style but ensure that you do not fall into its inherent "traps."

EXERCISES TO DETERMINE SEXUAL STYLE

First Exercise: Choosing the Right Sexual Style for You

Discuss the following questions. Do not try to be "politically correct" or to second-guess your partner. Be honest and forthcoming:

1. How important is sex in your life? How important is your sexual relationship?
2. In terms of affectionate touch, do you prefer kissing, holding hands, or hugging?
3. How do you distinguish affectionate touch from sensual touch?
4. How much do you enjoy sensual touch? Do you prefer taking turns or mutually giving and receiving?
5. What is the meaning and value of playful touch? Do you enjoy nicknames for your genitals and sexual activities? What is your favorite playful sexual scenario?

6. How much do you enjoy erotic scenarios and techniques? Do you prefer multiple stimulation or single stimulation? Taking turns or mutual stimulation? Using external stimuli (sex toys, videos, playing out fantasies)? Do you enjoy erotic sex as a route to orgasm or only as a pleasuring experience?
7. What is your preferred intercourse position? Man on top, woman on top, rear entry, side by side? What type of thrusting do you prefer? In and out? Circular? Deep inside? Fast or slow? Do you enjoy multiple stimulation during intercourse?
8. How much do you value afterplay as part of your couple sexual style?

Compare your answers with your partner's, clarifying both practical and emotional dimensions. Remember, you are not clones of each other. You want to maintain your individuality and not feel embarrassed or apologetic about your emotional and sexual desires. Your preferences and sensitivities are part of who you are as a sexual person and need to be integrated into your couple sexual style for you to be truly satisfied.

Divide your answers into three categories.

1. **Areas you agree on**. These will enhance your enjoyment and satisfaction. For example, you may agree that you want sexuality to play an energizing role in your relationship and that you value verbally sharing and bonding afterplay.
2. **Areas on which you can reach agreement**. Identify differences you can accept and even enjoy. The partner who more highly values sex agrees to be the initiator the majority of time. If you would rather engage in touching standing up and your partner prefers lying down or if the man prefers woman-on-top intercourse while she prefers side by side, you can integrate your preferences or take turns. Enjoy your partner's sexual preferences and responses. Remember, an involved, aroused partner is the best aphrodisiac.
3. **Differences to accept or adapt to**. Identify areas of differences. For example, sex may be the major means of connection for you while your partner emphasizes social activities; you love playful touch, but your partner is uncomfortable with playful touch; you want to use a vibrator during intercourse to help you be orgasmic, but he is put off by the vibrator; he wants to experiment with porn videos, which you see as degrading to women. It is not easy to deal with these differences, but there are two major coping strategies. One is to accept the differences without letting them turn into a power struggle. Instead, acknowledge

and work around them. It is crucial to recognize that differences do not mean rejection. The second strategy is to agree to enter couple therapy to understand the meaning of the differences, and find mutual solid ground for intimacy and sexuality.

To develop your comfortable, pleasurable, functional, and mutually satisfying couple sexual style, take personal responsibility for your sexuality and your growth as a unique, intimate team. Respectfully sharing emotional and sexual feelings and preferences increases understanding, empathy, and acceptance.

Second Exercise: Valuing Both Intimacy and Eroticism

This exercise facilitates being personal and concrete about the role and meaning of intimacy and eroticism for each of you and helps integrate intimacy and eroticism into your couple sexual style. While the usual starting point would be intimacy, as a challenge we will start with eroticism.

Let the woman begin. Share with your partner an experience when you felt desirable, sexy, turned-on, and really let go sexually. What was it about you, him, the setting, the mood, and external stimuli that allowed you to feel erotically charged? Share both the erotic scenario as well as what gave this experience special meaning. What did you do to feel and invite eroticism? How did your partner invite, facilitate, and elicit your eroticism? In terms of your arousal preferences, do you prefer partner-interaction arousal, self-entrancement arousal, role-enactment arousal, or a combination of arousal styles? How important are your partner's erotic feelings and response in creating your erotic receptivity and responsivity?

Next, it is the man's responsibility to design an erotic scenario. It is important not to make this "tit for tat" or to prove how erotic you can be. Rather, what are the erotic scenarios and techniques that you find the most engaging? Afterward, sit and talk outside of the bedroom setting. Make one to three requests of each other to enhance eroticism in your relationship.

Now, let us focus on intimacy. This time the man initiates first. What allows you to feel close, safe, warm, and emotionally and physically open? At its core, intimacy involves acceptance as well as affectionate and sensual touch—a way of being with each other in a warm, meaningful manner. Intimacy is about safety and closeness, which is a very different connection than eroticism.

What do you as a man value in a physical and emotional intimate experience? What types of touch facilitate intimate feelings: holding hands, hugging, lying together in your trust position, giving or receiving a sensual massage, enjoying a Jacuzzi together, cuddling on the couch, or lying together in bed before going to sleep? Instead of trying to impress or please your partner, honestly state what types of emotional feelings and expression facilitate intimacy for you personally. For some men, verbalizing facilitates intimacy; for others the key is silence or breathing in tandem. For some men, the important emotion is feeling safe, for others it is predictability, and for still others it is feelings of acceptance.

Then it is the woman's turn to initiate and share an intimacy experience. Again, this is not a question of who is "right" about intimacy. Don't try to impress or lobby your partner. Share with him your unique way of feeling and experiencing intimacy.

Next, have a couple discussion. What facilitates intimacy for you as a couple? Share your awareness and understanding of the different roles and meanings of intimacy.

The last phase of this exercise is the most challenging—how to integrate your new learnings into your couple sexual style. You want to experience both closeness and sexual vitality. Rather than fall into the power struggles of intimacy versus eroticism or my way versus your way, establish a couple sexual style that energizes your bond.

Third Exercise: Adopting a Comfortable, Functional Couple Sexual Style

Your couple sexual style is not "pure," but it is crucial to agree on the basic structure of who you are as an intimate and erotic team. Organize your couple sexuality so that it affirms your sexual voice and allows you to feel intimate and erotic.

Each partner states which one or two couple sexual styles would be the best fit as well as what couple sexual styles would not be right for them. This is not a rational decision-making exercise but an attitudinal, behavioral, and emotional commitment of who you want to be as a sexual team. Ideally, both partners would choose the same couple sexual style.

When there is not agreement, engage in a positive, focused emotional exploration of why the sexual style each of you prefers would be good for you as a couple. Do not go into demand/attack mode. Instead, share with your partner what the key elements are in your sexual voice, what you most value about being an intimate team, and your preferred balance of intimacy and eroticism. Listen empathically and respectfully to your partner's preferences, feelings, and values. Healthy relationships are based on a positive-influence process. Stay away from power struggles. Adopt a couple sexual style that is comfortable, functional, and works for both of you. You want to find genuine common ground in which sexuality will thrive. Within your couple sexual framework, you can individualize components so that it uniquely fits you as sexual individuals and as a sexual couple.

Fourth Exercise: Monitoring the Vulnerabilities of Your Chosen Couple Sexual Style

Each sexual style has its vulnerabilities (traps). You and your partner need to be aware of these so you don't fall into them. Commit to taking action to avoid these traps. Since you've already chosen your couple sexual style you don't have to do all four dimensions of this exercise, only the one relevant to your couple sexual style.

Complementary Couple Sexual Style There are two main traps to avoid. The first is taking your sexual relationship for granted. The second trap to watch for is letting your couple sexuality suffer when there is a change in your life circumstances—especially becoming parents. Awareness of these vulnerabilities is important, but what is even more important is the commitment to do something positive to counter them.

To avoid treating couple sexuality with benign neglect, you need to devote time and energy to your sexual relationship whether you've been a couple for 5, 20, or 40 years. We suggest that every 6 months you introduce a new intimacy, pleasuring, erotic, intercourse, or afterplay scenario. Then it's your partner's turn to initiate something new during the next 6 months. Ideally, each year two new sexual scenarios or techniques would be added to your complementary sexual style, ensuring that it remain vital and satisfying. Change could involve something relatively small such as trying a different lotion for a sexual massage, a different intercourse position or thrusting rhythm, or being sexual in the morning or early evening rather than just at night. Or you might implement a significant change such as going away for a couple weekend without children for the first time in 3 years, introducing a one-way (asynchronous) erotic scenario, or using a vibrator during couple sex.

For the second vulnerability, the challenge is to accept the lifestyle change while reestablishing a sense of emotional, practical, and sexual equity. Reinforce that the most important bond in your family is the bond with your partner. Remember, the role of intimacy and sexuality is to energize your bond and reinforce feelings of desire and desirability. Initiate a couple date to reenergize your intimate bond.

Traditional Couple Sexual Style There are two major vulnerabilities for your chosen sexual style. The first is that as the man begins to age in his 40s and 50s he is no longer able to function autonomously as far as erections are concerned and needs partner involvement and genital stimulation. The second trap is that the woman feels her needs for intimacy and touching are not validated; rather, they are overridden by his needs for intercourse.

In addressing these traps realize that as you age you need to rely on each other more to maintain sexual desire and satisfaction. Before sexuality becomes a crisis, our suggestion is that once every 3 or 6 months the woman initiates a sexual date and the man initiates an intimacy date with a prohibition on intercourse. You can respect traditional gender roles while adding positive dimensions to your chosen couple sexual style.

Soul Mate Couple Sexual Style The major vulnerability in your chosen couple style is that there is so much closeness that you de-eroticize each other. A second vulnerability is that the requirement for mutuality in sexual desire results in infrequent sexual encounters. To address the first trap it is important to reinforce each partner's sexual voice. A good way to do that is for each partner to initiate a playful sexual scenario. Couple sexuality can be "spiced up" by sexual playfulness. You can introduce sexual nicknames for genitals, use sex toys, or play out a creative sexual scenario. In terms of the second trap, while mutuality is a good thing, if every feeling and scenario must be mutual it becomes oppressive. A positive intervention would be for each partner to initiate a "selfish" sexual scenario every 6 months or even more frequently. This confronts the tyranny of mutuality. Soul mate couples need to be sure that playfulness and eroticism remain present so you continue as a sexually energized couple.

Emotionally Expressive Couple Sexual Style The vulnerabilities—and thus the interventions—for this fun and erotic couple style are totally different from those of the other sexual styles. The first of the two major vulnerabilities is in the heat of the moment saying or doing extremely destructive things (dropping "atomic bombs"). Second, the frequency and intensity of ongoing emotional and sexual drama wear out the partners and the relationship.

The intervention to stop the "atomic bombs" involves telling your partner one to three things that would devastate your trust in the person and relationship. As partners, you make an emotional commitment that no matter how hurt, angry, or drunk you are you will honor these boundaries. In terms of wearing each other out, be aware that although drama and unpredictability can elicit sexual desire, when your partner signals being emotionally or sexually overwhelmed you need to honor his or her request to tone down the intensity for the sake of your relationship.

CLOSING THOUGHTS

Finding a mutually comfortable, inviting, and functional couple sexual style is one of the best things you can do to promote sexual awareness and satisfaction. Your chosen couple sexual style promotes desire, pleasure, eroticism, and satisfaction. This ensures that sexuality will continue to energize your intimate relationship. Do not take sexuality for granted. Play to the strengths of your couple sexual style. In addition, be aware of the vulnerabilities and traps of your couple sexual style so you can monitor and confront these. You want sexuality to continue to reinforce feelings of desire and desirability and energize your intimate bond.

7

BRIDGES TO SEXUAL DESIRE

Arousal and orgasm have been the traditional focus of sex therapy. Masters and Johnson barely mentioned sexual desire. People believed that the way to build desire was to increase the incidence of orgasm. There is a positive relationship between sexual desire and function: people who enjoy sexual touch, experience arousal, create erotic scenarios and techniques, and celebrate orgasm report higher sexual desire. However, the essence of sexual desire has little to do with orgasm. People find that hard to accept, but it is true. The four components of sexual function are desire, arousal, orgasm, and satisfaction. Sex therapy has traditionally underemphasized desire and satisfaction and overemphasized arousal and orgasm. The new mantra for healthy couple sexuality is desire, pleasure, eroticism, and satisfaction.

Desire is the most important aspect of sexuality, especially in a marital or serious relationship. The key to enhancing desire is to understand the positive functions sexuality can play for the individual and couple. You are a sexual being from birth. Sexuality is integral to your identity as a woman or man. You are responsible for your sexuality and deserve to express sexuality in a way that enhances your self-esteem, relationship, and life. Sexuality is more than an individual behavior. Sexuality is a crucial component in your intimate relationship.

There are three primary functions of couple sexuality: sex as a shared pleasure; sexuality as a means to build and reinforce intimacy; and sex as a tension reliever to deal with the hassles and stresses of a shared relationship and life. Couple sexuality also has one optional function, which is to create a baby. Having a baby is a great impetus for desire when it is a planned, wanted baby and an inhibition of desire if there is fear of an unwanted pregnancy. Having children is a choice, not a mandate.

When sexuality goes well, it contributes approximately 15 to 20% to relationship satisfaction. The prime function is to energize your intimate bond and reinforce feelings of desire and desirability. When sexuality is dysfunctional, conflictual, or nonexistent, it plays an inordinately powerful 50 to 75% role, draining intimate feelings and causing major conflict. Sexuality, especially sexual desire and satisfaction, is a positive, integral element in self-esteem and your relationship. Conversely, sexual problems subvert self-esteem, devitalize your relationship, and threaten relationship security.

FEMALE–MALE DIFFERENCES IN SEXUAL DESIRE

Women and men learn about sexuality very differently. For women, sexuality has been tied to a relationship and to a cooperative, interactive process (a healthy learning) but has not been valued for itself (a negative learning). Sexuality has not been recognized as a positive, integral part of being a woman. Instead, female sexuality has been contingent on other aspects of life rather than being dynamic and strong in and of itself. Traditionally, female sexuality has emphasized intimacy and deemphasized eroticism.

Men have learned to value sexuality as a quality integral to masculinity (a positive learning) but also as a competitive act divorced from feelings and a relationship (a negative learning). The trap for male sexuality is that it has not been integrated into the man's life and relationship. Eroticism, intercourse, and perfect performance are overemphasized, while intimacy and nondemand pleasuring are deemphasized.

During adolescence and young adulthood, the traditional double standard favors male sexual desire. It is rare for men to report lack of desire (unless such issues as a fetish arousal, preference for masturbating with or without Internet porn, sexual trauma, or a sexual orientation issue are involved). Men experience easy desire, arousal, and orgasm during masturbation as well as during partner sex. However, in the long run the double standard subverts the sexual desire of men. When couples stop being sexual, no matter at what age, it is the man's decision in the great majority of cases. The man's assumption that he should be able to have sex anytime and anywhere and that erection should come easily, automatically, and autonomously ultimately undercuts male sexual desire because he cannot meet these unrealistic performance demands as he ages. The essence of sexuality is a cooperative, pleasure-oriented, intimate, interactive process.

Many women report major difficulty with inhibited sexual desire. One-third of adult women complain of low desire. For young women, fears of unwanted pregnancy and sexually transmitted infections, concern over being labeled *promiscuous* (a sexist term used mostly for women), worry about personal reputation and gossip, lack of affection, and disappointment in the partner or relationship can be factors in low desire.

Traumatic sexual experiences also can inhibit desire. These include not only child sexual abuse, incest, and rape but also being exhibited to, peeped at, harassed, ridiculed, or rejected. Women have always borne the brunt of negative sexual experiences. They maintained silence out of fear they would not be believed and because of the cultural tendency to blame the victim in these cases.

Warnings against sexuality (especially premarital and extramarital sexuality) have been aimed at women. The responsibility for avoiding negative sexual consequences (unwanted pregnancy, sexually transmitted infections, sexual assault) also has been the woman's burden. She has not been encouraged to value sexuality for herself, only in conjunction with a relationship. Although sexuality within the context of an intimate, secure relationship is ideal, that is not the learning context for most women (or men). Sexual idealism can undermine sexual desire.

With aging, there is often a reversal of female and male sexual desire. Women gain permission to be sexually expressive: She begins to "own" her sexuality, becomes aware of her conditions for satisfying sex, and develops a healthy, integrated "sexual voice." She becomes more assertive and makes requests to increase pleasure and arousal. Female sexual desire and arousal become easier and more predictable as the couple develops an intimate, interactive sexual style.

Meanwhile, male arousal is changing, too—becoming less predictable and more variable. The big difference is that male sexual response is no longer autonomous. He no longer has a spontaneous erection. Male sexuality becomes more like female sexual desire and arousal. Both the man and woman need pleasurable, interactive, erotic stimulation. Men who accept and enjoy flexibility and variability will not lose sexual desire. Those who long for the "good old days" and are distracted by a fear of sexual performance (i.e., getting and maintaining an erection) lose positive anticipation and sexual desire. Anticipatory anxiety and fear of performance failure are major inhibitors of male sexual desire. The challenge for males over 40 is to be "wise" men who are open to pleasure rather than "traditional" men who view intercourse as a pass–fail test.

BUILDING SEXUAL BRIDGES

There is a range of sexual experiences and a variety of ways to initiate sexual activity. Awareness of "sexual bridges" to replace old routine patterns is crucial. Initial sexual desire is driven by novelty, illicitness, spontaneous erections, and the passionate trappings of romantic love. The media—in movies, songs, and novels—presents an unrealistic, fantasy version of desire that is magical, filled with romantic love, passionate sex, idealization. In these fictions, there is nothing conscious or intentional about sexual desire; if sex is not passionate and dramatic something is wrong. According to this myth, sexual desire cannot be nurtured or enhanced; it is "hot" or it is not.

Using "bridges to sexual desire" to nurture intimacy and energize your relationship is realistic and healthy for you as a couple. Romantic love, propelled by passion, is unique to a new relationship. It almost invariably fades in a year or two. If sexuality is to continue to be a shared pleasure, you need to create and reinforce healthy sources of desire and initiation.

What are the most important sexual bridges? Foremost is a rhythm of being sexual. Sexual expression must be a regular, valued, energizing element in your relationship. The ability of both partners to freely initiate intimacy, pleasuring, eroticism, and intercourse is crucial. Touching both inside and outside the bedroom is a healthy source of desire, as is awareness that not all touching has to lead to intercourse. Sexual dates, planned or spontaneous, add a vital dimension to your relationship. Couples who value a range of sexual experiences—"quickies," nondemand pleasuring, romantic sex, sex during a stressful period, sex to affirm caring, sex to bridge an alienated phase—have a healthier sexual life than those who decree that both people need to be equally desirous, aroused, and orgasmic each time.

Fantasy is a major bridge to sexual desire for both women and men. Sexual desire often increases on vacation. Going away for a weekend without children facilitates desire. Use of external stimuli such as sexually oriented movies, romantic music, scented candles, sexy clothing or lingerie, X-rated movies, erotic novels, and mirrors can be legitimate and enhancing sexual bridges. Sex can serve as a celebration for a career success or as a consolation for a personal disappointment. Couples have sex after attending a wedding as a way to acknowledge the value and vitality of their marriage. Individuals and couples can build a variety of bridges to facilitate sexual desire.

Many people (men more so than women) have difficulty with the concept of intentionality in sex. Our culture puts inordinate emphasis on spontaneity and "horniness" as the "right" reasons for sex. We are in favor of love, spontaneity, and passion, but we believe there are even more healthy sources of desire. Sexuality can play a number of enhancing functions for you individually and as a couple. Sharing sensual and sexual touch is crucial for your intimate relationship. What happens in far too many relationships is that sex is treated with benign neglect as jobs, house, kids, extended family, friends, TV, and social and community activities take precedence. These activities are talked about and planned, whereas sex is left to the spontaneous, nonverbal realm. Sex is relegated to the last thing you do at night after walking the dog, paying bills, and watching TV. It becomes a mechanical habit rather than a vital, pleasurable connection. If sexual desire is to remain strong, you need to make it a priority and put time and energy into your sexual relationship.

One of the saddest findings is that nearly 40% of couples say that sex was best in the first 6 months of their relationship. Does marriage kill sex? Is there sex after marriage? We believe sexual intimacy, quality, and satisfaction can increase after marriage. Novelty, romanticism, and wantonness can be replaced by a mature emotional and sexual intimacy, by communication, by the establishment of quality sexual scenarios, by the freedom to be yourself as a sexual person and to enjoy a comfortable, functional couple sexual style. The key to sexual desire is to value sexuality, be aware of bridges to desire, maintain the rhythm of being sexual, play and experiment with erotic scenarios and techniques, and enhance anticipation and satisfaction.

The two "poisons" for sexual desire in an intimate relationship are a misplaced emphasis on "natural, spontaneous feelings" and the demand (pressure) to have intercourse. Romanticism and spontaneity make for great movies, novels, and songs, but they are terrible for marital relationships. If such fictions form the basis of sexual desire, then desire will weaken considerably within 2 to 5 years.

Bridges to sexual desire offer an approach relevant to the great majority of couples. There is no one right bridge or scenario that works for all couples. An erotic scenario or technique might empower some couples but be a turn-off for others. One way to think about sexual bridges is to view them like a smorgasbord or buffet—pick and choose what appeals to you most. You have the flexibility to choose what facilitates desire at a particular time and in a specific situation. Valuable bridges to desire include planning a sexual date, indulging in romantic or playful touching outside your bedroom, setting a sensual mood, taking turns initiating, dropping children at a friend's and coming home to be sexual, showering before bed so you are fresh for a sexual encounter, watching an R- or X-rated movie, offering a relaxing massage as a prelude to sexual stimulation, having a "quickie" after a stressful or disappointing day, using sex to celebrate a birthday or promotion, going on a sexual date on Sunday evening as a way to end the weekend.

BOB AND JEANNETTE

Bob and Jeannette wistfully recall their 14-month premarital period, especially when they met for weekends. Bob lived in Boston and Jeannette in Philadelphia. Every time they got together they were sexual, their passion as strong as their anticipation. They did not need to plan sexual dates; just being together was enough to ignite the sexual spark. The 5 months they lived together before marriage were less sexually exciting. They attributed that to distractions caused by wedding planning difficulties with in-laws. Shortly after marriage, arguments about sexual frequency and initiation patterns became frequent. Jeannette complained that Bob was always pushing sex, especially when they only had a short time.

Nine years later, with children ages 5 and 2, roles were reversed. Jeannette felt Bob avoided being sexual except for late at night. Both Bob and Jeannette looked forward to their yearly 1-week trip when they left the children with the grandparents. They also had one couple weekend getaway a year. Sex was a highlight of these trips, demonstrating they still had the capacity for pleasure and passion. Jeannette wanted a healthy sexual life but felt it needed to be experienced at home, not just on vacations.

Unfortunately, couples seldom do preventive marital maintenance, especially when it comes to sexuality. Sex is taken for granted and treated with benign neglect. It takes a crisis to get the couple's attention. A common crisis is an extramarital affair. Bob had the most frequent type of male affair—a high-opportunity, low-involvement affair while on a business trip. Sex occurred after working together all day and then having three drinks; it was an intense, erotic experience. Bob planned to keep it a secret because he was embarrassed and afraid of Jeannette's reaction. Also, Bob wanted to leave open the opportunity to repeat the indiscretion on subsequent trips.

Bob exemplified two adages: "Affairs are easier to get into than out of" and "Affairs take more time, require more energy, and are more complicated than you ever expected." The woman wanted much more than Bob bargained for. She demanded not only that he appoint her his special assistant but also that he be faithful to her and stop sleeping with Jeannette. She idealized Bob, which was flattering but scary. Bob had seen the movie *Fatal Attraction* and was afraid he had fallen into a version of it (luckily, a fear that proved to be unfounded). He was afraid the woman would follow through on her threats to call Jeannette and maybe file a complaint with the office manager. For a month Bob tried to finesse this situation. Finally, he chose to do the courageous thing and tell Jeannette what had happened and about the dilemma he was in. Jeannette was hurt and angry but not vindictive. Together, Bob and Jeannette met with the woman, and Bob apologized for his behavior. Although there were residual negative feelings on the woman's part, the crisis was defused.

Bob and Jeannette were left to deal with their marital issues, especially rebuilding their trust bond and revitalizing their couple sexual style. Rebuilding trust and sexual desire is a complex, gradual process—not the intense sexual catharsis portrayed in movies and love songs. Crucial to the process of reestablishing trust was their up-front agreement not to have affairs. If either of them found themselves in a high-risk situation, they agreed to talk before acting out. An agreement of this type, combined with the commitment to value your intimate bond, is the best strategy to prevent affairs.

Rebuilding sexual desire was a complex, often confusing, experience. Jeannette and Bob were romantics who wanted sex to arise spontaneously, easily, and passionately—just like in the movies (and in Bob's affair). While such spontaneity happens early in a relationship and during an extramarital affair, it is not the reality for an intimate relationship, especially for couples with children, careers, and a home. Couple time does not just happen; it needs to be consciously discussed and planned. Both spouses need to accept that you cannot compare marital sex with affair sex.

It was Jeannette who made the breakthrough. She insisted that during the week the TV stay off except for their favorite Thursday night show. This allowed them the time and space to connect as a couple. A number of those times together led to sexual encounters. Instead of Bob always being the initiator, Jeannette began initiating. Her style of initiation was quite different from Bob's. Jeannette didn't initiate verbally or in the bedroom. Jeannette's bridge to desire was playful/seductive touching in the kitchen, shower, or on the porch. She did not want to go into the bedroom until she felt turned on. This initiation scenario was fun and increased desire. She anticipated and valued sexuality, which in turn increased Bob's desire.

Bob was used to initiating late at night when cuddling gave him an erection. This was not Jeannette's favorite time, but she was open to "quickies." Bob preferred she be involved in the lovemaking. Jeannette said for that she needed to be more awake than she was at 11 p.m. Bob changed his initiation pattern. He put the children down for a nap or arranged for them to be watched by a teenage babysitter. He was surprised to discover that Jeannette did not insist that he be aroused and erect before they began. She preferred him to become aroused by her arousal and enjoyed helping him get turned on. This freed Bob to initiate teasing and playful touching to see whether it led to arousal and intercourse and to enjoy the connection either way.

They developed special erotic scenarios. Bob's scenario was being sexual on the jungle gym on a warm spring or fall night after midnight, when the children and neighbors were asleep. The sense of illicitness and adventure was a powerful aphrodisiac. Jeannette's scenario was being sexual in the shower. She enjoyed sitting at the end of the tub while Bob knelt during intercourse. Pleasuring and stimulation was erotic, and washing off after intercourse was easy as could be. They might engage in their special scenario once a month or every other month, but it was exciting to know they had a unique sexual scenario to look forward to.

EXERCISES THAT ACT AS BRIDGES TO DESIRE

First Exercise: Sexual Dates

You set dates to go to a movie, play bridge, go out to dinner. What about sexual dates? Setting time for a sexual date need not be formal or awkward. It can be romantic and fun. A sexual date allows you to anticipate being intimate as you would a sporting event or play.

As with other exercises, we suggest taking turns. Divide the week into two parts—for example, Saturday at 5 p.m. until Wednesday at 9 a.m. for the woman to initiate and Wednesday at 10 a.m. until Saturday at 4 p.m. for the man. This is the "ping-pong" system of initiation. After your partner initiates, it is your turn. If your partner did not initiate during this time, it becomes your prerogative to do so. The commitment is for each person to make at least one initiation per week.

When it is your "ping," set the time, place, and sexual scenario. Do it your way. Do not try to second-guess your partner or compare your way with his or hers. Make the initiation as inviting as possible. Be creative in your invitations. Examples include cooking a special dinner with sex as dessert, cuddling for half an hour in front of the fireplace before starting genital stimulation, calling before you leave work to suggest a sexual date, surprising your spouse by joining him in the shower, putting on your favorite music, bringing lotion to bed and spending 15 minutes giving your partner a sexual massage. Men can and do initiate creative sexual dates, contrary to the myth that romantic, seductive initiation is the woman's domain.

The woman can become comfortable with her ability to initiate. If sexuality is to remain a vital part of your relationship, learn to be open to creating and crossing bridges to sexual desire. Initiations could include waking your partner in the morning (or from a nap or in the middle of the night) by sucking on his penis and putting him inside you. You can share old pictures or letters to set the mood, rent your favorite R- or X-rated movie and fast-forward to the sexiest parts, ask your partner to put the children to bed and meet him in the bedroom where a scented candle is burning and you are wearing his favorite corduroy shirt. Get a babysitter and plan a hotel weekend in the city to roam through art museums, eat Italian food, and have sex without worrying about interruptions.

We cannot stress enough that sex does not just spontaneously happen. It requires thought, planning, and setting aside couple time. Approximately 80% of sexual encounters are planned or semiplanned. Enjoy spontaneous sexual experiences when they do occur, but don't fall into the trap of believing that somehow spontaneous sex is more genuine than intentional sex. Sexual dates are important bridges to desire.

Second Exercise: Overcoming Discrepancies in Sexual Desire

If couples had to wait until both partners were equally desirous, frequency of sex would decrease by at least half. It is the norm, not the exception, for one partner to desire and initiate sex more than the other. What poisons sexual desire is anger about nonsexual issues (which need to be dealt with outside the bedroom) and resentment over feeling sexually pressured. Under no circumstances is it acceptable to physically force or verbally coerce your partner to engage in sex. "Intimate coercion" has no place in your relationship. Sex is best when it is voluntary and pleasure oriented. Pressure and coercion lead to alienation and anger, and the ensuing resentment poisons sexual desire.

What can you do when one wants to have intercourse and the other does not? This exercise uses the "yes/no" technique to deal with desire discrepancy. Our culture socializes men to always say yes to sex, so the woman is stuck in the role of sexual gatekeeper. In fact, it is perfectly natural, normal, and healthy for men to say no to sex, and on occasion more than 80% have.

In this exercise, each partner has to say at least one "no." The focus is on expanding your repertoire of what is acceptable when there is a desire discrepancy. The quality of the intimate experience is more important than frequency of intercourse. Sexual intimacy is reinforced by caring about each other's feelings and sharing pleasure rather than perceiving sex as a goal-oriented power play.

This exercise requires a number of cycles rather than one structured experience. Each person will have several initiations. The initiator speaks from an awareness of what she wants—to feel desirable, attractive, and valued; unpredictability and playfulness; orgasm; time to be alone before erotic contact; multiple stimulation during intercourse; affectionate touch. Ask for and initiate activities you enjoy. The woman is aware that her partner will say no at least once and preferably more than once. This allows them to practice negotiating sensual and sexual alternatives. He will not just say no but will offer an alternative that both suits his fancy and addresses her needs. For example, if she wants a whole-body massage as a way of meeting her needs for sensuous time before erotic contact and he is lukewarm toward the idea of a body massage, he might offer to draw a bubble bath or suggest building a fire and talking and touching in front of the fireplace. If her initiations are co-opted because he is action oriented, she can offer a number of feeling-oriented, nonintercourse ways to intimately connect.

This is the major struggle in desire discrepancy. The woman has a right to request a range of sensual and erotic experiences without her partner contending that only intercourse is real sex. She can suggest manually pleasuring him to orgasm, that they engage in nongenital pleasuring, that he pleasure her and she'll decide if she wants a mutual sexual experience, that they have oral sex, that they share an activity (going for a walk, playing golf, going shopping) before being sexual, that he stimulate himself while she holds him. He can say no to suggestions he is not comfortable with, but he needs to say yes to at least one of her alternatives. There are many emotional, sensual, playful, and erotic ways to connect that may or may not evolve into intercourse.

A common male trap is using sex to meet nonsexual needs. In extreme cases, men use sex like alcoholics use alcohol—to deal with emotions from anger to boredom, from excitement to emptiness, from celebration to depression. You can learn emotional coping strategies to deal with nonsexual problems. Sharing feelings can be a better way to deal with sadness than having intercourse. Celebrating a merit bonus with couple friends can make more sense than using sex as a reward when the partner is not feeling sexual.

The most common issue in a problematic sexual relationship is inhibited sexual desire. At the other extreme, some men use sex compulsively to avoid dealing with issues and emotions. Hyperactive sexual desire results in an alienated relationship. Sexual bridges are meant to encourage pleasure and intimacy. Couple sexuality is subverted when sexual initiations carry negative emotions and compulsive sex demands.

The man is urged to personalize his sexual invitations. He is less likely to be distracted by nonsexual factors such as fatigue, hunger, anger, alienation, and anxiety about children. This can be a sexual strength, but it can also be a source of misunderstanding and strife. She complains he wants sex, not her. Making your sexual invitations and requests personal and caring will avert this problem. Sex is good, but not when it's at the expense of your partner or relationship.

Will the experience of saying no to intercourse and yes to sensual and erotic alternatives resolve all desire discrepancies? Of course not, but it will allow you to stay intimate friends and provide greater flexibility and degrees of freedom in expressing your needs for intimacy and sexuality.

Third Exercise: Sources of Erotic Desire

There are multiple sources of sexual desire; some are healthy, some less so, and some are poisonous. Healthy sources of sexual desire include, but are not limited to, sharing pleasure, feeling "horny," reinforcing intimacy, using sex as a way to connect, getting turned on by a fantasy or sexy movie, taking advantage of time away from kids, sharing loving feelings, celebrating a special date or anniversary, using sex as a tension reducer, enjoying the novelty of being at a hotel, making up after a disagreement, feeling erotic after sensuous caressing. Examples of unhealthy or destructive sources of sexual desire include proving something to yourself or partner, using sex to express anger or power, acting out a compulsive need, getting high so you can have sex, demanding sex after a physically abusive incident, acting out a self-destructive pattern (high-risk sex), using sex as a manipulation, and engaging in sex to run away from problems.

A persistent misbelief is that your partner should be the source of all sexual desire. According to this myth, if you fantasize about someone else or get turned on by seeing an attractive person, you are disloyal. In truth, fantasies and other external stimuli—movies, TV, novels, Internet, people on the street, sexual pictures or magazines—can be a healthy source of desire. Almost no one fantasizes about having intercourse in bed with his or her spouse in the missionary position. The essence of erotic imagery is that it entails socially undesirable acts, people, and situations. If people were prosecuted for their sexual thoughts and fantasies, almost everyone would be in jail.

Erotic fantasies are a major bridge to desire. Sexual fantasies can be misused, especially when they are compulsive, cause shame, or function as a wall to shut off your partner. However, most of the time and for most people sexual fantasies serve to increase desire, involvement, arousal, and orgasm.

In this exercise, each partner lists at least 3 and up to 10 sources of eroticism and desire. We suggest sharing at least two and keeping at least two to yourself. Sexual desire can be inhibited by sharing everything and describing fantasies in detail. Sex fantasies usually work better as private fantasies rather than playing them out. The typical outcome is awkwardness and disappointment, if not disaster. Sexual fantasies and real-life sexual behavior are very different domains.

Instead of waiting for desire to "naturally" occur or expecting all desire to come from your partner, use erotic cues and fantasies to fuel desire. A good example is a sexual daydream or the visual memory of an attractive person in a store. Allow that erotic image to "simmer" throughout the day so that at night it serves as a bridge to desire and sexual initiation. During the next month be aware of erotic cues and allow them to be a bridge for sexual initiation at least twice.

Fourth Exercise: Special Sexual Scenarios

People have favorite sports teams, music, movies. This is also true of sexual scenarios. We are not talking about "bread and butter" ways of having sex, but experiences that are "special turn-ons." One of the most interesting things about being a sex therapist is discovering the range of what individuals and couples find sexually inviting. There are the traditional romantic scenarios of dressing up, having a gourmet dinner with wine and candles, followed by tender, loving, prolonged sex on silk sheets. There are also the traditional erotic scenarios of going to a motel, watching X-rated videos, dressing in lingerie, and having sex under a ceiling mirror. For some, the key is external stimuli—sexy videos, covering each other's genitals with lotion, feeding your partner gourmet snacks and wine, playing out a dominance–submission scenario you download from the Internet, reading erotic fantasies aloud. Many people emphasize sexual techniques like simultaneous fellatio and cunnilingus ("69"), vibrator stimulation during intercourse, mutual manual stimulation while standing in front of a mirror, taking a 10-minute wine break and resuming stimulation, engaging in one-way sex to arouse your partner to total abandon, using multiple stimulation during intercourse, switching intercourse positions three times, using light bondage as an erotic turn-on.

Each partner initiates his or her favorite sexual scenario. An erotic scenario may need to be experienced two or three times before it becomes a genuinely satisfying part of your couple sexual style. Anticipating a special scenario is a powerful bridge to sexual desire.

CLOSING THOUGHTS

Sexuality cannot be phoned in. The flames of sexual desire must be nurtured and bridges to desire reinforced. Too many couples recall having their best sex when it was new, illicit, and youthful—as if sex ends with intimacy, commitment, and age. What a self-defeating view! Sexuality can remain a vital part of your relationship into your 80s. You can enhance the process by being aware of and maintaining bridges to sexual desire. The keys to desire are anticipation, freedom, and choice.

8

EROTIC SCENARIOS AND TECHNIQUES

We have emphasized the importance of nondemand pleasuring and the reduction of performance orientation to enhance sexual awareness and comfort. However, more is required to create arousal, eroticism, and orgasm. Sexual satisfaction involves the integration of intimacy, nondemand pleasuring, and erotic scenarios and techniques. This chapter explores a range of erotic scenarios and techniques.

People associate passion with a new, intense, volatile relationship in which sex is insistent and driven. Just being with your partner is a turn-on. Passionate sex is powerful and special; unfortunately, it is also unstable and transitory.

Erotic sex connotes the "fun and dirty" approach promoted by X-rated movies, Internet porn, sex shops, and kinky scenarios. Can intimate sex in a serious relationship be arousing and erotic as well? Is that unrealistic? We are convinced—theoretically, empirically, clinically, and personally—that sex can be exciting, erotic, satisfying, and integrated into your intimate relationship. Eroticism is not reserved for premarital or extramarital sex. Not only can sex in serious and marital relationships be erotic, but eroticism is essential if you want to maintain desire, vitality, and satisfaction. Ideally you have an emotionally intimate, secure bond that has a solid foundation in nondemand pleasuring. Erotic scenarios and techniques are the ingredients that add a sense of excitement, adventure, creativity, mystery, and vitality.

ENHANCING EROTICISM

Each couple develops a unique style of eroticism. There is no "one right way" to experience eroticism; a medley of choices is available. Be aware that it is not technique alone, or even primarily, that eroticizes sex. Sexuality is enhanced by spontaneity, playfulness, and experimentation but above all by awareness of erotic feelings and openness to creative expression. Sexual creativity emanates from three sources: awareness of feelings, thoughts, and fantasies; a dynamic process between you and your partner that includes touching, teasing, unpredictability, and non-verbal cues; and openness to experimentation with a variety of erotic scenarios and techniques. Sexual creativity involves acknowledging sexual feelings and desires and taking the risk to play them out. You do not have to give a Hollywood-level performance, but you do need to share and be expressive. Eroticism need not reach for the levels of passion and lust portrayed in movies or experienced at the beginning of a relationship. What eroticism does call for are creativity, energy, unpredictability, letting go, and enjoying orgasmic sex.

Routine, predictability, and alienation sound the death knell for sexuality, especially sexual desire. The typical sexual scenario for "Joe and Jane Average" is late-night sex. One person, usually the male, reaches to kiss or caress his partner and says, "Are you interested?" The scenario follows a predictable 5 to 10 minutes of foreplay, with the focus on getting her ready for intercourse. This is followed by 2 to 7 minutes of intercourse where he and sometimes she reach orgasm, a minute or two of holding and talking, and then sleep. Is there something wrong with this? Absolutely not. However, it is not the stuff of vital, erotic sexuality. Why should sex be relegated to the last thing at night after you have completed all the tasks of daily life like paying bills, putting children to sleep, cleaning up, and watching the late-night comedy show? When sex is taken for granted and given a low priority, it is hard to maintain eroticism and vitality.

When people think passion, excitement, and eroticism, they focus on premarital and extramarital affairs. Why are people willing to take emotional and sexual risks with a new person but not with their intimate partner? You have been brainwashed by the hype of movies, songs, and sex videos that extol novelty, illicitness, spontaneity, passion, and being swept away by sexual impulse. The message is that the best sex is intense, unthinking, spontaneous, overwhelming, and "bad." Erotic sex can and does exist in the context of a committed, intimate relationship. Intimacy and eroticism can and do complement each other. Erotic sex energizes your bond and adds a special element to your intimate relationship.

CREATIVE SEX AND MULTIPLE STIMULATION

Essential to maintaining eroticism are creative sex and multiple stimulation. Ideally, people are more creative in an intimate relationship than in an affair because the commitment and communication allow you to take risks and let go. You do not need the disinhibition of alcohol or an affair to give you permission to be sexually creative. Creativity can include spontaneity, but the basis of creativity is fantasizing, anticipating, and expressing.

There is no law that says only people having an affair can meet at hotels. One of our favorite stories begins with an opportunity to have an overnight babysitter for our children one cold February Sunday. Barry was conducting a workshop that afternoon, so we made plans to meet at a funky downtown hotel. Barry arrived first and signed the registration card. Emily arrived an hour later. The hotel clerk asked if Emily wanted to leave her name at the desk, reassuring her that "any name would be fine." Emily found it intriguing that the clerk assumed she was there for an affair. His reaction was typical: Why would a married couple meet at a hotel on a Sunday night? By introducing the unexpected into your lives, you can reclaim your right to erotic sex. Creativity enhances your relationship.

Our prescription for satisfying sex is integrating emotional intimacy, nondemand pleasuring, and erotic scenarios and techniques. Multiple stimulation is the most common erotic technique. This mutual, simultaneous involvement utilizes a range of erotic stimuli, allowing arousal to build to high levels before you let go and abandon yourselves to passion. Erotic scenarios and techniques can involve mixing manual and oral stimulation, including playing out a master-slave scenario in which the submissive partner is receiving three types of stimulation; having intercourse from the rear-entry position with her caressing his testicles while he stimulates her clitoral area; giving and receiving oral stimulation simultaneously; using erotic fantasies to augment the intercourse experience; burning incense and listening to your favorite jazz music as you engage in a seductive half-hour of gentle touching before switching to intense, rapid intercourse; engaging in mutual manual stimulation to orgasm as you watch an X-rated video; combining oral breast stimulation with manual clitoral stimulation while she orally stimulates him; utilizing vibrator stimulation during intercourse in the woman-on-top position while she verbalizes how turned on she feels. Multiple-stimulation scenarios are a great way to practice creative sex.

ARTURO AND MARGARITA

The crisis of a discovered extramarital affair is a common impetus for couples to enter marital therapy. Margarita was having an affair with a work colleague, and Arturo had short affairs when he traveled. These revelations shocked and saddened them. Friends and family members took sides and advised ending the marriage, but that was not what either Arturo or Margarita wanted.

A number of difficult issues needed to be addressed to revitalize their marital bond. Trust and sexuality were the most important. They committed to 6 months of couple therapy to rebuild their trust bond and develop a new couple sexual style. Through therapy, Arturo realized that sexual arousal does not exist in a vacuum. Margarita realized the importance of dealing with complex, emotionally difficult issues if loving feelings are to stay strong and resilient.

Arturo had been aroused and attracted to Margarita before marriage, but since the birth of their son he did not think of her in an erotic manner. The thrill of high-opportunity, low-involvement affairs is what turned Arturo on. Margarita had been vulnerable to a colleague who found her attractive and pursued a sexual relationship. Margarita resented Arturo's failure to affirm her sexual desirability. She viewed herself as an adult woman, spouse, parent, competent professional, and desirable lover—and she wanted Arturo to see her that way, too.

Strengthening emotional intimacy, rebuilding the trust bond, and nondemand pleasuring were necessary but not sufficient. Love, trust, and communication are not enough for erotic, vital couple sexuality. Margarita and Arturo had to learn to value marital sex and integrate erotic scenarios and techniques into their intimate relationship. This was a couple challenge, not the sole responsibility of either spouse. It is a joint responsibility to develop a couple sexual style that is intimate, erotic, and satisfying.

Arturo was enthusiastic about creating erotic scenarios. He was a visually oriented man and liked looking at pictures, videos, and attractive women on TV as well as seeing Margarita in sexy, seductive outfits. Although Arturo enjoyed nudity, he was more aroused by sexy clothing or seeing Margarita half-dressed. His emphasis on visual turn-ons had previously been off-putting to Margarita. She felt he wanted her to act as a sex object, while she wanted to be seen as a desirable sexual woman. Eroticism involves letting go and allowing a sense of abandon to prevail, but not at the expense of your partner or relationship. Margarita needed to trust that Arturo's visual turn-ons included her and served as a bridge to an involved, erotic experience. A key learning was that

Arturo's desire peaked when Margarita was dressed in a sexy blouse, no bra, and black panties. His arousal fed her arousal, resulting in a mutual erotic experience that evolved to passionate intercourse.

Most sexual experiences are not special. Even loving couples with no sexual problems are lucky if they have one to three special sexual experiences a month. Realizing that erotic feelings and marital intimacy can not only coexist but also be mutually enhancing was a major breakthrough for Margarita and Arturo. Experiencing eroticism while maintaining an intimate connection allowed them to "own" their sexuality. They didn't need affairs to experience eroticism. Feelings of desire, attraction, and sexual vitality energized their marital bond.

Margarita's erotic scenarios were quite different from Arturo's. The key for her was anticipation and a slowly building eroticism that burst into powerful sexual intercourse. Rather than one or two scenarios, Margarita developed four or five scenarios with a multitude of variations. The seductive build-up could occur almost anywhere, including the bedroom, but certainly was not limited to it. Margarita loved to play sexually in the car and on walks. One day when they left the children at his mother's, which was a one-and-a-half-hour drive, Margarita so turned Arturo on by her sexual playing that they pulled off onto a deserted road and had sex in the car. They joked and had fantasies about that experience for months afterward.

Margarita enjoyed the nights when Arturo took charge of the children's baths and bedtime stories because it gave her a chance to relax and read a novel (a favorite activity). She would put on music, pour a glass of wine, and change into an outfit that could easily be slipped out of. Taking care of the kids shortstopped Arturo's preoccupation with work, money, and sports. He looked forward to joining Margarita for pleasuring and music. Arturo was eager to have sex after 10 minutes but accepted Margarita's prolonged pleasuring scenarios. She preferred building arousal to a high level before proceeding to the bedroom and intercourse. At times she enjoyed completing the sexual scenario in the living room. Arturo reacted with a combination of arousal and worry that a child would awaken. Margarita was prepared to stop if that occurred. She valued the eroticism generated by sex play outside the bedroom and looked forward to the time she and Arturo would "be a couple again."

MISUNDERSTANDINGS ABOUT CREATIVE SEX

The concept of creative sex is vague enough to intimidate the most knowledgeable, sophisticated couple. What creative sexual scenarios are we missing? How do we prove we are liberated? Before HIV/AIDs, there was a new, chic sexual activity introduced (usually from California or New York) every 6 months. This became the "in" scenario. Several years ago, the scenario was triadic sex—two women and a man. The next way to prove you were sexually free was to have anal intercourse. Six months later, it was using handcuffs and neck collars to play out dominance–submission scenarios. Next came triadic sex with two men and a woman (to confront homophobia). Then there was the ultimate test of sexual freedom—being able to masturbate in front of a group to prove you were not ashamed. In our opinion, these are not indicators of creative sex but performances to prove something to yourself or others. Erotic sexuality involves freedom to feel comfortable, share pleasure, create turn-ons, and enjoy orgasm, not having to prove you are liberated.

The essence of creative sexuality is being aware of sensual and erotic feelings, thoughts, and fantasies and willingness to play them out with your partner. Having the freedom to share feelings is more important than scenarios and techniques. In our sexually supercharged culture, couples feel intimidated and not "good enough." The essence of creative sexuality is feeling and expressing arousal as sexual play, not as a performance or competition. The problem with most sex books (as well as movies and TV programs) is that they reinforce the image that only a tiny, elite group is sexually liberated.

Creative sexuality is relevant to the great majority of couples. It is about playing, sharing, and enjoying and has nothing to do with "keeping up with the Joneses" or meeting a sexual criterion set by a media sex guru or the McCarthys. Our mission in this book is to empower you to embrace creative sexuality, not feel intimidated by erotic sex performance.

A key question is whether spontaneity is crucial to creative sexuality. In our opinion, spontaneity is healthy but oversold. Once you have established a comfortable, arousing sexual scenario, it is easier to spontaneously reintroduce it. Spontaneous encounters add a special sexual charge. However, at the core of creative sexuality lie erotic experiences that have become part of your couple sexual style. These involve experimentation and verbal as well as nonverbal feedback. Once established, they can be spontaneously initiated and played out.

Perhaps this example will clarify the process. Jill was feeling amorous, recalling the quick but fulfilling sex with her husband, Vince, 2 days ago. She wanted to be with Vince again but this time desired a prolonged experience. Vince had a busy week but was open to a quick, passionate intercourse experience. Jill told Vince their 4-year-old daughter would be at a birthday party for 2 hours. She gave him a lingering kiss and said she wanted the whole 2 hours for them. As Vince drove off to do grocery shopping, his lips and penis had tingly feelings. As he walked the grocery aisles, he fantasized an erotic scenario. Vince volunteered to take his daughter to the party, which allowed Jill a respite. Vince came back to find her in a bubble bath. Although tempted by an invitation to join her, Vince found baths more relaxing than sexual. He preferred to soap Jill and take the opportunity to mix nongenital and breast stimulation. Jill shared with him how much his touching turned her on and then divulged her fantasy of making love in the family room. As Jill was putting on her favorite perfume and robe, Vince closed the shades, put the answering machine on, and chose three CDs.

Vince loved the stimulation position where he stood and Jill sprawled on the couch. Jill's favorite multiple-stimulation scenario was when Vince combined oral breast stimulation with manual clitoral stimulation while she orally stimulated him and he rhythmically thrust his pelvis. They switched from mutual stimulation to one-way stimulation then back to mutual. Jill was receptive to intercourse after she had orgasmed with manual stimulation and knew that Vince was highly aroused. Her "I want you inside me now" was a very stimulating invitation. For Jill and Vince, creative sex did not end with orgasm. Afterplay was an integral part of their sexual experience. Jill loved taking a nap or having Vince bring tea and fruit to bed and talking about their next couple outing.

As you read about Jill and Vincent's sexual scenario, you might be impressed or amused. Do not worry about their way; find your own creative scenarios.

GUIDELINES FOR EROTIC PSYCHOSEXUAL SKILL EXERCISES

What is erotic for one partner might be viewed as "kinky" or distasteful by the other. Experimenting with sexual scenarios and techniques is healthy, but you need to develop a clear commitment to noncoercive guidelines. Experimentation should not involve proving anything to anyone or making performance demands; it should not take place at the expense of your partner or be manipulative. Focus on increasing eroticism rather than performance, on requests rather than demands, on honesty instead of manipulation. Approach these exercises as mutual exploration; do not allow pressure or intimidation.

You do not have to prove you are sexually liberated or search vainly for the ultimate aphrodisiac. The best turn-on is an involved, aroused partner. The idea that you should find each erotic technique highly arousing is a form of sexual fascism. Discover what is inviting and erotic for you.

First Exercise: Multiple Stimulation

Traditionally, stimulation has been limited to foreplay. The man stimulates the woman so she is ready for intercourse. Stimulation should involve both giving and receiving pleasure, either taking turns (self-entrancement arousal) or mutual (partner-interaction arousal). Multiple stimulation extends this process to erotic stimulation in both nonintercourse and intercourse sex. Multiple stimulation is most effective when the level of arousal is moderate and building (at least a 6 on a 10-point scale). The best example is oral–genital stimulation. If arousal is a 4 or less, receiving oral stimulation is likely to increase self-consciousness for women as well as men, resulting in lowered arousal. However, if arousal is a 6 or 7, oral stimulation is likely to enhance erotic flow for both women and men.

Let the woman make the first initiation. She can set the rhythm of pleasuring so that both partners are involved in the process of arousal. We suggest you initiate multiple stimulation in the context of erotic, nonintercourse sex and encourage you to use multiple stimulation during intercourse in subsequent experiences. We provide the following roster of suggestions that you can try or modify. Or design your own. Examples of multiple stimulation include kneeling and facing your partner who is also kneeling, kissing, engaging in mutual manual stimulation, and requesting he use his tongue to caress your breast; you standing, he kneeling, utilizing manual vulva stimulation combined with oral breast stimulation as you verbalize a fantasy of his being your sexual slave; you lying on your side, he kneeling, rubbing his penis against your breast, manually stimulating your vulva while you fantasize about two men and two women stimulating you under a blooming tree; you lying on your back, he between your legs, his oral stimulation combined with simultaneous manual anal stimulation while you caress your breasts and verbalize how aroused you feel. Continue the multiple-stimulation scenario to orgasm if you desire.

When it is the man's initiative, he introduces his multiple-stimulation scenario during intercourse. Traditionally, males were supposed to need only thrusting during intercourse. Whether you need it or not, most men find that multiple stimulation during intercourse increases involvement and erotic flow. Examples of multiple stimulation include: from the man-on-top position, request that she caress your testicles while you stretch and lick her breast; from the rear-entry position, stimulate her vulva manually as she verbalizes erotic feelings and you fantasize; from the woman-on-top position, enjoy her growing arousal while playing with her breasts, she using circular thrusting movements; from the side-by-side position, she stroking your chest while you rub her buttocks and kiss each other's bodies.

Feel free to experiment with multiple-stimulation scenarios and techniques; request the combination that heightens arousal and erotic flow for you and your partner. Integrate multiple stimulation into both pleasuring and intercourse.

Second Exercise: Personal Turn-Ons

One of the most fascinating things about sexuality is the individual differences in what people find erotic. Sex magazines and pornography try to sell people (mostly men) on the idea that "dirty" and "kinky" scenarios universally turn people on. They are wrong. You do not have to prove you are sexually free, sophisticated, or uninhibited. Sex is not about performance or proving anything to your partner, yourself, or anyone else. Sexuality is about giving and receiving pleasure and experiencing arousal and eroticism. Turn-ons are very individualistic. Sexually one size does *not* fit all.

He takes the first initiative. Even more than multiple-stimulation scenarios, there are vast differences in personal turn-ons. The following are a few examples that can be used by either the man or the woman: slow, mutual touching and romantic kisses, followed by rapid, intense intercourse in which both partners rush to orgasm; playing out a fantasy scenario (master–slave, strangers having a first sexual encounter, the sophisticated lover meets the naive and impetuous partner, the whore and virgin); making love after watching *Gone with the Wind;* waking up to your partner orally stimulating you; switching intercourse positions multiple times before reaching orgasm; engaging in one-way sex (one person gives pleasure and orgasm without reciprocation); being sexual in the shower or right afterward so you are fresh for oral sex; reading a sexual fantasy aloud while your partner stimulates you following the fantasy script; using a special lotion or a scented candle to heighten sensations; the man giving oral sex so she can have as many orgasms as she wishes; having intercourse standing up or doing it while the woman is sitting on the kitchen counter; making erotic dates for your birthday or anniversary. At a later time, she can design and play out her personal turn-on. Remember, personal turn-ons are not a competition; your turn-ons are usually different from your partner's. It is not a question of "right versus wrong" or "kinky versus vanilla." Request and share sexual scenarios and turn-ons that heighten your eroticism.

Third Exercise: External Turn-Ons

People believe that being in love is all you need to feel sexual desire and arousal. If arousal is not spontaneous, it is a sign there is something wrong with you or your relationship. The tyranny of the "shoulds," especially "love should be enough," subverts sexuality. For sex to remain vital and erotic, feel free to utilize external turn-ons.

The woman initiates first. Here are some examples of alternatives couples have found erotic. Each person can veto anything they find negative, but we encourage you to be open and experimental. Examples of external turn-ons include being sexual in front of a mirror and enjoying visual feedback; using an erotic movie or your favorite scene from an R-rated movie; being sexual in areas of the house other than the bedroom; using vibrator stimulation as an additional source of erotic stimulation; being sexual on a deserted beach or private wooded area; having sex in a shower or bathtub; using play aides like a feather, silk sheets, or mittens; being sexual in the back seat of a car as a remembrance of adolescence; using accoutrements from bondage and discipline games such as loosely tied ropes or a paddle; going to a bed-and-breakfast, funky hotel, or upscale inn as a special sexual treat; using a new body lotion or scented candle to enhance the milieu; being sexual under the stars during a camping trip.

The man has his turn at initiation using external turn-ons. You are free to introduce what you want to experiment with. Each individual and couple have their unique set of turn-ons. It is not that couples need external turn-ons but that external stimuli add spice to your sexual relationship.

Fourth Exercise: Creative Couple Sexuality

Instead of taking turns with initiation, allow creative sexuality to be mutual. Each partner can contribute to an erotic scenario. This requires nonverbal and/or verbal communication. When each person's thoughts, feelings, and sexual expression flow, your arousal enhances your partner's. This is an extension of the give-and-get pleasure guideline.

Pick your favorite place to have a creative scenario (the den, bedroom, guest room). Do not plan a scenario in detail, but be open to feelings and requests; let it flow as a mutual co-created experience. Have favorite erotic turn-ons readily available if you decide to introduce them—lotion, a mirror, music, a sexy story, beads or feathers, a vibrator, scented candle. During the pleasuring allow yourselves to be as free and playful as possible. Be comfortable with a multitude of positions: standing, lying, kneeling, sitting. You can have your favorite music on, dance, wrestle, play strip poker, or participate in your favorite seductive touching game. Do not set up artificial barriers between sex play and intercourse. Allow creative sexuality to flow into creative intercourse. Experiment with positions, multiple stimulation, expressing erotic feelings. Allow intercourse to be a flowing experience. Creative sexuality does not end with orgasm. Enjoy creative afterplay in which you express, verbally and nonverbally, a range of affectionate, sensual, romantic, or playful feelings.

CLOSING THOUGHTS

Not only is there erotic sex in an ongoing relationship; this also is a vital aspect of intimacy. Intimacy and eroticism can be successfully integrated. You owe it to yourself, your partner, and your relationship to enjoy erotic sexuality that energizes your bond. Sexual vitality and eroticism are not relegated to the young or to illicit or new relationships. Eroticism deserves to be an integral part of your intimate relationship.

9

PLEASURING, EROTICISM, AND INTERCOURSE

Our emphasis on being an intimate team, feeling comfortable giving and receiving pleasure, and being aware of and responsive to erotic scenarios and techniques applies equally to intercourse. All too often couples consider pleasuring important only to "set the stage" for the "real thing." The traditional equation was that "sex = intercourse." Our view is that pleasuring, eroticism, intercourse, and afterplay are part of a continuous, flowing process. Intercourse is an integral part of the sexual experience, not an isolated activity. The best way to think about intercourse is as a special pleasuring experience that flows from eroticism.

ACTIVE INVOLVEMENT

Pleasuring that is slow, tender, rhythmic, and caring allows for a natural progression into eroticism and intercourse. Sexual intercourse is not a mechanical juxtaposing of two bodies; it involves the interaction of needs, feelings, and mutual pleasure. A traditional myth is that foreplay is for women and intercourse is for men. That cheats the individual and couple of a great deal of sexual pleasure.

The sexually aware couple enjoys the pleasuring process for itself, not just as foreplay. Pleasuring can be as enjoyable for the man as for the woman. It is not only acceptable but also preferable that both partners feel free to initiate intercourse. The woman can enjoy and gain as much (and sometimes more) from intercourse as the man does. Rather than assuming the role of passive recipient, she can initiate and be active throughout intercourse. By its nature, intercourse involves mutuality, reciprocity, and sharing. Intercourse is most enjoyable if you are attuned to the needs, feelings, and preferences of your partner. It is the natural culmination of an involving experience of sexual sharing that begins with communication (both verbal and nonverbal) and progresses to kissing, caressing, pleasuring, eroticism, intercourse, and afterplay.

INTERCOURSE TRAPS

The main traps couples fall into regarding intercourse are as follows:

- Separating pleasuring from intercourse
- Making intercourse a mechanical routine by doing the same thing each time
- Transitioning to intercourse at low levels of arousal
- Making intercourse simply a penis–vagina interchange that does not involve multiple stimulation

To counter these traps, keep in mind the "give-and-get" guideline. The best way to ensure a mutual experience is to give pleasure, which ensures that your partner is responsive. In turn, your partner's increasing ardor will increase your level of arousal. Each person's pleasure facilitates involvement, arousal, and erotic flow for both of you.

Too much emphasis is placed on both partners having orgasm during intercourse. Although orgasm is important and desirable, to make it a rigid goal is self-defeating. A healthier attitude is to consider orgasm during intercourse desirable only when both partners feel open to it. Two factors are crucial in understanding the relationship between intercourse and orgasm. First, female sexual response is more complex and variable than male sexual response. She might be nonorgasmic, singly orgasmic, or multi-orgasmic. Orgasm might occur during the pleasuring phase, intercourse, or afterplay. If the man demands that his partner have one orgasm during intercourse without requiring additional stimulation ("look Mom, no hands"), he is not accepting the variability and complexity of female sexuality. He is inhibiting her, as well as couple sexuality, from full erotic expression. Only one in four women follows the male pattern of having one orgasm during intercourse without additional stimulation.

The second factor is that there are nonintercourse methods of orgasm, including manual, oral, vibrator, and rubbing stimulation during pleasuring and afterplay. These are normal, healthy sexual expressions that can heighten your experience. One in three women never or very seldom experiences orgasm during intercourse. Female nonorgasmic response during intercourse is a normal variation, not a sexual dysfunction. Only about 10 to 15% of women are orgasmic 100% of the time during couple sex. The average woman who feels good about her sexuality is orgasmic in approximately 70% of sexual encounters. Intercourse where the woman is involved although not orgasmic can be a positive experience for both partners. Approximately two of three women are occasionally or regularly orgasmic during intercourse. The key for these women is multiple stimulation during intercourse, especially with additional clitoral stimulation by either partner.

AFTERPLAY

Whether or not intercourse results in orgasm, afterplay is extremely important. Traditionally, couples set orgasm as a goal, and once this goal was reached the sexual encounter was over. This orgasm cutoff point is a myth, both from a physiological and psychological viewpoint. Masters and Johnson described four phases of sexual response: excitement, plateau, orgasm, and resolution. From a physiological view, afterplay is important since it corresponds to your body's return to a less intense state (resolution). From the psychological viewpoint, an even stronger case can be made for the importance of afterplay. You have just shared an intense physical and emotional experience. Afterplay has been called "afterglow" because it is an emotional and symbolic means of showing you care about and value your partner. Pleasuring starts as a sensual experience, and afterplay ends the encounter as a sensual experience. Afterplay is almost as important to an intimate relationship as pleasuring. For many couples, afterplay is key for sexual satisfaction.

EXPERIMENT WITH POSITIONS

Satisfying sexual intercourse involves being experimental, playful, and innovative. All too often couples assume there is only one "right" way to engage in intercourse: man on top with no activity except thrusting. Within our culture, this is the preferred and most commonly used position. However, it is a myth that man on top is the only normal or correct position. Intercourse position is a matter of comfort, skill, and preference. Exploring a variety of positions does not mean you have to utilize esoteric skills or become acrobats or contortionists. Exploration and experimentation require knowledge of intercourse positions and their possible variations with an awareness of your own and your partner's desires, feelings, and preferences.

Without exploration and experimentation, you run the risk of performing stereotyped intercourse that becomes dull and unrewarding. When sex becomes routine, it turns into a mechanical chore rather than a sharing, satisfying experience. We emphasize slow, tender, gentle, rhythmic, flowing touching, but if each sexual experience fulfilled only these criteria sex would become boring and unsatisfying.

We do not want to fall into the trap of so many sex manuals by describing in great detail an endless variety of intercourse positions and variations. The mistaken message they often convey is that you have to prove yourself a masterful technician. When intercourse becomes a gymnastic feat, it also becomes a detached, impersonal, and unfeeling experience. Instead, be aware of choices and be an active, involved participant in the sexual experience. Focus on comfort and expand your repertoire rather than perform according to a rigid criterion. Playfulness and experimentation mean being aware of your desires and preferences and feeling free to express them.

Experimentation is based on feeling comfortable sharing with your partner and giving feedback. To reemphasize, sexual intercourse involves a sharing and mutuality that take into account the needs, feelings, and preferences of both partners. You can expand sexual awareness by exploring intercourse positions, variations, and multiple stimulation during intercourse.

POSITION VARIATIONS

Popular misconceptions involve two extremes—either that man on top is the only normal position or that sexual intercourse has no limits with regard to positions. In reality, the basic intercourse positions are few in number. We will describe four positions, all of which have interesting variations. Intercourse should not be used to prove something—be it sexual prowess, physical agility, or the ability to do it better than the book. Rather, you need to develop an intercourse style that is comfortable, functional, and satisfying for both partners. It doesn't matter what a book says or what others do.

To use the analogy of ice cream, some people prefer vanilla while others try two or three flavors. Some sample 9 or 10 but usually stay with 1 or 2, although once a month they try an exotic flavor. And there are those who try all 33 flavors and then make up their own. This reflects people's attitudes and individual preferences toward intercourse positions and variations. It is not a question of what is normal or abnormal; it is an acknowledgment of differences in style and preference and finding a flavor you both enjoy. The important question is what is right for you as a couple.

ROB AND ELAINE

Is it possible to have a successful sexual relationship if intercourse is unsatisfactory? Most people, including marital therapists, would say no, but they have not met Rob and Elaine. This late-20s couple was living together, considering marriage within a year, and had worked out a number of relationship issues, especially conflict regarding their two careers.

Rob and Elaine felt attraction and arousal. They began intercourse after a month of dating, but it had not gone well. They believed it was simply a matter of time and practice. Sex problems either get better or worse; they seldom stay the same. Although their nonintercourse erotic relationship became much better, intercourse became worse. They had erotic, nonintercourse sex between three and five times a week, with both Elaine and Rob experiencing pleasure, eroticism, and orgasm. However, in their once-a-month attempt at intercourse, the result was intromission and thrusting but minimal arousal for Elaine. Rob would reach orgasm, but Elaine never did.

Elaine felt that until this problem was resolved she was not ready to marry. Rob believed he and Elaine were a special couple and was committed to marriage. Although a private person, Rob agreed to seek couple sex therapy.

Rob did not receive adequate penile stimulation during intercourse. He complained of Elaine's passivity during intercourse in contrast to her being active during manual and oral stimulation. Elaine was frustrated because she was waiting for Rob to take the lead. He seemed indecisive and inept with intercourse. The only position they used was man on top, and during intercourse the only activity was Rob's thrusting. It is amazing how the learnings people have gleaned from pleasuring and eroticism fall away when they switch to intercourse.

Elaine became aware that intercourse was not solely Rob's domain. Intercourse was a shared, pleasurable erotic activity in which she had an active role. Rob learned to ask for additional stimulation and take an involved, experimental approach during intercourse. The therapist suggested psychosexual skill exercises to break their rigid pattern and introduced the concept of intercourse as a mutual pleasuring experience, They experimented with woman-on-top and side-by-side positions, alternated who controlled thrusting, used multiple stimulation during intercourse (including breast touching, testicle stimulation, and kissing), and Elaine flexed her pelvic muscles while Rob was inside her. These techniques, in addition to greater communication and the experience of intercourse as a mutual activity, increased pleasure, eroticism, and satisfaction. At the tenth therapy session, Elaine happily announced they had set a wedding date.

INTERCOURSE AS A NATURAL EXTENSION OF PLEASURING AND EROTICISM

Intercourse and orgasm have been overemphasized to the detriment of naturally developing sensual and sexual response. The natural transition from pleasuring to arousing, erotic intercourse can be smooth and flowing. Being aware of your partner's responsivity and sharing your sexual feelings are crucial.

A good guideline is to engage in pleasuring that deliberately does not end in intercourse at least once every 3 to 6 months or whenever you feel a need to be intimate but do not desire intercourse. It is easy to fall into the trap in which all touching becomes intercourse oriented and you lose appreciation of the pleasuring–eroticism process. Continue to enjoy nongenital sensuality, genital pleasuring, and erotic scenarios and techniques. Most couples find it better to make the transition to intercourse at high levels of erotic flow rather than at low levels of arousal (7 to 8 rather than 4 to 5 on a 10-point arousal scale). Intercourse is enhanced when it occurs as a choice and not as an each-and-every-time routine. The key is to view intercourse as a natural transition in the pleasure–eroticism process, not a pass–fail test separate from pleasure.

POSITION EXERCISES

First Exercise: Woman on Top

Talk about what you have learned during nongenital touching, genital pleasuring, and other desire and eroticism exercises you have tried. In particular, share feelings about the nondemand orientation and the transition from pleasuring to erotic flow. Do not fall into the trap of making intercourse a pressured, goal-oriented task.

Discuss previous experiences, if any, with the woman-on-top position. Expunge the common myth that the man should always be the sexual initiator and dominant figure. Having the woman on top allows the couple to experiment with a position that encourages her to initiate and be active. In addition, it is recommended for treating sexual dysfunction that can occur in both partners (i.e., nonorgasmic response and premature ejaculation). At first glance, the woman-on-top position may seem threatening. In reality, it neither threatens nor impinges upon feelings of femininity or masculinity. It enables both partners to be active and expressive and build on each other's arousal. It allows the man to enjoy receiving pleasure rather than having to assume the role of active, controlling partner. This can expand his awareness and enhance feelings of masculinity and sexuality.

The woman can begin as pleasure-giver. Switch to mutual pleasuring, utilizing manual and oral stimulation, allowing the stimulation to be caring and rhythmic. The transition to intercourse should be unhurried and flowing. He can lie comfortably on the bed, with you straddling his upper thighs, your knees bent.

Do not immediately proceed to intromission. Continue with pleasuring, allowing excitement and erotic flow to build. Though he is in a passive position, he is free to actively touch and stroke you, to manually stimulate your vulva or move his penis around your mons and clitoral area. Initiate intromission when both of you are feeling aroused. An advantage of this position is that you can guide his penis into your vagina and control the depth of penetration. You can gently and unhurriedly insert his penis by sliding back on it at about a 45-degree angle. Utilize whatever type of thrusting you find arousing—slow up-and-down, circular, rhythmic in-and-out, or any combination thereof. He can request the type of movement and speed that is comfortable and arousing for him. Experimenting and giving feedback is the best way to establish mutually enjoyable intercourse.

The man can utilize his greater freedom to caress, stroke, and fondle your body throughout intercourse. Multiple stimulation during intercourse facilitates arousal for both partners. He can stimulate your clitoral area manually. Many women find it easier to be orgasmic during intercourse with additional clitoral stimulation whether by his hands, your hands, or a vibrator. Another advantage of the woman-on-top position is better ejaculatory control, so that both partners can enjoy prolonged sexual intercourse (2 to 7 minutes). Be aware of and enjoy cues from eye contact and facial expression. This is an excellent position for nonverbal and verbal communication; make the most of this opportunity.

One of the most cited disadvantages of the woman on top is that his penis can slip out of your vagina. We suggest experimenting with loss of penile containment. Rather than reacting with anxiety or panic (a trap for the man), use this break to engage in additional pleasuring; when arousal is high, proceed with a second intromission. Losing penile containment does not have to be a fearful event. Rather than trying to reinsert immediately, enjoy manual or oral stimulation. When you both feel aroused and desirous of coming together, return to the woman-on-top position, with penile reentry driven by erotic flow. Occasional loss of containment is to be expected in this position since he does not control coital thrusting. The reason so many couples exclusively use the man-on-top position is that it is easiest for him to guide intromission and maintain penile–vaginal containment. Staying with the man-on-top position for security inhibits sexual playfulness and pleasure.

Many couples have a difficult time with the transition from intercourse to afterplay. This transition can be comfortable and flowing rather than an abrupt stop followed by something totally different. Intercourse typically ends when the man has an orgasm. Achieving orgasm by both partners at each intercourse is a poor criterion for sexual satisfaction. Generally, at each intercourse the man will have an orgasm. However, this is not always true, especially for older males. The woman might be nonorgasmic, singly orgasmic, or multiorgasmic. Female sexual response is more complex and variable. Typically the woman is orgasmic in 70% of couple sexual encounters, with only about 10 to 15% of women orgasmic at each sexual encounter. You might be orgasmic during pleasuring, intercourse, or afterplay. When your partner pressures you to have an orgasm during intercourse, you feel invalidated and frustrated.

At the point when he ejaculates, you might already have had an orgasm (or several orgasms) or you might feel the need to be orgasmic. If you do not desire orgasm, decrease movement, stay in the woman-on-top position for at least a minute, hold and touch, and share feelings. Sharing feelings is very different from clinically analyzing and rating the experience. The latter promotes resentment about being judged and results in emotional alienation. Switch to a comfortable afterplay position where you can see and touch each other. You may want to have tissues or a towel nearby so you can wipe off the semen, or, if you are comfortable with the feel of the semen on your body, let it be.

Once you find a comfortable position, be aware of your own and your partner's resolution ("coming down") reactions. Share how you feel and what you would like; be playful, hold, rub his chest, run your fingers through his hair, talk. Afterplay can be a special bonding time. Sometimes you become rearoused and desire a second intercourse. If this happens, fine. However, do not push yourselves. Second erections are less easy to attain and second orgasms less fulfilling for the man. Afterplay is an intimate sharing experience, only occasionally oriented toward rearousal.

When the woman desires an additional or first orgasmic experience after the man ejaculates, it is important that she clearly and assertively request this. One partner should never insist that the other has an orgasm. This is one of our few absolutes in sexuality. We have seen the negative results of this pressure. The man partially loses his erection after ejaculation, so continued intercourse movement can be irritating to his penis. Continue intercourse only if it is comfortable for him.

There are several alternatives to help you reach orgasm: he can use manual clitoral stimulation, including manual intravaginal stimulation, while at the same time orally stimulating your breasts; you can rub your pelvis against him; he can do cunnilingus; you can manually stimulate yourself; he can use vibrator stimulation. You can combine and vary these techniques. After orgasm, continue to hold and touch. Even if—and sometimes especially if—one or both partners has not been orgasmic the afterplay experience is important. Instead of feeling unfulfilled or frustrated, afterplay offers a positive way to end the sexual experience.

It is normal that some intercourse experiences are mediocre, and at least a few will be downright failures. On average 5 to 15% of sexual encounters are dissatisfying or dysfunctional. Accept this. Do not expect each experience to be memorable. Being able to laugh about a not-so-great intercourse is a crucial ingredient in healthy couple sexuality.

There are several variations of the woman-on-top position, as there are for other intercourse positions. You can lie directly on top of him, be in a semikneeling position, or sit up with your face away from his. Share feelings; discuss what you liked and did not and what to refine so you can enjoy greater pleasure in the future. Remember, the first try at anything (recall your first experience with nongenital pleasuring) can be awkward. It takes practice and feedback to feel comfortable with intercourse positions and techniques.

Second Exercise: Man on Top

Man on top is by far the most popular intercourse position among American couples. If you use it often or exclusively, discuss what aspects are particularly enjoyable. Some commonly mentioned advantages are that it allows face-to-face interaction that facilitates verbal and nonverbal communication.

Many couples find kissing during intercourse highly enjoyable, and the man-on-top position easily allows this. Intromission is smoothest in this position and penile containment easy to maintain. It is also the best position for couples who are trying to get pregnant. The man can control thrusting, and this position allows for deep, sustained vaginal penetration after he ejaculates. If you are not using the man-on-top position to advantage, discuss how you might experiment with variations so that intercourse is mutually enjoyable.

Spend more than your usual amount of time with pleasuring, Continue until the woman signals or initiates movement toward intercourse. Allow arousal to erotic flow before beginning intercourse. Although at times minimal pleasuring followed by quick, vigorous intercourse can be erotic, one of the biggest mistakes couples make is to begin intercourse before they—especially the woman—feel sufficiently aroused.

She lies comfortably on her back with legs apart and knees slightly bent. She can elevate her pelvis by putting a pillow under her buttocks. You can partially support yourself by placing your knees or arms on the pillow or bed. Do not make your partner uncomfortable by requiring her to support your full body weight. When you remove body weight, the couple is freer to share the rhythm of pelvic movements. In this exercise, you control the type and speed of coital thrusting.

Once in the man-on-top position, do not immediately proceed to intromission. You can rub your penis around her vulva and clitoral area. She can focus on the pleasurable feelings and sensations of your penis and can take the initiative in guiding you into her vagina. Begin coital thrusting with a slow, steady, rhythmic movement. Initially penetration should not be deeper than 1.5 inches (roughly two finger joints) into her vagina. Keep the thrusting slow and rhythmic. As arousal builds, you can gradually increase the depth of penetration and rhythm of movement.

Multiple stimulation can occur throughout intercourse. A common mistake is to cease other stimulation as soon as penetration occurs. You and she can kiss; you can fondle her breasts and she can scratch your back; you can massage her buttocks while she plays with your chest or testicles. As she becomes aroused, do not abruptly increase thrusting. Slowly increase the rhythm. Notice your reaction to rhythmic, steady thrusting. Compare that with short, rapid stroking. Does multiple stimulation throughout intercourse increase your involvement and arousal?

When you ejaculate, increase sensations by thrusting deeply into her vagina. During ejaculation most men cease movement and focus on the sensations of climax. Be aware of your excitement and pleasure during ejaculation.

After ejaculation, stay in this position for a minute or so. Look at your partner and communicate feelings about the experience you just shared. In afterplay, you might want to explore a playful mood rather than emphasizing comfort or intimacy. You could have a pillow fight, tickle each other, or play a frivolous game with your hands.

Experiment with position variations, including having her legs fully elevated and resting on your shoulders; put a pillow under her buttocks to adjust the vaginal angle or have your partner lock her legs around your body. Man on top is the most common position because it has advantages for both partners. Feel free to experiment with variations in pleasuring, intercourse, and afterplay so that you can fully experience and enjoy the man-on-top position.

Third Exercise: Side by Side

Side-by-side intercourse is viewed by sophisticated couples as the most enjoyable and arousing position. However, this position does not come naturally. It takes a good deal of working together and communicating as well as tolerating awkwardness and unsuccessful tries.

There are many variations of the side-by-side position. We will focus on the "scissors" variation. Before beginning, agree that you will use this exercise to explore and experiment rather than become frustrated with yourself or your partner. A single attempt will not afford the necessary opportunity to experience its benefits. You are likely to feel self-conscious and unsure at first.

Begin with mutual pleasuring; enjoy giving and receiving pleasure simultaneously. Feel free to move and change pleasuring positions. Notice some are smooth transitions (e.g., from the man stimulating the woman's breast to the couple kissing and holding), while other changes punctuate the rhythm of pleasuring—for example, after lying side by side and holding each other, she disengages and moves behind him to caress his back and buttocks. Both smooth and distinct transitions can be erotic and add variety.

The easiest way to move into the scissors intercourse position is from the woman-on-top position. Penile intromission is challenging (and many find it impossible) from the scissors position. From the woman-on-top position, you kneel, and move slightly forward on his chest. As you move forward, he helps place your extended leg behind you. Raise your other leg in a bent-knee fashion over his upper thigh (approaching the level of his waist). On the side where your leg extended, his leg is extended parallel to yours. Put your head by his shoulders, and together roll to the side-by-side position. We suggest not having the penis in your vagina the first time you try this. In rolling, the penis sometimes slips out. To prevent this, when the couple rolls, he can hold your buttocks so the penile–vaginal connection is more secure.

If while moving into the side-by-side position or during intercourse you lose penile connection, do not panic. Return to the female-on-top position, and use the transition to touch and rebuild pleasure and erotic flow before returning to the side-by-side position.

Take advantage of the potential provided by the side-by-side position. Since you are facing each other, use eye contact and facial cues to convey pleasure. You have greater freedom of movement because you do not have to support your partner's body weight. Use that freedom to enjoy a variety of coital and touching movements and experience the sensations of whole-body contact. To increase comfort, use pillows under your head or back. Place pillows on the bed so they are in easy reach after you transition to the side-by-side position.

Take advantage of access to your partner's body. From this position, more than any other, you can utilize multiple stimulation during intercourse. It is easy to shift which partner directs the rhythm of coital thrusting. The partner controlling thrusting can at the same time be pleasured nongenitally and genitally. In subsequent experiences try variations—for example, have the partner controlling the thrusting also do the pleasuring. At least once, change the person directing coital thrusting. Switch rhythm or type of thrusting to be in tune with your needs. This is especially important for the woman. You can freely engage in coital thrusting to increase your level of arousal. This is an excellent position for ejaculatory control, so he can enjoy arousal without worrying about premature ejaculation.

In the side-by-side position, you are free to enjoy intercourse and not push for rapid orgasm. Remember, it is not mandatory that both partners achieve orgasm during intercourse. It is easier for the woman to have orgasm first because there is a good deal of pelvic and indirect clitoral stimulation. If you desire further orgasms after his ejaculation, he can utilize manual stimulation. Some couples enjoy doing this from the side-by-side position, while others switch to a pleasuring position in which he has more freedom of movement.

One of the most harmful myths is that simultaneous orgasms are superior and the ultimate in sex. Setting simultaneous orgasm as a goal is a major mistake. Orgasms last 3 to 10 seconds, so striving to achieve perfect timing distracts from the mutual experience of pleasure and eroticism. It is frustrating if the goal of simultaneous orgasm is not achieved, which it usually is not. Accept simultaneous orgasm as enjoyable if it occurs, but do not set it as a goal. Some couples enjoy the experience, others do not feel simultaneous orgasm lives up to its press, and still others find it a disappointment.

The side-by-side position is excellent for afterplay. Continue to touch and share feelings of caring and connection. If you wish, you can sleep in this position.

Side-by-side intercourse takes getting used to. To realize its benefits, you need to refine, play, and experiment. Feel free to explore variations of side-by-side intercourse.

Fourth Exercise: Rear Entry

Discuss negative reactions you might have to the rear-entry position. People confuse rear-entry intercourse with anal intercourse. Rear entry means the positioning is altered, but the penis is in the vagina. This is not anal intercourse, in which the penis is inserted in the woman's anus—although there is nothing abnormal or kinky about anal intercourse. It is a variation in sexual technique that one in five couples experiment with and that 5% use as a regular part of their lovemaking. Since HIV is most easily transmitted through anal intercourse, we strongly advise couples not to use this unless they are absolutely sure both partners are HIV negative. If you engage in anal intercourse, use a condom or take care to wash the penis with soap before placing it in her vagina. Vaginal infections are caused when anal intercourse is followed by vaginal intercourse without adequate hygienic measures.

A misconception about rear-entry penis–vagina intercourse is that it represents a bestial orientation, since many animals use rear-entry positioning. In reality, there is nothing primitive or animalistic about rear-entry intercourse. In some cultures with a liberated sexual climate the rear-entry position is a favorite.

Another myth is that rear entry is a homosexual position or that people who use it are "latent homosexuals." What makes an act homosexual is the gender of the partners involved, not the technique used.

With those misconceptions aside, be aware of the advantages and discoveries available with the rear-entry position. A major advantage is that it allows the man considerable freedom in pleasuring the woman. Your hands are free to caress, fondle, and stroke her body both in back and front. The sensation of your body against her buttocks is sensual and erotic. You are free to massage her mons and clitoral area during intercourse, making this an excellent position for multiple stimulation. A side variation of the rear-entry position is comfortable and minimally exerting. Side rear-entry is a recommended intercourse position during the later months of pregnancy.

This exercise focuses on the side rear-entry position. Don't lose sight of the fact that the emphasis is on exploring and experiencing rather than testing your sexual prowess. Communicate, share feelings, and experiment to discover how rear-entry intercourse can enhance your sexual relationship.

Begin with a shower or bath, being particularly aware of the buttocks as you wash them. Allow pleasure to be a free-flowing mutual experience. Be playful. You can run your fingers through her hair, draw an imaginary circle on her body while kissing it, or tickle her feet. She might lightly fondle your chest, stomach, shoulders, and genitals as she lies behind you with her body resting against your back. When both of you are feeling aroused, position yourself behind her. As you lie next to her, you can caress and fondle her breasts, neck, stomach, buttocks, and mons.

With both partners lying on their left side, they bend their right legs, she extending her left leg to a comfortable position. Extend your left leg behind you and bend it slightly. When you are settled, lift your body high enough to guide intromission. As you guide your penis into her vagina, she can shift her body to help establish penile containment. Some women prefer to reach behind and guide intromission. Let intromission proceed slowly. If you have difficulty, do not panic or feel pressure. Remember, you are learning and exploring.

Begin slow, rhythmic thrusting, being careful not to penetrate too deeply since in this position the vaginal canal is shorter. Deeper penetration is an advantage of the kneeling rear-entry position. She can guide your manual caresses over her body and change thrusting by moving her pelvis in harmony with your rhythm.

As intercourse continues, caress her clitoral area, which can heighten arousal and culminate in orgasm. Be aware of whether she desires orgasm during intercourse because once you ejaculate you are unable to maintain penile containment. If you do ejaculate before she is orgasmic, you can use manual stimulation so she can have her first or additional orgasms. It is not mandatory that both partners experience orgasm at each encounter. Remember, orgasm as a pass–fail performance test subverts emotional and sexual satisfaction.

The afterplay period is important in making this an integrated experience. Change positions so you have eye contact as you come down together. Discuss what you value about the experience. Perhaps you enjoy the feeling of her buttocks against your genitals or touching her back during intercourse; perhaps she enjoys simultaneous manual and penile stimulation or buttock stimulation. Explore and experiment with variations of rear-entry intercourse, including with the woman kneeling or sitting on you while you are lying on your back.

CLOSING THOUGHTS

Intercourse is a special erotically charged experience for both partners—a natural extension of the shared pleasuring–eroticism process. Feel free to experiment with additional intercourse positions such as woman sitting/man kneeling or both standing. Intercourse is best when integrated with pleasuring, eroticism, and afterplay. It is least pleasurable and potentially destructive when viewed as a performance test.

10

SEXUALITY AND AGING

A biological fact of life is that our bodies are continually changing. While development is intensely studied in children and adolescents, much less study and research has been devoted to the aging process, especially as it affects sexual desire and function. Sexual changes with aging occur gradually, involve large individual differences, and are multicausal and multidimensional.

Your body changes in ways that affect your sexual response, body image, feelings, and sexual self-esteem. Our youth-oriented culture focuses on the passionate, performance-oriented aspect of sexual encounters. Little attention was paid to the effects of aging on sexual function until the pioneering work of Masters and Johnson. The result is that the area of sexual expression in persons 60 and older is myth ridden, poorly understood, and neglected. Couples who desire to continue pleasurable sexual function need to be aware of your bodily changes and changes in your partner. You need to communicate and develop a positive attitude toward sexuality and aging. The more aware, comfortable, and knowledgeable you are about aging and sexuality the better. This includes psychological, biological, social/relational, and psychosexual skill factors. Knowledge is power.

MYTHS ABOUT SEX AND AGING

There are myriad myths about sex and aging. A prevalent fallacy is that when a woman enters menopause (typically between the ages of 45 and 55) her desire for sex ends. The older woman who values sexual pleasure and intercourse is viewed as an anomaly or "oversexed." Menopause—a topic shrouded in myths—involves changes in hormonal functioning as well as the cessation of the menstrual cycle and the ability to conceive a child. However, the need for affection, sensuality, pleasure, and eroticism continues, perhaps at an even greater rate since contraception and fear of pregnancy are no longer factors inhibiting sexual desire.

The man who does not get an immediate, strong erection or feels a lessened need to ejaculate might believe the myth that he is "burned out" sexually. The need for direct penile stimulation and taking longer to get an erection are normal, natural concomitants of aging. It is untrue that a man has only so many ejaculations and then runs out, although at 60 you may no longer feel the need to ejaculate at *every* sexual opportunity. Regularity of sexual expression throughout adulthood is the best way to promote continued sexual function after age 60. The famous adage "use it or lose it" is based on scientific fact.

Another myth is that sex is for the young and beautiful. According to this misconception, as you get older and lines develop around your eyes, your skin wrinkles and weight increases, sexual desire disappears along with sexual desirability. While this could not be further from the truth, what is true is that when people become self-conscious they develop a self-defeating attitude that becomes a self-fulfilling prophecy. The good scientific news is that you can enjoy sexuality in your 60s, 70s, and 80s.

A particularly prevalent myth is that it is the woman who stops being sexual. In reality, in over 90% of couples, when sexuality ceases it is the man's decision. He becomes frustrated with erection and ejaculation problems and decides sex is just not worth it. Sex is more of an embarrassment and frustration than a pleasure. He says to himself, "I don't want to start something I can't finish." So he avoids all sensual and sexual contact. It is a sad, unnecessary loss for the man, woman, and couple.

As we age, our need for warmth, affection, self-esteem, pleasure, eroticism, and orgasm continue. Being sensual and sexual is a sign of positive psychological adjustment to aging.

CHANGES WITH AGING

In the aging process there are regular, normal, predictable changes in your body, including decreased genital vasocongestion (blood flow to your genitals), which affect your sexual response. However, the changes that accompany aging can be incorporated into your self-image without losing sexual self-esteem.

Develop a positive outlook about your sexuality and communicate this to your partner. Although your body reacts more slowly as you age, the need for sensual pleasure and healthy sexuality is still very much alive. Sexual response is different, not worse. Whatever your age, the basic need for touching, warmth, and intimacy does not diminish; indeed, with aging, these needs increase. Life is a balance of physical, psychological, social, and sexual components. It makes sense that social, psychological, and sexual factors will become more important as your physical state changes. Sexual response may be less physically intense, but it becomes more cooperative, interactive, and intimate for the aging couple. Sexuality continues to be an integral, positive force. With aging, you need each other more, and couple sexuality becomes more human and genuine.

For a woman, changes during and after menopause are gradual. The walls of your vagina become thinner and less elastic, lubrication is slower and lessens in volume, and your vagina does not expand as rapidly. If there are distressing symptoms, such as painful intercourse or uterine spasms after orgasm, we urge you to consult a gynecologist or endocrinologist with expertise in hormonal management of menopause and the aging process. Hormone replacement therapy is more likely to focus on specific interventions such as an estrogen-based cream rather than systemic, ongoing hormone therapy. Make it clear to your physician that continued healthy sexual expression is important to you. Unfortunately, too many physicians believe myths about sexuality and aging or are too embarrassed to discuss sexual function and problems with people over 50. With men over 50, the physician will offer a pro-erection medication rather than talk with him about psychological, health, and relational factors that involve sexuality with aging.

It is not aging itself that decreases sexual function but rather illness and especially side effects of medications. We specifically recommend scheduling a consultation as a couple with your internist or specialist (cardiologist, neurologist, oncologist, endocrinologist, or psychiatrist). You are not asking for sex therapy but how to be an active, involved patient, to address the illness, to minimize the side effects of medication, and to explore whether there are changes in medication or health habits that can promote healthy sexuality.

Psychologically, the most important resource is to see sex and aging as a challenge, not as a loss, which seems to be more the case for men, and to adopt the approach of "beating the odds." You can feel more sexually motivated if you learn to build on your partner's arousal. Relationally, view your partner as both your intimate and erotic friend. Equally important is use of psychosexual skills. These include transitioning to intercourse at high levels of erotic flow rather than as soon as he has an erection, having the woman guide intromission, and using a vaginal lubricant before a sexual encounter or incorporating it into the pleasuring scenario.

ADELE AND JAMES

The most enjoyable couple Barry ever had the privilege of working with were Adele and James. Adele was 64 and James 67. They had been married for 43 years and had three grown children and four grandchildren. They loved, respected, and trusted each other and valued their marital bond. They had an admirable marriage and interesting, full lives. Both continued part-time employment, so they had the freedom and money to pursue interests in travel, community activities, and grandchildren. They were cooperative in sharing parenting before it became vogue. They were affectionate with the kids, although not open or communicative sex educators. They kept in close contact with their adult children and grandchildren.

Unfortunately, their sexual relationship had always been difficult. James had a chronic problem of premature ejaculation. Foreplay was relatively brief and uninventive. Although Adele enjoyed the symbolism of sexually coming together, intercourse was unrewarding for her. They were affectionate, but the concepts of nondemand pleasuring and eroticism were totally foreign to them.

James and Adele regretted their poor sex life, though neither spoke of it so as not to highlight difficulties and make the spouse feel bad. Occasionally they would read in a popular magazine or hear at a church group about the importance of communication for a sexual relationship. Although they felt closer for a week and pledged to try harder, this resolve soon fizzled out. Twenty years previously when the media highlighted the importance of female orgasm, Adele and James decided that must be the problem. They concentrated on Adele achieving orgasm. When she became orgasmic, Adele was pleased and James felt they were on their way to a satisfying sexual relationship. However, after 2 months that impetus also came to a standstill.

Adele and James consulted Barry after hearing him discuss sexuality and aging in a presentation about intimate marriage. Their intercourse frequency was once a month, with minimum pleasuring or sexual play. Adele and James were a committed, communicative, affectionate couple with a solid base from which to develop an intimate, interactive sexual relationship. Therapy started by putting a prohibition on intercourse and introducing nongenital pleasuring exercises. James and Adele took to these experiences like ducks to water. When genital pleasuring was added, the transition from sensual to sexual was smooth. Within a month Adele was regularly orgasmic with manual and rubbing stimulation. When intercourse was reintroduced as an extension of pleasuring, Adele used a lubricant as part of the pleasuring–eroticism process, which facilitated the transition to intercourse. James was surprised and pleased to find he now had better ejaculatory control—a bonus of aging and a comfortable sexual relationship. The process of pleasuring facilitated a slower, more intimate couple sexual style that generalized to intercourse. After 3 months of sex therapy, James and Adele not only had a better sexual relationship than the majority of people in their 60s but also a more intimate and erotic relationship than most couples in their 30s.

MEDICAL FACTORS AND INTERVENTIONS

Anything that affects physical health will affect sexual health. As you age, you are dealing with more illness and are taking more medications, many of which have negative sexual side effects. In addition, your physical body is less efficient. The three systems that most impact sexual functioning—hormonal, vascular, and neurological—operate less efficiently. Therefore, we emphasize the importance of enhancing psychological, relational, and psychosexual skill factors in maintaining healthy couple sexuality.

Maintaining healthy habits—especially getting sufficient sleep and exercise and eating properly—is crucial. Eliminating smoking is important because smoking affects vascular function, which impacts sexual response. Drinking moderately or not at all becomes a factor because alcohol is a central nervous system depressant that also inhibits sexual function.

The Viagra commercials initiated a media campaign that medicalized male sexuality. While that campaign overstated the drug's promise, Viagra, Cialis, and Levitra are positive resources. However, they are not "magic pills" that return a man to the erections of his 20s. For both men and women, testosterone—the hormone that most influences sexual desire—can be valuable if medically needed, especially in gel or patch form. For many women, estrogen supplements used in patch or cream form also can be a valuable resource. However, these medical resources need to be integrated into your couple sexual style, not relied on to ignite passion. Requisite for a vital, integrated sexuality as you age are intimacy, nondemand pleasuring, erotic scenarios and techniques, and positive, realistic expectations.

SEXUAL GAINS WITH AGING

In discussing perceptions and feelings, we encourage you to emphasize gains, not dwell on losses. Changes in the rate and speed of sexual response mean that you spend more time with pleasuring and enjoy gradually building excitement. Slower response allows you to be a loving couple and enjoy a variety of pleasuring scenarios and erotic techniques. Aging couples find that sharing intimacy and eroticism is a more fully involving experience than the predictable sex of their 20s and 30s. They enjoy the flexibility and variability of sensual, playful, erotic, and intercourse touch. We call this the Good Enough Sex (GES) model. GES in no way implies inferiority; rather, it promotes acceptance of a variable, flexible pleasure-oriented approach to intimacy and couple sexuality based on realistic expectations of the varying circumstances that occur in every stage of life.

The psychosexual skill exercises presented in this chapter facilitate comfort with age-related changes in your body. Sharing and communicating are crucial. There are two overriding guidelines. The first is to support your partner as she or he strives to positively adapt to sexual changes. The second is that each of you guide your partner by clearly and directly expressing your needs and desires as you explore sexual expression that includes, but is not limited to, intercourse and orgasm.

First Exercise: Sensual Time

Discuss the major sexual change that occurs with aging—namely, the increase in length of time needed for arousal. An erection that was fast, automatic, and autonomous at age 20 now takes longer, needs partner stimulation, and is not completely "hard." For the woman, there is a major decrease in vaginal lubrication and an increase in the time to arousal and lubrication; thus, the majority of women over age 45 use additional lubrication. Although your body is a less efficient sexual machine, it does provide you the opportunity to enjoy being sensual, giving, and flexible lovers as you adopt the variable, flexible GES approach.

Begin by taking a relaxing, sensuous bath or shower. As you lie together, be aware of your partner's body and of feeling emotionally close and connected. Allow touching to be sensual, warm, nondemanding, and flowing. Intermix nongenital and genital pleasuring. Be aware of your own and your partner's gradually growing sexual responsivity. Accept the sensations rather than trying to force or speed up arousal. Instead of reaching into the vagina to check on lubrication, you can gently massage her inner thighs, breasts, back, and shoulders. Use a hypoallergenic lotion (baby oil, aloe vera lotion, Astroglide, K-Y) as an additional lubricant. The man should not focus stimulation on the labia, clitoris, or vagina until she is receptive and moderately aroused (a 6 on the 10-point arousal scale). She can teasingly touch and caress his penis and genitals and enjoy his slowly building erection (accept its firmness; do not compare it to that of a 20-year-old athlete). Women are used to arousal coming from a giving, interactive partner. Instead of mourning the loss of automatic, autonomous erections, the man can learn to enjoy "grown-up erections" that come from being receptive and responsive to her stimulation rather than wish for the autonomous "show-up erections" of his 20s.

Enjoy your partner's building arousal. Touch in a nondemanding manner; enjoy the relaxed, sensuous atmosphere, which compares favorably to the demanding, goal-oriented approaches of youth. When both of you are feeling aroused, you can proceed to intercourse or stay with these good feelings. If you choose the latter, while holding and touching discuss your reactions and feelings to the lengthening time of sexual receptivity and response. If you proceed to intercourse, be sure to set aside time to discuss feelings about your comfort, pleasure, arousal, and erotic flow pattern. How do you feel about the man's less firm erection? Do you miss the quicker, heavier flow of vaginal lubrication? Can you accept your partner's slower, more variable, flexible arousal cycle? Can you enjoy this less predictable, more playful couple sexuality? Integrate these changes into your feelings about yourself as a sexual person and the two of you as a sexual couple.

Second Exercise: Sexual Advantages

Now that you have a sense of enhanced pleasure and understand how the lengthened time for arousal can heighten your sexual experience, you can focus on changes during eroticism and intercourse. The major changes for the woman are thinner and less flexible vaginal walls, decreased lubrication, and diminished intensity of orgasm. For the man, erection takes longer and requires direct penile stimulation, ejaculatory control is easier, and he no longer needs to ejaculate at each intercourse. In addition, erection requires more stimulation for rearousal and quickly decreases after ejaculation.

Discuss changes in your body's responsiveness, and ask questions about your partner's changes. Allow the discussion to be frank, explicit, and honest. Do your experiences follow the information presented on age-related changes, or are they different? Remember, each person and couple is unique. The woman wants to know how he feels about stimulating her when her arousal is slower. How about sensations of vaginal containment? How does he feel about her orgasmic response? Does she enjoy helping him get an erection? How does she feel about changes in erectile ease and predictability? How does she feel when he ejaculates? He also can inquire about her reaction when he does not ejaculate. With aging, female sexual response is easier and more predictable than male sexual response. How do each of you feel about this? It is a reversal of traditional sexual socialization and experiences. Can you welcome and embrace it?

It is important to accept natural body changes, to support your partner in making positive adaptations, to view sexuality in a broad-based manner, and to accept intercourse as part of your sexual repertoire rather than as the main (or only) act. Be open to experiences that are available as a result of the aging process, specifically his ability to better control ejaculation and her ability to maintain arousal. Sexual arousal becomes a more interactive, cooperative experience. Enjoy this gradual, mutual whole-body sensual and sexual arousal.

Use pleasuring techniques—nongenital and genital touching, oral stimulation, pleasuring positions, whole-body contact, multiple stimulation—to facilitate your arousal. Enjoy the gradual build-up, and take pleasure in observing your partner's mounting excitement. Be supportive, warm, giving, and loving. Enjoy your more interactive sexuality. A great advantage of aging sexuality is that it's more human and genuine; you have increased need for each other sexually.

Demanding that the man get an erection increases pressure, which increases performance anxiety and dampens arousal. Instead, the woman can use a variety of manual and oral stimulation techniques. As his subjective arousal builds, so will his erection. He can deal sensitively with the slowness of her lubrication, accepting that she may be subjectively aroused although her physiological responses are more extended. Do not raise her anxiety, which decreases arousal and lubrication, but continue with sensual and sexual touching. Pleasuring naturally leads to heightened arousal. Experiment with K-Y or a hypoallergenic lotion for additional lubrication. Self-consciousness is antierotic. Focus on positive feelings and sexual sensations. Enjoy the pleasuring process and erotic flow.

Before initiating intercourse, be sure both of you are receptive and aroused. Do not pressure yourself or your partner. Intercourse is not a performance test. Even if the man's erection is not completely hard, it is firm enough for penetration. Let her guide intromission. She can caress your penis and actively facilitate insertion. She can direct coital thrusting to enhance feelings and sensations. During intercourse continue slow, tender, rhythmic movements. Enjoy the warm and erotic feelings. Instead of focusing solely on penis–vagina contact, engage in multiple stimulation. Touching, fantasizing, and caressing during intercourse is an effective arousal technique for old and young alike.

You can savor the entire experience and avoid the youthful trap of expecting and demanding rapid genital release. She can enjoy being orgasmic whether before, during, or after intercourse. Notice that orgasm is a whole-body sensation rather than an intense, focused genital experience. As you ejaculate, enjoy the feelings that have developed throughout pleasuring and intercourse. Focus on sensual and sexual feelings throughout your body, and accept the less commanding genital sensations. Celebrate heightened sharing, flexibility, and variability. Sexuality and aging facilitate an integrated, broad-based sexual experience. Sex may be less physically intense, but it is more intimate and satisfying. GES is what keeps sexuality alive and satisfying into your 80s.

To complete the experience, bask in the afterplay phase. While holding and touching, discuss how pleasuring, eroticism, and intercourse can continue as a vital part of your intimate relationship. Sexuality as we age can be just as or more satisfying than when we were in our youth, even though sexual function is more variable and flexible.

Third Exercise: Erection and Ejaculation

This exercise focuses on making a positive adjustment to two of the more threatening aspects of the aging process—the man's less predictable erection and the lessened need for ejaculation. During youth, erections were easy, automatic, and autonomous, with ejaculation accompanying each intercourse. Even if a young man is fatigued, drinks too much, is not aroused, or becomes stressed or ill, he considers lack of erection or ejaculation to be a failure.

Typically, men are not knowledgeable about changes in erection and ejaculation with aging. The sexually functional woman accepts a built-in variability in her arousal and orgasm experience. While orgasm is integral to her sexuality, she learns to accept and enjoy nonorgasmic experiences and does not consider this as negative or a failure. However, she is used to you ejaculating every time and overreacts when you do not. She can support you in making a positive adjustment to variable, flexible patterns of erection and ejaculation. Embracing GES is easier for your partner than for you.

What you learn to accept is that it takes longer and requires more direct penile stimulation to obtain an erection. Arousal and erection are dependent on psychological awareness, couple intimacy, partner stimulation, and learning to "piggy-back" your arousal on hers. You can have pleasurable intercourse without feeling the need to culminate in orgasm each time.

You learn to adopt the approach your partner has experienced for the past 30 years. You can be affectionate, sensual, playful, and erotic and can enjoy those dimensions as valuable in themselves. Erection and ejaculation happen when the flesh is able, but their absence is not indicative of a lack of sexual interest or pleasure. Erection, intercourse, and ejaculation are not the sole factors in sexuality for the older man. You can experience a different, more genuine sexuality than the sex of your 20s. Don't just accept but also embrace GES as offering first-class sexuality for you and your relationship.

This exercise is best done a day or two after an ejaculation when you are feeling little or no ejaculatory demand. Enjoy pleasuring, arousal, and intercourse. Both partners focus on making the interaction arousing and on prolonging stimulation; introduce your penis into her vagina under her guidance and enjoy the total sexual experience. Be aware, though, there is no demand or desire to ejaculate. Your penis is responsive to stimulation, and you enjoy arousal and erection. There is pleasure on intromission and during intercourse. If she is aroused and desires orgasm, you can enjoy her sexual satisfaction, whether during intercourse or with manual, oral, or rubbing stimulation.

Experiment with ways to make this a positive experience. You might cease intercourse and receive manual stimulation, roll over and hold her, ask her to give you a whole-body massage using lotion, or sit, touch, and talk. Make this a pleasurable experience in which you enjoy a broad range of sensual and sexual activities, including intercourse. The trap for the man is to feel that the experience is worthless if you do not ejaculate—and to push yourself to ejaculate. The trap for the woman is to commiserate about the man's "failure" or push you to ejaculate in order to prove to both herself and you that she is still sexually desirable. This is self-defeating. Your partner can have a positive experience without orgasm, and so can you.

Your sexual relationship will be enhanced if you both feel positive about nonorgasmic experiences. Ejaculating only when there is a desire for orgasm, and accepting it as normal if you do not ejaculate, will do much to enhance enjoyment of sexuality into your 60s, 70s, and 80s. A reality of sexuality and aging is role reversal: female arousal becomes easier and more predictable than male arousal. Learn to enjoy your body's changes and accept them instead of fighting them.

Are the sexual techniques you used to help her be orgasmic acceptable and enjoyable for you? Feel free to experiment with scenarios and techniques that allow both partners to enjoy a broad-based, flexible GES experience that does not depend solely on erection, intercourse, and ejaculation.

Fourth Exercise: A Special Sexual Time

Set aside 2 hours or more. You may want to include a glass of wine or one mixed drink. You could put on music, turn on an erotic video, recite your favorite poems, look at special pictures, or read romantic or sexual stories.

Take a sensuous bath or shower and lie in bed nude. The man can begin by caressing the woman's body and, while touching, describe how it looks and feels. If at any point you feel uncomfortable, you can interrupt and check on what he meant or is feeling. Focus not on what you have lost but on here-and-now feelings about your body image, desirability, and sexuality. You trust his perceptions and feelings and listen to what he says about the lovely, sensual parts of your body. You are aware of and accept bodily changes and a new body image. There is more to sexual self-esteem than a young, firm breast. Even if it has grown heavier, it is still your breast and a desirable part of you. If the man accepts your bodily changes gracefully, this facilitates your ability to think of yourself as an attractive, sexual woman. So does his expression of loving support, conveyed both verbally and by touch. The fact that you know he enjoys touching you enhances sexual intimacy. The essence of adult sexual desire is touch, not visual stimuli.

Switch roles and let the woman caress the man's body while being aware of and commenting on changes. Be open and honest in acknowledging differences in your bodily responses while she shows support, affection, and caring. Accept changes in your body tone, the wrinkles on your skin, the gray hair. You are not in training to be a sexual athlete or a movie star. Be aware of differences and relish the positive experience of prolonged pleasuring, sensual feelings, and openness to erotic scenarios and techniques. Erections take longer to achieve and there is greater need for active stimulation, but arousal is maintained by "give-and-get" pleasuring. Rather than the aging process obliterating sexual expression, it is building and reinforcing whole-body feelings. Sexuality is an involved, cooperative sharing in a giving, intimate relationship.

Intercourse can follow an extended period of pleasuring. Give and receive multiple stimulation before and during intercourse to enhance involvement, pleasure, arousal, and erotic flow. After the sexual encounter, embrace the feelings of closeness. Afterplay could involve sharing a drink, a talk, or a pillow fight. Then return to touching. You will not get a second erection, nor will you desire a second ejaculation. She is aware of a lessened need for arousal and orgasm. However, the need for touching and pleasure remains strong. Allow your second coming together to be a sensuous, whole-body experience that can overcome fears and negative feelings about attractiveness and sexual desirability.

GUIDELINES FOR SEX AFTER 60

- You are a sexual person throughout your life, no matter your age. Age does not cause sexuality to cease.
- Key to maintaining a vital sexuality is to integrate intimacy, nondemand pleasuring, and erotic scenarios and techniques.
- Contrary to popular mythology, when couples stop being sexual it is the man's decision in over 90% of cases. Because he finds sex frustrating and embarrassing, he makes the decision unilaterally and conveys it nonverbally.
- Sexuality is more likely to remain functional and satisfying when both the man and woman value a variable, flexible, pleasure-oriented couple sexual style rather than an individual performance-oriented, pass–fail intercourse test.
- With aging your hormonal, vascular, and neurological systems function less efficiently, so psychological, relational, and psychosexual skill factors become more important in maintaining a healthy, resilient sexuality.
- The best aphrodisiac is an involved, aroused partner. You turn toward each other as intimate and erotic allies.
- The "give-and-get" pleasuring guideline has particular value for the aging couple. This promotes mutual stimulation, multiple stimulation, and accepting asynchronous sexual experiences.
- The major physiological changes in male sexual response are that it takes more time and more direct penile stimulation to obtain an erection, your erection is not as firm and more likely to wane, and there is a lessened need to ejaculate at each sexual encounter.
- The major physiological changes in female sexual response are diminished vaginal lubrication that usually necessitates using a vaginal lubricant, thinner vaginal walls, increased time and stimulation required for arousal and orgasm, and less intense orgasmic response.
- Estrogen creams for women, Viagra for men, and testosterone for both men and women are not "magic cures." However, they can be positive, valuable resources for sexual functioning when integrated into your couple intimacy, pleasuring, and eroticism style. These need to be prescribed and monitored by a physician.
- Positive, realistic expectations are crucial in maintaining a healthy sexual relationship. Do not compare sexuality in your 60s to the sexuality you experienced when you were 20. Focus on quality and pleasure, not quantity and performance. The good news is you can be sexual when you are in your 80s.

- Sexuality is more than genitals, intercourse, and orgasm. Sexuality involves affectionate, sensual, playful, erotic, and intercourse touch. Not all touch can or should result in intercourse. Couples who enjoy the GES model report high levels of desire, pleasure, eroticism, and satisfaction.
- A crucial factor, especially for women, is accepting your body image. Traditionally, female sexual desire and sense of attractiveness have been contingent on everything being perfect. Self-acceptance, especially for older people, promotes partner acceptance and vital, resilient sexuality.
- Maintaining a regular rhythm of sexual contact is crucial. The average frequency of sexual activity after 60 is once a week. When couples are sexual less than every 2 weeks, self-consciousness and anxiety replace comfort and positive anticipation. A key to satisfying sexuality is to maintain a pleasure-oriented connection, which includes intercourse and orgasm but emphasizes a broader, more flexible approach to pleasure, eroticism, and satisfaction.
- Satisfying sexuality requires partners to maintain a pleasure-oriented connection. The variable, flexible couple sexual style advocated by the GES approach includes valuing sensual, playful, erotic, and intercourse touch.
- Couples who cling to the traditional male–female double standard are vulnerable to less satisfying sexuality. Emphasizing male–female equity and being an intimate sexual team facilitates healthy sexuality.
- You can appreciate and enjoy the role reversal where female sexual response becomes easier than male response. He learns to "piggy-back" his arousal on hers, a crucial psychosexual skill. Remember, sex is about sharing pleasure; it is not a competition or performance.
- Most women use a lubricant to facilitate intercourse and reduce the likelihood of dyspeurnia (painful intercourse). Additionally, the female can guide intromission, which makes sense since she is the expert on her vagina. This also reduces male performance anxiety.
- The man needs to accept his mature penis and its response rather than compare it to the easy, predictable, autonomous erections of his 20s. Enjoy your body, your partner's body, and the sexual experience rather than maintain a rigid focus on erection and intercourse as a test of your manhood.
- Replace the concept of *perfect* intercourse performance with the GES model. Eighty-five percent of encounters will flow to

intercourse. Both partners can be comfortable with at least one and ideally both of these alternative scenarios: an erotic, nonintercourse scenario to high arousal and orgasm for one or both partners, and a warm, sensual, cuddly scenario.

• Sex after 60 is a more intimate, genuine, and human than sex in your 20s. Enjoy these new feelings and experiences and focus on becoming intimate and erotic allies.

CLOSING THOUGHTS

The years from the 60s to the 80s constitute one of the most significant times in life for enjoying feelings of caring, sensuality, and variable, flexible sexual expression. Sexuality in those over the age of 60 is normal and healthy. The best way to ensure sexual function and satisfaction is to stay actively involved in sensual and sexual pleasuring and refrain from making performance demands. Enjoy and appreciate your body, your partner's body, and couple intimacy. The integration of intimacy, nondemand pleasuring, and eroticism reaches fruition with aging. Allow GES to be a positive part of your relationship in your later years.

11

YOUR SEXUAL VOICE

Sexuality is an integral part of who you are. A healthy attitude includes regarding sex as a positive aspect of your personality and expressing sexuality in a manner that enhances your life and intimate relationship. You and your partner are sexual in similar and complementary ways that can enhance your bond as respectful, trusting people who value your intimate relationship.

This perspective differs drastically from the traditional Victorian or double-standard views that many people grew up with. Negative learnings about sexuality—especially that sex is "exciting but dirty" and that men and women are from different planets sexually—inhibit sexual desire and function. Sexuality is a way to express your human need for touching, sharing, pleasure, and eroticism. This need is equally valid for the woman and the man.

You can increase awareness of and comfort with sexuality. This is not a demand to be sexual and perform at any time or in any situation. That sexual pressure is traditionally placed on the man. It is as dehumanizing a view of male sexuality as the traditional female imperative to not be sexual at any time, in any situation, or with any person other than her husband—and even then not be carried away with passion. You can learn to be comfortable and accepting of yourself as a sexual person. It is your choice to be sexual at a time and in a manner that allows you to genuinely celebrate intimacy, pleasure, and eroticism.

How do people learn about sexuality? There are many sources, but the prime one is through touch. The touching you received as an infant from your mother and father is important; so is your own touching to explore your body. Before the age of 6 months, most children discover the positive sensations of touching their genitals. Was playing with your penis or vulva accepted by your parent as normal and healthy, or were your hands slapped and told, "No, that's dirty"? We do not blame parents for adult sexual problems; your parents acted according to what they knew. Only in recent years have sex educators and researchers advocated acceptance of childhood sexual curiosity and exploration. We believe that as an adult you can undo negative learnings and build a healthy sexual awareness and comfort. You can create your own adult sexual voice.

Children's touching themselves is likely to include both nongenital and genital touch. They are experiencing positive feelings and have an important lesson to teach adults. Sensuality is the basis of sexuality. Children feel they are entitled to the warm, comfortable feelings of sensual touch. Genital exploration and stimulation are a natural extension of sensual touch.

Masters and Johnson, the pioneer sex researchers, point out that you cannot will or force sexual response. No person and no book can make you become sexually aroused or have an orgasm. The potential for sexual response is natural and lies within you. What you can learn is awareness of sensual and sexual touch, how to nurture sexual desire, the importance of clear and direct communication, active involvement in giving and receiving pleasure, and openness to eroticism. Be positive about your sexuality, not inhibited by the "roadblocks" that interfere with healthy sexual expression. The most common roadblocks are anticipatory anxiety, performance anxiety, trying to impress your partner, goal-oriented sex, forcing sexual response when you are not turned on, using sex as a weapon in an argument or power struggle, using sex in a manipulative manner, and doing something sexually that you are not comfortable with or that violates your values. Sex is not a performance or a spectator sport, nor should you seek to prove something to yourself or your partner. Performance orientation inhibits desire, pleasure, eroticism, and satisfaction. Sexual awareness is facilitated by being open and receptive to affectionate, sensual, playful, erotic, and intercourse touch. The essence of sexuality is giving and receiving pleasurable touch.

SUSAN

Susan is a good example of a person who was controlled by inhibited sexual desire. She is 32, divorced, and has custody of her two children. She received little sex education other than the jokes and stories of friends. As an adolescent, Susan was attractive and popular but felt pressured by boyfriends. Although she enjoyed the attention, affection, and excitement of touching, she felt ambivalent and held back. This pattern is typical of the dating experiences of adolescent and young adult women. The woman fears being taken advantage of. She is concerned about pregnancy, sexually transmitted infections, and being labeled promiscuous.

Susan's most powerful negative learning came from the double standard. The man assumed the role of initiating and pushing sex. He was supposed to be sexually knowledgeable and experienced. This put Susan in the position of fending off sexual advances and not saying what she wanted or making requests. She was afraid of leading her boyfriend on and being labeled a *tease*. When she was expressively sexual (making sounds or engaging in pelvic thrusting), her partner told her that was not the "right" thing to do. Susan became embarrassed and altered her sexual responsivity, which diminished her desire and arousal.

Susan became pregnant at 18 and entered into a fatally flawed marriage. She did not feel in control of her life and regarded sex as the culprit. Four years later, after a relationship that focused on her second husband's sexual needs rather than on hers and resulted in another unplanned pregnancy, he left her for another woman.

Susan was suffering from low self-esteem, depression, and difficulties coping as a single parent. Neither of the ex-husbands nor her parents provided financial resources. Luckily, she had the support of a women's group and entered a career training program. At 32 Susan was professionally competent, financially functional, and responsible for herself. Unfortunately, she had not transferred these attitudes and behaviors to her sexual life. She was merely repeating adolescent experiences and felt they were not worth the effort. She did have male friends but had not had a sexual relationship in 4 years. When a friendship with a man became romantic, Susan panicked.

Susan consulted a female psychologist with a specialty in relational and sexuality issues. The therapist emphasized that Susan had a right to choose whether or not to be sexual but that when she did sexuality could enhance her life and relationship. She consulted a gynecologist and chose the birth control pill. Rather than striving to be orgasmic, Susan focused first on being comfortable with her body and self-image. She engaged in a self-exploration/touch program that improved her sexual self-esteem. Susan utilized sexual fantasies to enhance self-stimulation, enjoying images of men servicing her as if she were a powerful queen. Susan learned to view herself as an attractive woman and was able to be assertive and tell her partner what she wanted practically, emotionally, and sexually. For the first time, Susan was looking forward to being an involved, active sexual person, with touching and sexuality playing a positive, energizing role in her life and relationship.

SEXUALITY AS A CHOICE

Both men and women are entitled to make choices about sexuality, including choosing to be nonsexual. You can enjoy sex without having to prove anything to yourself or your partner. You do not have to apologize for or defend your choices. You deserve sexual comfort, pleasure, eroticism, and satisfaction.

Sexual desire means that "you want to." You can nurture and enhance sexual thoughts, images, and fantasies. A key to sexual desire is positive anticipation. Feeling that you deserve to enjoy sex and can anticipate pleasure is crucial for sexual desire. Use fantasies to anticipate and rehearse a sexual encounter. Fantasies are psychological turn-ons that facilitate desire and receptivity to touching, pleasure, and eroticism.

The cultural stereotype is that women need encouragement to be sexual but men do not. According to tradition, the man needs nothing emotionally or sexually; he could have sex with any woman, at any time, in any situation. What a terribly demanding, and demeaning, myth! It is especially burdensome for the man with inhibited sexual desire. Desire problems are a secret he tells no one, especially male friends, for fear of ridicule. It would be easier to admit to an erection problem than to disclose you feel low or no sexual interest. The man does not even tell his wife or partner what he is feeling; he avoids sex by working too hard, drinking too much, blaming his partner, or having another headache.

Men need to be more accepting, less critical, and less demanding of themselves sexually. Young men experience anxiety, guilt, and confusion about sex, but rarely do they have problems with desire or arousal. This is because adolescents learn to masturbate early and learn to view sex as a way of confirming masculinity. In addition, young men use sexually explicit fantasies. Male sexuality is tied to youth, illicitness, and automatic, autonomous erections. For a middle-aged man, these sources of sexual desire lose their strength, and men often fall into the trap of viewing themselves as "over the hill."

You can develop a new, healthier way of understanding yourself as a sexual man. You need to rid yourself of the pressure to be a "stud" who can induce sexual desire and produce an erection at will. As you age, you become less a sexual athlete and more of an involved lover. Which is more important: that you get an erection without needing your partner's touch or that you enjoy the give and take of sexual sharing? As you age, sexual desire and arousal become a shared, cooperative experience. This can be a great advantage for you and your intimate relationship.

You can feel masculine and sexual as you age as long as you accept bodily changes and adopt healthy attitudes. Of special importance is to value shared pleasure rather than feel you have to perform for your partner. Do you give yourself permission to believe that it's normal not to feel turned on sometimes? Are you entitled to say no to sex? You are a sexual person, not a sexual machine.

ALEX

Alex is a 51-year-old married man who has experienced inhibited sexual desire for the past 4 years. Alex talks wistfully of experiences as a young man when sex was the major thing on his mind and he had erections whenever he saw a woman. He had several premarital partners and married Darcy when he was 27. Alex reported a lessening of sexual desire at age 30, after 3 years of marriage and two children. In his 30s and 40s Alex had sex once or twice a week. When he was out of town, he would occasionally go to a prostitute (he practiced safe sex) or massage parlor because he felt that is what "real men" did. He considered his sex life average and moderately satisfying but gave sex a low priority.

About 4 years ago, Alex's oldest son began living with his girlfriend. Alex had ambivalent feelings. He liked the woman and was glad his son was in a stable relationship, yet he was worried about their "living together" rather than marrying. Alex envied his son's sexual relationship because he felt "used up" sexually. Rather than discussing this with Darcy, male friends, or a therapist, Alex decided to remedy the problem by having an affair with a younger woman as a "tonic." As often happens, the affair provided sexual excitement but caused major problems. Alex felt used by the woman in many ways, including financially. When the affair was discovered by a friend and reported to Darcy, it provoked a strained and embarrassing 6-month period. For the next 3 years, sexual desire disappeared from Alex's life. He would occasionally have sex at Darcy's initiation but had difficulty maintaining an erection. This frustrated and depressed Alex and increased his sexual avoidance. He would occasionally masturbate, especially after a poor experience with Darcy, to reassure himself that physiologically everything was functional.

Alex came to therapy after reading an article about inhibited sexual desire. His first question was, "Am I normal?" Alex was seen individually and then with Darcy. The therapist helped Alex clarify what he valued about sexuality and the benefits of revitalizing marital sexuality. Alex had negative self-esteem as a middle-aged man. He did not anticipate sex and believed the myth that the best sex was "youthful and illicit"—like his son's. The core issue was that Alex had lost his erectile confidence. This resulted in a pattern of anticipatory anxiety, performance-oriented intercourse, frustration, embarrassment, and avoidance.

Self-defeating attitudes and the unrealistic goal of returning to youthful sex are major causes of inhibited sexual desire in middle-aged men. These have to be confronted and replaced with healthy attitudes and new strategies, including nondemand pleasuring, erotic scenarios and techniques, and developing a cooperative, give-and-take intimate relationship. This puts new life into couple sexuality and allows you to adopt an attitude of sexual challenge rather than mourn the loss of youthful sexual vigor. Sexuality becomes pleasure oriented, intimate, erotic, and interactive, including being less predictable. In other words, the challenge is to adopt the Good Enough Sex (GES) model rather than stay stuck in the traditional, sex-performance approach.

As Alex's interest and desire returned, his erectile comfort and confidence also returned. If it had not, Cialis, a pro-erection medication, might have been used as an additional resource to rebuild comfort and confidence with erections. In the past few years, physicians have used Viagra as a "magic pill" for desire, erection, and everything else sexual. It would not have "cured" Alex, however. Men have to make attitudinal, psychological, and psychosexual skill changes if a pro-erection medication or another medical intervention is to be successfully integrated into couple sexuality. Alex learned to value Darcy's sexuality and their give-and-take stimulation. They did not have that in their 20s, so in many ways sex in their 50s was more involving, better quality, and more satisfying. Their therapeutic experiences inoculated Alex and Darcy from sexual problems in their 60s and beyond.

EXERCISES: ENHANCING AWARENESS OF YOUR SEXUAL SELF

The focus of the psychosexual skill exercises in this chapter is to help increase awareness of what you personally value about sexuality and identify ways to enhance desire. In addition, you need to identify blocks and inhibitions to sexual desire that can be confronted and changed. The exercises are learning and exploring experiences, not performance tasks. You cannot fail at an exercise. They are aimed at helping you become aware of what you can celebrate about yourself as a sexual person.

First Exercise: Sexual Self-Esteem

Set aside at least a half-hour when you have privacy and are not distracted or worried. Give yourself permission to focus on the sensitive, yet crucial, topic of your sexual self-esteem. You might want to sit in a comfortable chair, have relaxing music in the background, and keep at hand something on which to jot notes to yourself. Begin by doing a personal historical inventory:

1. Where did you first hear about sexuality? From parents, friends, religious education, siblings, on the street, through reading?
2. Was sex presented as good and exciting or as evil and fearful?
3. What were your parents like as a marital and sexual model? Were they affectionate with you and your siblings?
4. What do you remember about touching and exploring your body as a child? Was it okay, or were you told this was bad?
5. What about sexual play with children in your neighborhood or with siblings or cousins?
6. When did you first explore your genitals? Did it feel good, or were you anxious and guilty?
7. When did you carry self-exploration through to masturbation?
8. Did you enjoy being orgasmic?
9. For men, what was your reaction to your first nocturnal emission (wet dream)?
10. For women, what was your reaction to your first menstruation? Was it a transition into womanhood or a source of embarrassment?
11. How old were you when you started dating?
12. Did you think of yourself as attractive and a good person to go out with?
13. Were initial dating experiences good for your self-esteem, or did they cause unhappiness and feelings of rejection?
14. Did you enjoy being affectionate—holding hands, kissing, hugging?
15. Was touching and sexuality an easygoing part of your relationship, something to be experienced and explored? Or was sexuality a double-standard battleground where the man was trying to prove something and the woman was pressured and stressed?
16. When was the first time you were sexually aroused with a partner?
17. What about your first orgasm with another person? Did you feel good about this experience?

18. First intercourse is an important learning for both men and women, and it is often a disappointment. What was it like for you?

19. By the time they reach 25 years of age, 95% percent of people recall at least one sexual experience that caused them to feel bad, confused, guilty, or traumatized. In addition to the trauma of incest, rape, and child sexual abuse, other negative experiences include guilt over masturbation or fantasies, having an unwanted pregnancy or sexually transmitted infection, being sexually humiliated or rejected, being peeped on, exposed to, or sexually harassed. What were your most negative sexual experiences?

20. Does this still cause guilt or flashbacks, or have you processed and accepted negative experiences so they do not affect your sexual self-esteem?

21. What are your attitudes and feelings about being a sexual adult?

22. Do you feel good about your body?

23. Do you feel responsible for yourself sexually?

24. Do you use effective contraception?

25. Roughly 4 in 10 people contract a sexually transmitted infection (herpes, chlamydia, genital warts, gonorrhea, syphilis, crabs). Do you think of this as a medical problem to have diagnosed and treated, or do you see it as a punishment for sex and put yourself down as a "bad person"?

26. Have you had an unplanned, unwanted pregnancy as approximately one of three women has?

27. How did you handle this dilemma?

28. Has it left any psychological scars?

29. What have you learned about yourself and creating a healthy relationship?

30. What aspects of a partner do you most value?

31. What makes for a good sexual relationship?

32. What was your best sexual experience?

33. How has your sexual self-esteem developed in your present relationship?

34. Has it been nurtured and reinforced or has it been subverted and lost its positive focus?

35. Do you "own" positive sexual experiences—that is, feel you deserve to enjoy them?

36. How can you improve sexual desire, pleasure, eroticism, and satisfaction?

As you complete this self-guided sexual history, be aware of the positive and negative elements of your sexual development. All of us have a sexual history. We have never met a person who did not have bad experiences, negative learnings, or regrets. You can learn from these and honor the experiences but not let them control present individual and couple sexuality. You are responsible for your sexuality. With increased awareness and understanding, you can have a healthy sexual life in the present and future. You owe it to yourself and your relationship to develop positive sexual self-esteem.

Second Exercise: Body Image

Our culture is obsessed by physical attractiveness and youth. Look at the ads in magazines and on TV—attractive, youthful, stylishly dressed men and women selling everything from soap to cars. It is as if to consider yourself attractive, you have to look like a movie or TV star. It's a self-defeating concept!

Positive body image is integral to sexual desire. You can accept yourself as an attractive person without having a perfect body. We are opposed to people undergoing plastic surgery every 2 years. We are equally opposed to the person who no longer attends to personal hygiene, does not shave, gains 60 pounds, and wears rumpled clothing. Seeing yourself as a sexual person involves accepting your body and emphasizing components that increase your self-acceptance and sense of attractiveness.

Set aside at least an hour of private time. Lay out three clothing outfits—a formal outfit, an informal outfit, and one you consider sexy. If possible, have access to a full-length mirror. Wash and groom yourself in a manner you find attractive. Put on your formal outfit and look in the mirror. What do you like best about your appearance? Do you see yourself as an attractive adult who takes care of yourself? Think of the compliments you have received when you were dressed formally; instead of dismissing them, realize you are an attractive person.

Put on your sexy outfit. It could be a dressy ensemble, a swimsuit, an unbuttoned shirt and pants, or a favorite nightgown or PJs. As you look in the mirror, experiment with changing your hairstyle, facial expression, or stance and posture. Enjoy different aspects of your body image; do not be embarrassed or inhibited about being expressive in front of a mirror. Give yourself permission to experience different dimensions of yourself and your body. See yourself as a desirable, attractive person.

Switch to your informal outfit. You do not need to be dressed formally or seductively to have an attractive self-image. Some people like a clean-cut, well-pressed image; others prefer a low-key, informal image; still others like to look distinctive and unique. What is your style preference? Give yourself permission to promote positive changes in your body image, especially your sexual self-esteem.

Be aware of the images, clothes, and attitudes that add to your feeling of being an attractive, sexual person. Focus on these at least twice a week for the next month as you reinforce an image of yourself as a sexually desirable person.

Third Exercise: Sexual Fantasies

If people were to know about your sexual fantasies, they would be shocked and you would be embarrassed. True or false? The socially desirable answer is false, but the reality is true. More than any other element of sexuality, erotic fantasies are your private domain. Even more than masturbation, fantasy is a private experience. Why? Fantasies by their very nature involve socially unacceptable thoughts, images, people, and situations. We do not fantasize about having intercourse in bed with our spouse. We fantasize about sex with a movie star, our best friend's spouse, an exotic person, a stranger, someone of the same sex, a relative. We fantasize less about intercourse, more about oral sex, being tied up, raping or being sexually coerced, performing simultaneously with four people who admire your sexual prowess, simultaneously engaging in oral and anal sex, being in a threesome with our spouse looking on in horror or fascination. In our fantasy we do not have sex in our bedroom but on a beautiful beach, in the office with everyone looking on in envy or disgust, in front of a 30-foot fireplace, on a movie set. People's erotic fantasies would be embarrassing and humiliating if publicly discussed. The source of sexual desire and arousal lies in this "forbidden fruit" aspect of sexual fantasy.

The essence of sexual fantasies is their illicit, creative, unpredictable nature. This is what makes fantasies an erotic turn-on. Fantasy and behavior are very separate realms. Fantasies are not meant to be experienced in reality but to be relished as harmless, exciting, sexually arousing images. Fantasies serve as a bridge to initiate sex and to heighten arousal. Fantasies are very problematic when the person obsesses about one scenario, experiencing high levels of eroticism combined with high levels of shame and secrecy. Secrecy, shame, and eroticism form a poisonous combination.

Give yourself permission to focus on a range of fantasies and images without judging or putting yourself down because they are "kinky," "weird," or "lustful." Enjoy erotic fantasies and images; allow yourself to feel sexy and "horny." People pair fantasies with masturbation. You can use your imagination or material like Internet porn, erotic stories, or a video you find to be a turn-on. The most common source of erotic material is Internet sex sites. You might be turned on by visual material, stories, or mental images. Use what works for you. Go with the fantasy; let it carry you rather than you direct it. Sexual fantasies have a life of their own, with a strong emotional, irrational component. As you experiment with sexual fantasies, do not become obsessed with just one. The mind is your private X-rated cinema. Enjoy the variety; it is free. Learn to enjoy fantasies for what they are: a positive part of sexuality that is a bridge to desire, eroticism, and orgasm. Erotic fantasies are the most common form of multiple stimulation during couple sex.

Fourth Exercise: Erotic Scenarios

One of the nicest things about being a child was your birthday, when everything was designed to please you. That seldom happens as an adult. We suggest couples designate "caring days," when your desires and emotional needs are given special attention. This is almost never done in the sexual arena. This exercise gives you permission to experience your favorite sexual scenario.

Plan a day to enhance your sexual desire. You might start with breakfast in bed, then take a walk in the woods, have a midday nap, listen to your favorite music, enjoy your partner's affection and caring, be surprised by an inexpensive gift or a bottle of wine, get a full-body massage, go to a movie, have dinner at a new restaurant, delight in a long, luxurious bath. Where does sex fit in? It could be in the morning, before or after your nap, in the early evening, or at the end of this special day.

What would be a special erotic scenario for you? It could involve being stroked and caressed for as long as you desire, experimenting with an oral sex position you have read about but were too bashful to try, being stimulated in front of a mirror where you enjoy visual as well as tactile stimulation. What about playing sexually for 10 minutes, taking a bath, then being submissive to your partner's every desire, perhaps using two intercourse positions you have not tried for ages (sitting facing each other, rear entry, standing up, the woman sitting on the man)? Would you enjoy multiple stimulation—him orally stimulating your breast and with one hand stimulating your clitoral area and the other hand stimulating your anal area? Some couples like active, abandoned sex where she "attacks" him and strokes his penis hard, sucks intensely during fellatio as he rapidly thrusts his pelvis, after which they engage in intercourse involving deep, fast, rhythmic thrusting. Other couples prefer a sexual scenario that is slow and tender with lots of intimate, loving verbal exchange. Choose your erotic scenario, play with it, enjoy it. You do not have to limit the scenario to one special day; enjoy eroticism in your ongoing couple sexuality.

CLOSING THOUGHTS

Sexual desire is not something you either have or do not have. Desire is a multidimensional set of attitudes, behaviors, and feelings that reflect you as a sexual person. Sex is an affirming aspect of life, and sexuality is an integral part of your personality. You are responsible for your sexuality and can build positive sexual self-esteem. Learn to express sexuality so it enhances your life and intimate relationship.

12

COUPLE SEXUAL DESIRE

Feeling comfortable as a sexual person and assuming responsibility for your sexuality can enhance your life and intimate relationship. Your partner can neither bestow nor force sexual desire on you. You are responsible for your sexuality and sexual desire.

Our culture is dominated by fantasy images of sex. Attraction means instant sexual compatibility and eroticism; sex is always highly passionate orgasmic magic! Being swept away by romantic love is a seductive myth. The reality is that romantic love and passionate sex seldom last even until marriage. The images and concepts presented by the media (novels, songs, movies) are counterproductive for couples trying to renew or maintain a vital sexual bond.

We propose a positive, realistic approach to developing and maintaining sexual desire in your relationship. This helps you attain and maintain a sense of yourselves as an intimate, erotic couple. Sex is a healthy sharing between two people who are aware, comfortable, and responsible. Emotionally and sexually intimate teamwork is not easy to attain or maintain, but it is very worthwhile and satisfying both in itself and as a relationship energizer.

TALKING SEX

If you are like most couples, you have had both exciting and disappointing sexual experiences. Other than joking or perhaps blaming, you have not honestly and openly shared sexual attitudes, feelings, and experiences. You justify this by saying that you do not want to remove the mystique from your sexual relationship. It is true that you can talk and analyze a sexual relationship to death, making sex so clinical and self-conscious that it lacks all semblance of fun. However, most couples err on the other end of the continuum—not having any discussion of sexual feelings, preferences, or eroticism.

Most couples do not have a comfortable sexual language. "Proper" terms such as *penis, vagina,* and *intercourse* seem formal and lifeless, whereas "slang" terms such as *prick, pussy,* and *fuck* can have an angry and derogatory ring to them. An alternative is to develop your own sexual language. What could you call your penis or vagina? What is a comfortable word or phrase for intercourse? Do *making love, getting together,* and *having sex* sound appropriate? Or do *getting it on, screwing,* and *doing the dirty* work better? Develop a sexual language that allows you to communicate your wishes in a clear and inviting manner.

You need to be comfortable sitting and talking clothed if you are to be comfortable in the nude being sexual. Talking, kissing, and touching in affectionate, nondemanding ways provide a solid base for your sexual relationship. Holding hands or walking with an arm around your partner's waist is an important element of intimacy. Sexuality encompasses more than genitals, intercourse, and orgasm. The base of sexuality is touch. To build sexual desire is to develop a pleasing, sensuous, intimate way of being with each other and enjoy nondemand pleasuring.

Accepting yourself as a sexual person enhances your attractiveness. Being an aware, responsible sexual partner facilitates becoming a sensual, erotic, satisfied sexual couple.

ALICE AND BRENT

Alice and Brent had a satisfying sexual relationship but allowed it to dissipate by taking sex for granted and not nurturing intimacy or eroticism. It surprised and embarrassed them that they'd become sexually dysfunctional because they had prided themselves on being sexually liberated and sophisticated. They had lived together for 8 months before marriage. Alice was 27, and Brent 26. They fondly recalled staying up half the night making love in their studio apartment. In the intervening 13 years they had grown and matured in many ways. They bought a townhouse with a lake view, had two children, held well-paid jobs (although Brent felt stuck in his career), and took pride in their personal and couple accomplishments.

Unfortunately, after 2 years of marriage their sexual life became unsatisfactory, and in the past 3 years they had become a nonsexual couple. They had unsuccessfully attempted to reverse this course by a number of poorly thought out, half-hearted efforts. These included buying a sophisticated sex book and trying one of the dramatic scenarios—being sexual in front of an open window, going to a "sex motel" with X-rated movies and a vibrating bed, and having a group sex experience at an ocean resort (which was risky in terms of sexually transmitted infections and HIV, although they used condoms). Brent and Alice even had affairs to see if that would make a difference. The affairs proved to be more complex and disruptive than either had bargained for. Again the generalizations about affairs proved true: They are easier to get into than out of, and they take more time and psychological energy than expected. Affairs are not a healthy way to solve a sexual problem, although many people with sexual problems use an affair to get a sexual "charge" or to gain reassurance that they are sexually desirable.

Alice and Brent sought sex therapy several years later than would have been advisable. A good guideline is that if a sexual problem lasts for more than 6 months it will probably not spontaneously go away, and you should seriously consider consulting a therapist. In assessing the problem, an important factor that emerged was the erosive state of Brent and Alice's marital bond. Respect, trust, and intimacy are the core elements of the marital bond. Respect lies in the acceptance of each other's weaknesses and vulnerabilities as well as strengths and stellar characteristics. Trust is based on the belief that your spouse has your best interest in mind. Even when angry or disappointed, you trust that neither of you would purposely do something to hurt the other. Sexual intimacy is not the prime factor in marriage but is a positive, integral part. The functions of sexuality are to share pleasure, to reinforce and strengthen intimacy, and to reduce tension in order to help you cope with the stresses of job, children, house, and a shared life. When sex is problematic, it undermines your relationship and robs it of emotional energy. When sex functions well, it contributes positively to relationship vitality and satisfaction. When it becomes dysfunctional or nonexistent it can drain 50 to 70% of the energy out of your relationship and rob you of intimacy and connection.

Alice and Brent's marital bond had been badly strained by frustration, discouragement, and misunderstanding, but it was still intact. As long as your couple bond is viable, sexual problems can be successfully dealt with. However, if the bond has been severed, it is hard to resurrect sex. Sex cannot save a nonviable relationship.

The first focus of therapy was for Alice and Brent to view their inhibited sexual desire as a couple problem. This allowed them to assume mutual responsibility and stop the blaming cycle. Inhibited sexual desire was the joint enemy, and it would take a team effort to break the avoidance cycle. The team approach served as the foundation from which to build a couple sexual style that was functional and satisfying. Whether a new or revitalized relationship is involved, the partners need to build comfort, attraction, trust, and sexual anticipation.

Alice and Brent found sex therapy very helpful. They were committed to revitalizing their intimate bond and willing to communicate and engage in psychosexual skill exercises to reach that goal. Progress was neither easy nor straightforward. Both positive experiences and learning from mistakes were necessary to rebuild and strengthen their sexual relationship. Alice and Brent realized that sexual desire is not automatic. They needed to build bridges to desire, anticipate sexual encounters, stay away from behavior that poisoned desire, and set aside time to be a sexual couple rather than dream of the perfect spontaneous sex portrayed in movies. They committed to nurture intimacy, pleasure, eroticism, and desire in their marriage.

DEVELOPING AND MAINTAINING SEXUAL INTIMACY

Becoming a sexual couple is a process that takes time and energy. Your sexual relationship needs continual nurturing. Sexuality cannot be taken for granted. Comfort, attraction, and trust must be reinforced if sexual desire and satisfaction are to be maintained.

In traditional marital therapy, sexual dysfunction was seen as a symptom of a relationship problem. If an underlying emotional problem in a relationship was successfully dealt with, so the reasoning went, the sex problem would spontaneously be cured. In fact, many couples have a trusting, respectful, committed relationship but experience sexual problems due to lack of information, performance anxiety, poor psychosexual skills, poor sexual communication, or a history of unsuccessful experiences, guilt, and blaming. The more specific the sexual dysfunction, the greater the need to focus directly on sexual comfort and psychosexual skills. The best examples are premature ejaculation or ejaculatory inhibition in men and nonorgasmic response and painful intercourse in women.

The most frequent sex dysfunction involves problems of sexual desire. Rather than positively anticipating sex and feeling you deserve sexuality to nurture your relationship, you are caught in the cycle of anticipatory anxiety, tense and performance-oriented intercourse, frustration, embarrassment, and avoidance. Inhibited sexual desire or struggles over sexual frequency are the most common reason for couples to enter sex therapy.

Relationship problems can interfere with sexual desire. Common problems include poor communication, lack of respect, anger over past events, frustration over relationship roles, power struggles, disappointments and resentments, disagreements about finances, child rearing conflicts, and being turned off by your partner's behavior concerning drinking, smoking, eating, or cleanliness. Sometimes a problem revolves around a specific practical issue such as disparate times of going to sleep, not having a lock on the bedroom door, or conflict about contraceptive use. Couples who experience complex individual, relationship, and medical problems are advised to seek sex therapy (resources are listed in Appendix A).

Refrain from feeling pressure to keep up with the Joneses sexually. Develop your unique sexual style. It is crucial to put time and psychological energy into nurturing your intimate relationship. Key elements in reviving sexual desire are positive anticipation, building bridges to sexual desire, and the conviction that sexuality deserves to be a pleasurable, satisfying part of your life and intimate relationship.

EXERCISES

First Exercise: Comfort

A first step in becoming a sexual couple is developing a comfortable, nondemand approach to touch and sensuality. How can you enhance sexual comfort? Begin by setting aside at least two occasions for this exercise, one in your bedroom and a second time in the family or living room. Although most of the psychosexual skill exercises involve nudity, this exercise begins with clothes on.

Sensuality involves being receptive to and enjoying nondemand, nongenital touching. Sensuality means touching for its own sake, not as a goal toward arousal, intercourse, or orgasm. Being open to the joys of slow, tender, caring, rhythmic touching is the basis of sexual response and is essential for maintaining desire in your relationship.

This exercise takes place in your bedroom with clothes on and focuses on nonverbal communication, with the woman as initiator. Traditionally, women have not had permission to initiate sensual or sexual activities. You can initiate this exercise in the morning, in the late afternoon on a rainy weekend, or early in the evening. We suggest not doing it right before bed when you are tired and do not have the energy or focus to engage in sensual exploration. Begin by taking a bath or shower and playfully washing each other. Towel dry your partner in a slow, caring fashion, and proceed to the bedroom. Put on clothing you feel comfortable with; it could be pajamas or an informal outfit.

How personalized is your bedroom? Does it have valued mementos? Is it decorated the way you like? Is there sufficient light? Is it a comfortable room to be in? Orchestrate the milieu to increase sensuality. You could burn a fragrant candle or put on music to romanticize the atmosphere. Be sure you are not too warm or cold.

Touch for yourself; do not try to second-guess your partner. Give yourself permission to experiment with a variety of ways to touch, hold, and caress. Use your fingertips, palms, both hands, or only one. Do not limit yourself. Use your legs; rub your body against his; let your lips or tongue explore his body. He can take off as much or as little clothing as you prefer. Some women find they are more comfortable if initially he keeps his eyes closed; others enjoy keeping eye contact throughout. Try it both ways. Which do you find more sensual? Explore and enjoy his body from the hairs on his head to the soles of his feet. Be aware of at least two areas you enjoy touching. Do not be surprised if there are body parts you do not like; this is not Tom Cruise made up to look perfect on a movie screen, but your live partner with a scar on his kneecap, a roll of flab on his midriff, more hair than you like on his back. Switch roles and let him explore your body to redevelop sensuality and comfort.

The bedroom is one thing; being comfortable in the living room or family room can be quite another. Do the second part of the exercise in the next day or two. Since this exercise is done in the nude, ensure that you will have privacy and not be interrupted by neighbors or children. An intimate relationship erodes because of lack of quality couple time. Couples discuss and problem-solve about practical, external problems but take little time for personal, intimate feelings and communication.

Make this your special time. Would you rather talk in the kitchen, living room, or family room? Would you like a cup of tea or glass of wine? Would music in the background enhance or distract from communication? Sit comfortably, facing each other. Nonverbal components of communication—especially eye contact, body posture, facial response, and touch—carry a message as important as words. Is talking enhanced by holding hands, having your arm around your partner's shoulder, playfully touching your partner's hands, or caressing your partner's face and neck?

How do you talk as a sexual couple? Is it comfortable to use proper words or to employ slang? Do you have a private sexual language? Can you share emotional feelings and intimacy as easily as you make sexual requests? Can you discuss what pleasuring and intercourse techniques increase sexual responsivity? To be an intimate couple, you need to be able to discuss both emotional and sexual feelings and preferences.

Share your fondest memory of being sexual. Take the risk of being vulnerable and discuss how you felt during and after that experience. The only time most couples are nude is in the bedroom is while having sex. Being nude, touching, and talking comfortably in the living room, den, or kitchen can be a liberating experience. Enjoy the freedom and openness of nondemand pleasuring and talking while nude outside your bedroom.

Is it helpful to touch while clothed in the bedroom? How do you feel about touching while nude outside the bedroom? Touching both inside and outside the bedroom is an excellent way to nurture sexual desire. Conclude this exercise by making requests and suggestions to make your sexual relationship, especially initiating sexual encounters, comfortable and inviting.

Second Exercise: Couple Sexual Attraction

Sexual attraction is not static. It is not some "magic" quality that either you have or you don't. Sexual attraction is a dynamic process between two people that waxes and wanes. Attraction is affected by myriad factors. Physical attractiveness is but one factor; it is certainly not the only one or even the most important one. Turn-ons vary for each couple, contrary to the media myth that there is a perfect, youthful body type that turns everyone on or a sexual technique that works for everyone. You can increase sexual attraction to each other and for each other.

Start this exercise clothed in a comfortable, private setting conducive to communication. Set aside at least 45 minutes that could extend 2 hours if you wish. Present yourself in a manner that you feel is attractive; choose an outfit you particularly like, shave, fix your hair, brush your teeth, dab on your favorite perfume or after-shave. Do the kinds of things people do to get ready for a date but usually don't do in a relationship they unfortunately have taken for granted.

Discussing attraction can be awkward, so we suggest a semistructured communication exercise. Let the woman begin. Tell your partner at least five (and up to 15) things you find attractive about him, being as clear and specific as possible. You might find his slightly balding head attractive or like his new glasses, the way he jogs, his arms and hands, how he looks in a suit and tie, his laugh, the tenderness he displays when putting the children to bed, how he handles a household emergency, the look in his eyes before initiating sex, how responsible he is about paying bills, the sounds he makes when he has an orgasm, his newfound skill at cooking, the muscles of his legs, how caring he was when his aunt died, how enraptured he is with classical music yet can still enjoy country, the way he orally stimulates you, how generous he can be with his time when someone needs help, his penis when he is aroused, how he puts up a tent when you go camping. Be honest in disclosing what you find attractive—physically, sexually, and psychologically. He listens and acknowledges his positive qualities; he does not shrug them off or minimize them.

Now pick one, two, or at the most three things you want him to change that could increase his attractiveness for you. Do not just state the problem. Make a specific request for change. Say, "I'd like you to cut your hair one-and-a-half inches shorter and comb it at night," rather than, "I don't like your hair; do something about it." Say, "When you initiate, kiss me and stroke my arms before you touch my breasts," not, "You come on too strong." Say, "Talk and play with each child individually," rather than, "I get angry because you never pay attention to the kids."

Let us suggest two guidelines about requests. First, request things your partner can actually change. For example, if he is 6 feet tall, you can't say you are attracted to men over 6 feet 5 inches. You can suggest that he carry himself more positively by walking tall and forcefully. Second, frame this as a "request" not a "demand." Your partner can agree, modify, or say no, and there will be no punishment or negative consequences. A healthy relationship is based on acceptance and a positive-influence process, not demands, ultimatums, or threats.

Switch roles and have the man share what he finds attractive about his partner. You may like the way she wakes you up with a kiss, that people view her as super-organized, how she purrs when her back is scratched, that she can fix broken items, the shape of her breasts, what a good athlete she is, how wet she becomes when she is aroused, how she sings to the children before bedtime, how seductive she looks in a see-through nightgown, how she cheers you up after a bad day, how her nipple gets erect after you lick it, the way she pads around the house in bare feet, how attractive she looks when dressed for a night out, the care she takes planning family picnics, the effort she makes in picking clothes for the children, how she moves when she is sexually turned on, how assertive she is with neighbors. What is special about your partner that you value and find attractive?

In addressing the one to three requests for change, feel free to make them either sexual or nonsexual. What will increase your partner's attractiveness for you? Remember, it is a request, not a demand. Say, "I want you to sit with me once a month and plan big purchases," not, "You don't care anything about money except spending it." Say, "I want you to try orally stimulating me when I'm standing," not "Stop being so hung up about oral sex." Say, "I wish you would initiate sex by stroking my chest when you wake up on a weekend morning," rather than, "You never initiate." Remember, these are requests for things your partner can change, not things your partner can't change. In terms of response to requests, she can accept, modify, or say no. A request connotes acceptance without a threat of negative consequences, while a demand says I don't accept you and if you don't agree to change there will be big problems. This is especially important in terms of sexual scenarios and techniques. There is no place for "intimate coercion" in your couple sexuality.

After discussing the process of maintaining and enhancing attraction you can end the exercise or engage in touching, which could lead to intercourse.

Third Exercise: Trust and Intimacy

A major value of your intimate relationship is trusting that your partner is on your side, has your best interest in mind, and would not do anything intentionally to hurt you. Trust is a central ingredient in your intimate relationship. Communicate how you feel about the level of trust in your relationship, both in the past and at present. If it is not as high as you want, what can you do to increase trust? What "trust vulnerabilities" does your partner need to be aware of? What can each of you do to increase trust? Trust is not something that occurs automatically; it takes time to allow feelings of trust to develop and be expressed both verbally and physically.

You can establish a "trust" or "safe" sexual position where you feel cared about and secure. This involves being nude in the privacy of your bedroom. Personalize your bedroom. Have a special light that gives a warm glow, a favorite erotic book or love poem by the bedstand, thick curtains so there is privacy, a full-length mirror to increase visual stimuli. Do you enjoy hanging out and talking in your bedroom? Caress your partner's face and recall a time when you felt vulnerable and your partner was there for you.

You have experimented with nondemand positions to increase receptivity, sensuality, and responsiveness. Develop a safe or trust position that facilitates feelings of intimacy, trust, and security. You might lie side by side holding each other, your bodies touching from the tips of your toes to your forehead. Try a position where he is sitting up with his back supported and you are lying with your head on his lap while he strokes your hair. Another trust position is lying next to each other, holding hands and being silent. Some couples use a "spoon" position where you lie with your chest against his back, put your arms around him, and breathe in unison with his rhythm. In another position, he lies on his back and you nestle your head against his shoulder, your faces close so that you can maintain eye contact. A trust position some couples value is sitting facing each other, keeping eye contact, putting one hand on your partner's heart. What adds to your sense of trust? Body contact, eye contact, being comfortable, feeling secure, being enveloped, talking, silence? Find at least one position where you feel intimate and trusting. Develop your unique trust position that establishes a solid base of physical security and connection.

In subsequent sexual experiences, when you become anxious, depressed, frustrated, or angry, utilize this trust position as a "port in the storm." Rather than ending a sexual experience on an anxious or frustrated note, switch to your trust position as a way of anchoring yourself. You can choose whether to continue the exercise or end the experience from your trust position. This helps you remain connected and realize you can depend on each other. You trust you are an intimate team and your partner "has your back."

Fourth Exercise: Couple Sexual Scenario

When a relationship is new, there is strong anticipation of being sexual, even if the quality of sex is not particularly good. Sex serves as an affirmation of your desirability and desire to be a couple. Romantic love and passionate sex energize a new relationship and make it "magical." There is the thrill of sexual exploration as well as energy that goes into making your relationship exciting and erotic.

After the initial romantic love and passionate sex phase has dissipated, it takes most couples 6 months to develop a couple sexual style that is intimate, functional, and satisfying. Part of the process is crafting couple sexual scenarios, the focus of this exercise. As a reminder, you are not a machine, so it is normal in the best of couples to occasionally have mediocre or negative sexual experiences. A sign of a healthy couple is your ability to accept this and not overreact to negative experiences.

What do you value most in a sexual experience? Each individual develops their sexual scenario. Let the woman introduce her scenario first. At another time the man can develop his.

When is your best time to be sexual? When waking up? After the morning paper? At noon? Before or after a nap? Before dinner (sex as an appetizer) or after dinner (sex as dessert)? In the evening? Most couples have sex late at night, but it is interesting that few people say this is their favorite time.

How do you set your preferred sensual and sexual mood? Do you listen to music, go for a walk, talk, light candles, drink wine, take a bath, have 15 minutes of time alone and then come together, meet your partner at the door and lure him into the bedroom? As a prelude to being sexual some couples enjoy doing together things like shopping, working in the garden, going for a run, or sharing feelings. Many couples start touching and playing in the living room or den and do not move to the bedroom until both are turned on. Others prefer to start in the privacy of their bedroom. What is your favorite way to begin a sexual scenario? Remember, there is no right or wrong; it is your preference.

Once the scenario is under way, what is your favorite script? Do you like to take turns, or do you prefer mutual stimulation? Do you verbally express sexual feelings, or would you rather let your fingers do the talking? Do you prefer a slow build-up, or would you rather begin intercourse as soon as you are aroused? Do you like multiple stimulation or one erotic focus at a time? Do you make use of all your senses—touch, taste, smell, hearing, sight—or does one element (observing your partner's arousal, hearing soft moans, smelling an erotic perfume, feeling sexual movement) turn you on? Develop the sexual scenario the way you want. Your partner is open to your guidance.

How do you transition from pleasure and eroticism to intercourse? Some people prefer to begin intercourse at moderate levels of arousal, but many prefer not transitioning to intercourse until they are highly aroused. Do you want to initiate the transition, or do you want your partner to? Who guides intromission? Do you prefer multiple stimulation during intercourse rather than a sole focus on thrusting? What is your preferred intercourse rhythm and type of thrusting (short, rapid thrusting; slow up-and-down thrusting; circular thrusting; changing intercourse positions)? Do you prefer being orgasmic during intercourse, or do you feel greater pleasure in being orgasmic during erotic nonintercourse sex?

How would you like to end the scenario? Afterplay is the most neglected element of the sexual experience. Your needs and desires are important here, too. Do you like to lie and hold each other, sleep in your partner's arms, engage in playful tickling, have a warm kiss, take a walk, read poetry, nap and start again, talk and come down together?

When it is his turn to create a sexual scenario, he is free to design his own, which could be similar to or totally different from hers. Many men fall into the trap of trying to outdo their partner. Sex is neither a competition nor a performance. Be yourself; develop an initiation, script, and afterplay scenario that is erotic, special, and satisfying for you.

GUIDELINES FOR REVITALIZING AND
MAINTAINING SEXUAL DESIRE

- Positive anticipation and feeling you deserve sexual satisfaction in your intimate relationship drive sexual desire.
- Each person is responsible for his or her desire, with the couple functioning as an intimate team to nurture and enhance desire. Revitalizing sexual desire is a couple task. Guilt, blame, and pressure subvert the erotic process.
- Inhibited desire and conflicts over desire discrepancies are the most common sexual dysfunction problems, affecting one in three couples. Desire problems drain intimacy and good feelings from your relationship.
- One in five married couples has a nonsexual marriage (being sexual less than 10 times a year). One in three nonmarried couples who have been together 2 years or longer has a nonsexual relationship.
- The initial romantic love/passionate sex relationship phase that fires desire lasts less than 2 years and often less than 6 months. Desire in an ongoing relationship is maintained by developing a comfortable, functional couple sexual style.
- The essence of sexuality is giving and receiving pleasure-oriented touching. The prescription to revitalize and maintain sexual desire is intimacy, pleasuring, and eroticism.
- Touching occurs both inside and outside the bedroom. Touching is valued for itself and does not always lead to intercourse.
- Couples who maintain a vital sexual relationship can use the metaphor of touching as having "five gears." First gear is clothes-on, affectionate touch (holding hands, kissing, hugging). Second gear is nongenital, sensual touch, which can be done clothed, semiclothed, or nude (body massage, cuddling on the couch, holding and caressing, touching when going to sleep or on awakening). Third gear is playful touching that intermixes genital and nongenital touching, clothed or unclothed; romantic or erotic dancing; touching in the bath or shower, on the couch or in bed; whole-body massage; playing strip poker or Twister. Fourth gear is erotic touching (manual, oral, rubbing, or vibrator stimulation) to high arousal and orgasm for one or both partners. Fifth gear integrates pleasurable and erotic touch that flows into intercourse as a natural continuation of the pleasuring/eroticism process.
- Both the man and woman value affectionate, sensual, playful, erotic, and intercourse experiences.

- Both the man and woman are comfortable initiating touching and intercourse. Both feel free to say "no" and suggest an alternative way to connect and share pleasure.
- A key strategy is to develop "her," "his," and "our" bridges to sexual desire. This involves ways of thinking, talking, anticipating, and feeling that invite being sexual.
- Sexuality has a number of positive functions for your relationship—a shared pleasure, a means to reinforce and deepen intimacy, and a tension reducer to deal with the stresses of life and your relationship.
- The average frequency of sexual intercourse is from four times a week to once every 2 weeks. For couples in their 20s, it averages from two to three times a week and for couples in their 50s once or twice a week.
- Personal turn-ons (fantasies, special celebrations or memories, feeling caring and close, anniversaries or birthdays, sex with the goal of pregnancy, initiating a favorite erotic scenario, being playful or spontaneous, sexuality to celebrate a career success or soothe a personal disappointment) facilitate sexual anticipation and desire.
- External turn-ons (R- or X-rated videos, music, candles, sex toys, visual feedback from mirrors, being sexual outside the bedroom, a weekend away without the kids) facilitate anticipation and desire.
- Nondemand pleasuring can be a way to connect physically, a means to share pleasure, or a bridge to sexual desire.
- Intimate coercion is not acceptable. Sexuality is neither a reward nor a punishment. Sexuality is voluntary and pleasure oriented.
- Realistic expectations are crucial for maintaining a vital sexual relationship. It is self-defeating and harmful to demand equal desire, arousal, orgasm, and satisfaction each time. Realistically, 35 to 45% of sexual experiences are very good for both people. Twenty percent are very good for one (usually the man) and fine for the other, while 15 to 20% are okay for one and acceptable for the other. Be aware that 5 to 15% of sexual experiences are dissatisfying or dysfunctional. Couples who accept occasional mediocre or dysfunctional experiences without guilt or blaming and try again when they are more receptive have a vital, resilient sexual relationship. Satisfied couples use the guideline of Good Enough Sex (GES) in order to adopt positive, realistic sexual expectations.
- Contrary to the myth that "horniness" occurs after not being sexual for weeks, desire is facilitated by a regular rhythm of

sexual activity. When sex happens less than twice a month, you can become self-conscious and fall into a cycle of anticipatory anxiety, tense and unsatisfying intercourse, and avoidance.

- Healthy sexuality plays a 15 to 20% positive, integral role in your relationship, with its main function to energize your bond and generate special feelings of desire and desirability. Paradoxically, the negative role of conflictual or nonexistent sex has a more powerful affect on your relationship than the positive role of good sex.

CLOSING THOUGHTS

Developing a couple sexual style and building bridges to sexual desire are crucial. Even more important, and more challenging, is maintaining sexual desire and a satisfying sexual relationship. Emotional and sexual intimacy needs continual nurturing. The most important guideline is to set aside "couple time" to be together and share feelings rather than dealing as a team only with the practical concerns of jobs, house, children, and money. If sexuality is to remain vital and satisfying, it requires communication, spontaneity, experimentation, and a sense of playfulness. Commit to making your intimate erotic relationship a priority.

Sex is not the most important component in your couple relationship, but it is integral and special. Sexuality functions as a shared pleasure, a means to build and reinforce intimacy, and a tension reducer to help deal with the hassles of everyday living. A vital sexual life energizes and makes your bond special. If sex is allowed to stagnate, it devitalizes your relationship. You have invested a good deal in becoming a sexual couple; continue to devote the time and energy to maintain sexual desire, intimacy, pleasure, eroticism, and satisfaction.

13

FEMALE PLEASURE AND EROTICISM

Until fairly recently, it was assumed that men were infinitely more sexually desirous and responsive than women. Sex was the woman's duty, not her pleasure. At best, according to this traditional view, sex was tolerated because it allowed affection and intimacy. The woman was not expected to anticipate sex or to enjoy intercourse. After all, sex could be painful and was a source of pressure. The idea that women could enjoy sex more than men was heretical.

In truth, empirical research has found many more similarities than differences in female and male sexual response. Women and men have similar capacities for desire, pleasure, eroticism, orgasm, and satisfaction. Actually, women have the opportunity to be more sexually expressive because they have the potential to have several orgasms (approximately 1 in 5 women have a multiorgasmic response pattern).

Give yourself permission to enjoy healthy sexual expression. Sexuality is as worthwhile for women as for men. As a couple comfortable with intimacy, pleasuring, and eroticism, you'll find that sexuality energizes and reinforces your intimate relationship. Traditional female sexual socialization emphasized intimacy and nondemand touching but not eroticism. Valuing eroticism is an integral component of healthy female sexuality.

In helping you understand, accept, and enjoy your sexuality, the goal is not to foster competition between partners. "The war between the sexes" has done great damage to women, men, and relationships. When the woman and man are sexually aware, they can share and enhance sexual communication and satisfaction. Massive misunderstandings regarding female sexuality have proven to be a major inhibiting factor in developing a couple sexual style. Unfortunately, findings about female sexuality, especially orgasm, have not been well presented to the public. The crucial fact to keep in mind is that female sexual response is more complex and variable than male response. It is not better or worse, more sexual or less sexual, but it is more flexible and variable.

VARIATIONS IN AROUSAL

Typically, the man has one orgasm, which occurs during intercourse. Although there is considerable variability in psychological feelings of enjoyment and satisfaction, male orgasm is a stereotyped response. Not so with female sexual response. Women may have no orgasm, one orgasm, or many orgasms. Orgasm might occur during pleasuring, intercourse, or afterplay. There can be considerable variation in your feelings of satisfaction. For example, there are times you might enjoy sex a great deal even though you are nonorgasmic. Orgasm in and of itself is not a good measure of sexual satisfaction. This is not to say that orgasm has no importance; it is a positive, integral component of female sexuality. However, it should not become a performance demand or be used as a test of femininity or sexual worth.

Learning to enhance arousal and be orgasmic is a gradually developed psychosexual skill that you, individually and as a couple, can understand and accept. Arousal and orgasm are not mysterious processes that must be conquered to prove you are sexual. Through self-exploration exercises and nongenital and genital pleasuring experiences, you have established a base of understanding and acceptance. Exercises in this chapter build on and extend that base. The focus is on pleasure and going with your erotic flow as a couple.

JAN AND MEL

Jan was 43 and had been married to Mel, her second husband, for 5 months. Her first marriage had ended in divorce 3 years previously. Jan was orgasmic on self-stimulation and was often orgasmic during partner sex. As soon as intercourse ended, Mel asked whether Jan had an orgasm, which was a major turn-off for her. If she said yes, whether true or not, Mel felt he had fulfilled his masculine role. Jan was less worried about orgasm (although she certainly enjoyed and valued orgasm). She was more concerned about her difficulty feeling sexually desirous, responsive, and aroused.

Jan had read a good deal about female sexuality and wanted to communicate her feelings and concerns to Mel before their sexual relationship became a major problem. She felt comfortable with and attracted to Mel, and both were committed to creating a satisfying, stable marriage. The question was whether she could trust him to be sexually cooperative and giving. Some men see the woman's sexual difficulty as a personal challenge, which puts a tremendous performance demand on her (and him). If she does not perform according to his expectations, he berates her for being "frigid." When a sexual difficulty is not resolved, the man blames the woman, which adds to her self-blame and feelings that she is "defective" or "broken."

Mel listened to Jan's perceptions and feelings in an understanding, respectful manner. He wanted to be there for her and share sexual pleasure. Mel no longer felt the burden of responsibility for "turning her on" but was open to her guidance and requests. Jan needed to be her own person and take responsibility for her desire, pleasure, eroticism, and orgasm—to develop her "sexual voice." She wanted freedom to express herself (make requests, utter sounds, move her body) without fear of being judged by Mel. Typically, it takes 6 months for a couple to develop a sexual style that is comfortable and satisfying. For Mel and Jan, it took 10 months, but it was well worth the time and energy invested.

Both partners in an intimate relationship need to increase their awareness of the woman's sexual receptivity and responsivity pattern. Increasing arousal and eroticism is a shared experience, not one for the woman to do alone or for the man to do for her. The focus is not on orgasm but on increasing pleasure and eroticism. If she is orgasmic, that is wonderful; orgasm is the natural culmination of increased sexual involvement, pleasure, and erotic flow. If she is not, sex can still be highly pleasurable and satisfying.

EXERCISES

First Exercise: Trust

This exercise focuses on increasing sexual trust. Dating patterns in our culture teach the woman not to trust the man but to be guarded and defensive in her sexual expression. She learns not to show arousal because of fear that her partner might take advantage of her. Many, in fact most, women have felt disappointed or hurt in a sexual relationship. Such experiences further reinforce the wall of vigilance and distrust. Whether the negative experience involved being harassed, cheated on, humiliated, or raped, our culture has long condoned sexual mistreatment and abuse of women. Such cultural attitudes and negative feelings can inhibit sexual expression even though you are now in an intimate, trusting relationship. Talk with your partner about how your trust has grown as a result of the nondemand sensual and genital pleasuring exercises and the sexual desire and couple sexual style experiences. Note especially the importance of giving and utilizing feedback, both verbal and nonverbal.

Start by bathing together. He can be particularly indulgent of your feelings, washing you gently and tenderly. He takes a big, fluffy towel and pats you dry. To accentuate feelings of trust, you can close your eyes and let him lead you to the bedroom, feeling that you are safe and in good hands.

Assume the pleasuring position called the "vulnerability" position. He positions himself comfortably against a wall, headboard, or cushions, with his legs spread. You position your back against his chest with your legs within his. You can place your head on his shoulder. His hands have easy access to your neck, breasts, stomach, vulva, and thighs.

Both partners keep their eyes closed so they can focus on warm, intimate, trusting feelings. His touch is slow, tender, caring, and rhythmic. As the woman's comfort increases, he can gently open her legs and put them over his. There is almost total body contact, which facilitates emotional and sexual intimacy.

With your legs spread, your vulva is open and exposed. A woman is taught not to sit that way, yet being completely open and receptive is totally healthy in your intimate relationship. You can focus on feeling cared for and trusting, so different from feeling vulnerable and inhibited. Allow yourself to feel responsive and experience pleasure and arousal.

Pleasuring intermixes nongenital and genital touching, with the rhythm of touching in unison with your pace and arousal. Enjoy pleasurable stimulation in the context of a nondemanding, trusting, and caring connection. As you become responsive and aroused, continue the rhythm of stimulation. A mistake men often make is to increase the speed or focus of stimulation to try to bring you to orgasm. What often occurs instead is that you lose your rhythm, arousal is decreased, and you no longer feel erotic flow. You feel frustrated and it seems that he is making demands on you, while he feels he has failed as a lover or blames you for being nonresponsive. The key to female eroticism and orgasm is continued stimulation maintained in a consistent rhythm. Your partner follows your movements and rhythm. You are the expert on your body, receptivity, responsivity, eroticism, and erotic flow.

Whether your arousal is low, moderate, or high, he accepts this rather than demand that you respond as he would like you to. Simply enjoy the sensuous, trusting, and caring feelings. The focus, after all, is to build feelings of trust and comfort without a sexual demand.

End this exercise by breathing together. He lies comfortably on his side. You lie in back of him, your head against his upper back and your breasts touching his back. Follow the rhythm of his breathing. As you breathe together, be aware of intimate, trusting feelings. Verbally share these feelings and allow yourselves to drift off to sleep. The core ingredients for female sexual response—trust, receptivity, and responsiveness without demand or inhibitions—are on solid footing in this scenario. While intimacy, trust, and pleasuring are not sufficient for orgasm, they are necessary in a serious or marital relationship.

Second Exercise: Vulva Exploration

You can share, as specifically as possible, your milieu for being receptive and responsive to sexual stimulation. Taking responsibility for your "sexual voice" is essential for increasing arousal. Verbalize your desire for sharing pleasurable and erotic experiences.

It is easy for you to become distracted and to turn off sexually. Tell your partner the turn-offs to avoid so this does not inadvertently occur. If in the midst of a sexual interaction you lose erotic flow, return to comfortable, pleasurable touching. Most women are able to regain receptivity and arousal, although others find it difficult. At a later time, outside the bedroom, you can discuss with your partner how to deal with the waxing and waning of arousal in a cooperative, pleasurable manner rather than in an angry, resentful, or accusatory mode.

Start with a bath or shower. Make it a relaxing, sharing experience. He begins as pleasure-giver. Keep your eyes open to facilitate communication, or, if you wish, close them to become more in touch with your bodily sensations and feelings. Arrange yourselves in a position where he leans against either the headboard or wall with his back supported by a pillow or cushion. Position your body between his spread legs, lying on your back and facing him, with your legs bent and resting outside his thighs. He has easy access to your open vulva as well as your breasts. You can touch him if you desire, but keep your focus on accepting touch and building your pleasure and arousal.

He touches you nongenitally, in a slow, tender, rhythmic manner. Genital touching is gradually integrated with nongenital touch. You can guide him by putting your hand over his, by modifying your movements, or by making verbal requests to alter the rhythm of touching. By making clear requests, you take responsibility for your pleasure. He might use a light, teasing touch, moving from your neck to your vulva, then around your abdomen and thighs in a flowing movement that leads to your breasts, using the type of breast stimulation to which you are most receptive and responsive. Touching covers your entire body, not just your vulva.

Stimulation of the vulva can begin as light and teasing. As you become aroused and begin to lubricate, he gently puts one or two fingers into your vagina and spreads the vaginal lubrication throughout your vulva, especially around your clitoral area. Continue nongenital and genital pleasuring. Neither partner demands or forces. Accentuate sensual and erotic feelings.

Your clitoris is the area with the most nerve endings and erotic sensations. The sole function of your clitoris is sexual pleasure. Exploration of your clitoral area can be confusing because the clitoris is small and during arousal is covered by the clitoral hood. You can take your partner's hand and guide him in touching and stroking your labia. Take his finger and move it around your clitoral area in a gentle, exploratory manner. Most women prefer indirect stimulation around the clitoral shaft rather than direct clitoral stimulation, which can be too intense and even painful (the disappearance of the clitoris under the clitoral hood is your body's way to facilitate pleasure and avoid pain).

Some women react negatively to vaginal insertion, which can be a turn-off if there is a low level of arousal. It would be as if you rhythmically stroked his penis when it was flaccid. Rather than building arousal, it increases self-consciousness and physical irritation. Too often men initiate vaginal insertion and then forget about continuing other pleasuring techniques. Most women find vaginal pleasuring to be stimulating only when there is at least a moderate level of arousal and additional pleasuring, especially clitoral and breast stimulation.

With his index finger, he can explore intravaginally to help you identify and determine areas of vaginal feeling and response. Close your eyes so you can focus on vaginal sensations. While exploring your vagina with one hand, he continues sensuous nongenital touching with his other hand. If at any time either partner feels pressured or uncomfortable, return to nongenital pleasuring.

Conceptualize your vagina as a clock with the section closest to the clitoris as 12 o'clock and the part closest to the anus as 6 o'clock. He can insert his index finger within your vagina to approximately two finger joints. Contrary to popular myth (which has it that the deeper the insertion, the greater the feeling), insertion of two finger joints— about one-and-one-half inches, at about 8 o'clock—reaches the section of your vagina adjacent to the pubococcygeal muscle. This is an area of special vaginal sensations for some women. Contrary to the myth about a magical G-spot as the source of vaginal orgasm, the anterior wall of the vagina, when stimulated, increases arousal for some (but not all) women.

He can gently but firmly move his index finger (or a second finger, if you desire) around your vagina. This movement is slow so you can identify sensations and feelings. Give verbal and nonverbal feedback to guide him during intravaginal stimulation. Touching certain areas of your vagina can be uncomfortable or painful. This might be due to tears in the vaginal wall or to vaginal dryness. Discomfort can be alleviated by using a lubricant or exercises to strengthen your pelvic muscles. If you do experience chronic pain, consult your gynecologist. Vaginal pain can be caused by infection, physical abnormalities, or estrogen deprivation. Pain also can be caused by spasms of the vaginal introitus (opening) that make intromission either impossible or very difficult. Pelvic or vaginal pain is a frequent sexual complaint that needs to be assessed by a gynecologist. It is most likely to be successfully treated by using pleasuring exercises under the guidance of a sex therapist or with psychosexual skill exercises monitored by a physical therapist with a subspecialty in female pelvic floor musculature.

Vaginal pain often reflects lack of subjective arousal and lubrication or your partner's being rough and demanding rather than open to your feedback and requests. Use of a hypoallergenic lotion or estrogen cream can enhance lubrication, especially for women 45 and older. Gynecologists recommend K-Y because it is sterile, but many women prefer abalone lotion, aloe vera lotion, or another pleasant-smelling lotion from the drugstore or a specialty store. Be sure the lotion is water-based and will not irritate or infect your vagina.

Stimulation of specific areas of your vagina can be arousing. Some women find stimulation of two finger joints at four o'clock and eight o'clock particularly erotic. Others report greater vaginal feeling with pressure on the anterior wall. Some women report relatively little intravaginal feeling. There is no right or normal response. What counts are your sensations and feelings.

Tell your partner when you feel aware of and comfortable with your vulval, clitoral, and intravaginal sensations and feelings. You might try this exercise on several occasions, using different positions to explore clitoral and vaginal responsivity. Many women find they enjoy clitoral, labial, and mons stimulation more than vaginal stimulation. Experiment with different combinations of touch, rhythm, and pressure to determine your pattern of sexual receptivity and responsiveness. Feel free to discuss and experiment with erotic scenarios and techniques to increase vulval, clitoral, and vaginal responsiveness.

Third Exercise: Multiple Stimulation

This exercise includes use of a lotion to increase sensual feelings. Choose a lotion whose touch and smell you enjoy. Pleasuring can begin with both partners lying down, facing each other, with eyes open.

Intermix nongenital and genital pleasuring. It is particularly important for you to feel free to guide your partner toward engaging in the manual or oral stimulation you find most pleasurable and erotic. Continue stimulation until you feel excitement and arousal. Your partner can check when and how you want to focus on erotic stimulation. This exchange can be verbal ("Do you feel into it?" or "Is this good?") or nonverbal (touching your vulva, using his hand to close your eyes, using a signal you mutually agree on). If you respond in the negative, continue pleasuring, allowing it to be mutual, and end the experience in a sensual manner. Afterward, discuss what each of you can do to facilitate comfort, trust, sensuality, pleasure, and eroticism.

If your response is positive, he can kneel by your side. He helps you move into a comfortable, receptive position; that is, stretch your legs out, put a pillow under your head, place your arm by your side. He can orally stimulate you (by kissing, licking, or taking small bites) from the top of your head to your mons. At the same time, he can manually stimulate you from your mons to the bottoms of your feet. Stimulation can begin as light and teasing, and then in a natural, rhythmic—and, most important, *slow*—flow it can become more focused, directed, and erotic. He can orally stimulate your breasts by kissing, licking, or sucking while at the same time manually stimulating your labia and clitoral shaft. If you find manual intravaginal stimulation arousing, that, too, can be added. Some women find finger stimulation inside their vagina (especially the anterior wall) adds to arousal, although if you are not already aroused it can be irritating and a turn-off. Stimulation should be consistent, in rhythm with your movements and feelings. You are free to direct his touching and set the rhythm. Remember, it is your arousal and erotic flow that is the driver in this exercise.

Contrary to the myth of male responsibility for the sex experience, no one knows more about female arousal and eroticism than you. Neither partner should demand or try to force sexual response. Pleasure and eroticism are the natural result of accepting, guiding, requesting, and building on sensual and sexual feelings. Give yourself permission to let go and abandon yourself to eroticism. You can be "sexually selfish" and allow yourself to be erotic and expressive. Enjoy eroticism and embrace subjective arousal and erotic flow.

Fourth Exercise: Quiet Vagina

Over a glass of wine or cup of coffee, discuss the attitudinal and behavioral changes you have experienced thus far. What are your feelings about embracing your individual "sexual voice" and integrating eroticism into your couple sexuality? Share feelings, perceptions, experiences, hopes, desires. Is your partner comfortable with your sexuality, or is he threatened by it? Are you trusting and accepting of erotic feelings, or do you feel vulnerable or inhibited? Is orgasm a goal of overwhelming importance, or is it a natural consequence of sexual responsiveness? Are receptivity, pleasure, eroticism, erotic flow, and orgasm a natural, developing process or something that you feel pressured to achieve? Are you comfortable being active and responsible for your sexuality? Have you stopped trying to prove something to yourself or your partner?

Begin this exercise with mutual pleasuring, using nongenital and genital touching as well as manual and oral stimulation. Allow feelings of sexual responsivity and arousal to build. Develop a comfortable, pleasurable, erotic rhythm. Allow each partner's arousal to be a turn-on for the other. Sometimes you are the initiator and pleasure-giver, sometimes he is, and often there is mutual give-and-take. Utilize slow, tender, caring, rhythmic, flowing touching to increase feelings of openness and receptivity. It is exciting to be aware of and embrace the responsivity of your partner; enjoy this variation on the "give-and-get" pleasuring guideline. See each other's arousal as a plus, not as a competition or pressure. You can "piggy-back" your arousal on your partner's arousal.

When both partners are feeling aroused, move to the woman-on-top intercourse position. Avoid immediate intromission. Explore sensations and feelings; play with your partner's penis, rubbing it around your vulva. This is a good position for both verbal and nonverbal communication. It gives you a greater range of movement than other intercourse positions and enables your partner to stimulate your breasts as well as touch and caress your thighs while you take his penis and rub it around your labia, clitoral shaft, and vaginal opening. Be together as a couple; enjoy receiving and giving pleasure. You can determine when to initiate intromission; wait until you are feeling highly aroused and desirous. Typically women (and men) initiate intercourse too early in the arousal cycle.

Intromission is accomplished by sliding back on the penis at a 45-degree angle. You can guide intromission. Once intromission occurs, practice the "quiet vagina" exercise. Guide his penis to the most sensitive parts of your vagina and enjoy penile sensations with minimal movement. Engage in slow, nondemand thrusting. Be aware of feelings in your vagina and throughout your body. Think of his expressiveness as a response to your pleasuring and eroticism. His penis is something for you to play with and enjoy.

The quiet vagina can also be enjoyed by the man, who feels its wet warmth and enjoys slow, nondemanding sensations. Continue the quiet vagina for 5 to 10 minutes, and longer if you wish. During this time touch each other and be aware of a range of sensual and sexual feelings, especially feelings of being cared for and sharing sexuality.

This time, or in subsequent experiences, you can proceed from the quiet vagina to active thrusting. However, resist reverting back to the old intercourse pattern. Slowly increase the amount of movement. You can initiate and guide the rhythm and type of coital thrusting.

In subsequent exercises, experiment with different movements and positions and enjoy the variety of sensations. You can try in-and-out thrusting, circular thrusting, or up-and-down thrusting. You can vary the speed and rhythm of movement. You can try side-by-side, man-on-top, and rear-entry intercourse. Contract your pelvic muscles while his penis is inside you. Be fully accepting of the feelings of his penis in your vagina.

During intercourse he can stimulate your clitoral area manually while his penis is inside you. Many couples find that simultaneous clitoral and vaginal stimulation enhances eroticism and sexual response. Experiment with several variations. He can use his hand, you can use your hand, or you can utilize vibrator stimulation.

Afterward, discuss the quiet vagina experience. Share what you particularly enjoyed—his penis, initiating intercourse, guiding intromission, slower thrusting, multiple stimulation during intercourse, combining vaginal and clitoral stimulation. He can share his feelings—how it felt to be passive during intercourse, how your vagina felt to his penis, how to incorporate multiple stimulation during intercourse, variations of woman-on-top and other intercourse positions he would like to experiment with. He reassures you that your being sexually active and assertive is not a threat. Be aware how you as a couple can integrate multiple stimulation before and during intercourse.

GUIDELINES FOR FEMALE AROUSAL AND ORGASM

- You are responsible for your desire, arousal, and orgasm. Developing your "sexual voice" is a positive —and personal— challenge. It is not the man's responsibility to "give" you a great sexual experience.

- Together, you and your partner can develop an intimate, interactive couple sexual style that promotes desire, pleasure, eroticism, orgasm, and satisfaction.
- Receptivity and responsivity to pleasurable and erotic touch facilitate arousal and orgasm.
- Arousal involves both subjective components (feeling responsive and turned on) and objective components (vaginal lubrication and physical receptivity to intercourse).
- "Foreplay" is widely regarded as the man stimulating the woman to get her ready for intercourse. This increases self-consciousness and performance anxiety by invalidating the woman's sexual voice and turning what should be a mutually enjoyable, erotic encounter into a command performance. The experience of "pleasuring," which emphasizes sharing touch and eroticism, facilitates desire and arousal.
- Arousal and eroticism can lead to intercourse, but intercourse is not necessary for a satisfying sexual experience. A key concept is to transition to intercourse at high levels of arousal (erotic flow).
- Develop your "sexual voice"—verbally and nonverbally making requests and guiding your partner.
- The prescription for satisfying sexuality is intimacy, pleasuring, and eroticism. Traditionally, female sexual socialization has underplayed eroticism, which is integral to your arousal and orgasm.
- Be aware of your preferences—single versus multiple stimulation; pleasurer–recipient versus mutual stimulation; when and how to transition from sensual to erotic stimulation; your conditions for a vital, satisfying sexual experience.
- Feel free to initiate the transition from pleasuring to intercourse and to guide intromission.
- Women who prefer multiple stimulation during pleasuring/eroticism usually prefer multiple stimulation during intercourse. You are free to utilize additional clitoral stimulation with his or your hand, request breast or anal stimulation, use erotic fantasies, or switch intercourse positions.
- Many women are interested in using medications, when they become readily available, to enhance sexual desire and response. Medication can be a valuable resource, but it is not a panacea for inhibited desire or sexual response. The pro-sexual medication or physical aide needs to be integrated into your couple sexual style of intimacy, pleasure, and eroticism.

- Many women, especially after 45, use some form of estrogen cream or a water-based lotion to enhance lubrication and facilitate intercourse.
- You are free to make requests of your partner (for prolonged pleasuring, attention to your pace of arousal, multiple stimulation) and engage in preferred erotic techniques (vibrator stimulation, his or your fingers for clitoral stimulation during intercourse, cunnilingus to orgasm) to enhance arousal and orgasm.
- Remember, sexuality is not about proving anything to your partner, yourself, or anyone else. It is about experiencing and sharing intimacy, pleasure, and eroticism.

CLOSING THOUGHTS

As a woman, and as a couple, you can be comfortable and accepting of vital, integrated female sexuality. Awareness, pleasure, arousal, and eroticism continue to grow as you engage in sensual, playful, erotic, and intercourse experiences. It is important that both of you understand and accept the variability, flexibility, and complexity of female sexual response. Intimacy and mutual enjoyment are better criteria of sexual satisfaction than orgasm.

14

FEMALE SEXUALITY

Becoming Orgasmic

Female orgasm: "the Big O." There has been more talk and articles written about orgasm than any other area of female sexuality. In their aftermath, they usually leave more questions than answers: Are you less of a woman if you do not have an orgasm each time? Is simultaneous orgasm the ideal? Are there differences between vaginal and clitoral orgasms? Is it the man's responsibility to give the woman an orgasm?

SEPARATING THE MYTHS FROM THE FACTS

Old repressive myths have been replaced by new performance myths, touted in sensationalistic articles and case reports—such as the belief the woman *must* have an orgasm each time, the tenet that orgasm is the *only* measure of satisfaction, the primacy of the G-spot orgasm, or the belief that being multiorgasmic is superior to having a single orgasm.

So-called sophisticated males feel they have failed as lovers if their partners are not orgasmic each time. This is as harmful a sex myth as the one that said the woman was not supposed to enjoy sex. Orgasm is an integral part of female sexuality, the natural culmination of sexual involvement, pleasure, and eroticism. The woman takes primary responsibility for experiencing orgasm.

However, orgasm cannot be willed or demanded. The irony is that the more you (and your partner) work to achieve orgasm, the less likely it is to occur. Female orgasmic dysfunction is caused by demands and pressure (from yourself or your partner) in the same manner that male erectile dysfunction is often caused by performance anxiety.

Here are some scientifically and clinically valid facts and guidelines about female orgasm:

- It is unrealistic to expect automatic arousal and orgasm during each sexual encounter. Only one in four women experiences the traditional male pattern of having one orgasm during intercourse without additional stimulation.
- Female sexual response is more variable and complex than male sexuality. You may be nonorgasmic, singly orgasmic, or multi-orgasmic, which might occur during pleasuring, intercourse, or afterplay, depending on your preferences and pattern. On average, the woman is orgasmic during 70% of sexual encounters.
- Orgasm is integral to the comfort/pleasure/eroticism cycle, not something separate from it. The psychophysiological orgasmic response, a series of genital muscle contractions that last from 3 to 10 seconds, is the same whether it occurs through manual, oral, intercourse, vibrator, or self-stimulation. However, there are differences in psychological satisfaction depending on values, expectations, mood, preferences, degree of stimulation, and partner support.
- The distinction between *vaginal* and *clitoral* orgasms is not scientifically valid. Orgasm is a response to indirect clitoral stimulation and is experienced the same way whether his penis is in your vagina or stimulation is done by hands, tongue, rubbing, or vibrator.
- Multiple orgasms are experienced by 15 to 20% of women.
- Very few women (less than 10%) learn orgasmic response during intercourse. The great majority have their first orgasm through masturbation, by manual stimulation, with the use of a vibrator, through cunnilingus, or during afterplay.

Each woman develops her unique style of being orgasmic. Setting an arbitrary criterion of good or bad orgasms is scientifically incorrect and psychologically self-defeating. Multiple orgasms are not necessarily better or more satisfying. Striving for G-spot orgasm, deep-vaginal orgasm, or simultaneous orgasm is an example of making sex a performance-oriented activity rather than an experience of shared pleasure. Do not fall into the male trap of pressuring yourself to be orgasmic each time and judging sex as a failure if you are not. In truth, less than 15% of women are orgasmic during each couple sexual encounter.

You do not need to have the "right" orgasm to prove something to yourself or your partner. Orgasm is a function of being comfortable with and responsible for your sexuality, being aware and receptive to stimulation, letting go and allowing yourself to climax. Responsibility includes using your "sexual voice" to make requests and guide your partner. Your partner does, of course, need to be caring, cooperative, and sharing, but he cannot "make" you have an orgasm, nor is he responsible for your orgasm.

THE ROLE OF MASTURBATION

Self-exploration/masturbation is one of the best ways of learning to become orgasmic. Men rarely have problems being orgasmic, in part because of their masturbation experiences. The woman who is aware of her arousal and orgasm pattern finds it easier to transfer this to partner sex. Traditionally, women have been anxious or guilty about masturbation. In reality, the majority of women masturbate, and frequency actually increases after marriage. Masturbation is not the only route for learning to be orgasmic, but it is a direct, effective, and the most common way to learn about your body, pleasure, eroticism, and orgasm. Most women find masturbation a more reliable way to be orgasmic but prefer couple sex and being orgasmic during couple sex.

ORGASM DURING PARTNER SEX

In learning to be orgasmic with a partner, start by examining your assumptions about sexuality. A healthy attitude includes being accepting of and feeling responsible for your sexuality. The guideline for vital sexuality is to integrate intimacy, nondemand pleasuring, and eroticism. You have a right to be sexually aware, make requests, value eroticism, enjoy high levels of arousal, go with the erotic flow, and experience orgasm.

What are your conditions for good sex? How important is being respected by your partner and respecting him? Do you trust your partner and your relationship? Do you feel good about the balance of power in your relationship? Are you happy with the quality and quantity of affection? Are you active and responsive during pleasuring? Are you involved in manual, oral, and rubbing stimulation, or do you hold back waiting for intercourse? Can you be orgasmic during erotic, nonintercourse sex, or do you not value that experience? Do you enjoy intercourse as an erotic experience, or are you trying to perform? Is your preferred orgasmic pattern with manual, oral, rubbing or intercourse stimulation? If you are aroused after your partner has ejaculated, are you comfortable asking for additional stimulation to be orgasmic with afterplay? Be aware of blocks that inhibit your natural arousal, erotic flow, and orgasmic response. In examining these dimensions, be in touch with your sexual values, feelings, and preferences.

MEDICAL INTERVENTIONS AS AN ADDITIONAL RESOURCE

Can medical interventions facilitate female desire, arousal, and orgasm? Yes, but not as a substitute for your sexual voice, your bridges for desire, taking responsibility for pleasuring and eroticism, and valuing multiple stimulation before and during intercourse. The most effective additional resources do not require a prescription or use of lubricants and vibrators.

A major cause of sexual dysfunction is side effects of medications, especially psychiatric and hypertensive medications. This does require seeing an internist, family practitioner, or a specialist (gynecologist, endocrinologist, or sexual medicine specialist) who can conduct a detailed medical history and exam, with special emphasis on evaluating these side effects and your hormonal, vascular, and neurological systems.

Major medical interventions include testosterone replacement (often in patch or gel form), estrogen supplements, and medications in the testing stage to enhance desire and sexual responsivity. None of these directly affects orgasm, but they can help facilitate the desire and arousal phases of your sexual response

SHERRI

Sherri was a 37-year-old divorcee beginning a new relationship with Charles. She had been caught in the middle of the sexual revolution during her high school years. The learning she received from parents and church emphasized female virginity and the double standard. Sherri's older brother had received a very different sexual socialization, which gave him permission to experiment without feeling guilty.

When Sherri entered college, she was bombarded by the sexual liberation and feminist movements. The transition from the 18-year-old conservative and cautious Sherri to the 19-year-old experimental and free-wheeling Sherri was extreme and unsettling. She recalls her college years as "sex, drugs, music, and liberation." By junior year, she was having orgasms through masturbation and, by senior year, orgasms during cunnilingus. After college, she was involved in a series of dating relationships. Her adult years included times of personal growth intermixed with bouts of depression and lack of direction in her life.

Partly due to insecurity and partly to peer pressure, she made an unwise marital choice. Sherri was intimidated by her husband's questioning why she had orgasms only through oral sex. He decided to "help" her by refusing to do cunnilingus so she would have orgasms during intercourse. Sherri felt alienated and disrespected. Her sexual desire decreased, and her orgasms disappeared.

After the divorce, Sherri felt negative about herself, men, and sex. She had ambivalent feelings about the dating scene. In one of her caustic moments, she said that single men were either "drunks, neurotics, or gay." For a 2-year period she dated only married men because they were considerate, but she tired of the "other woman" role. Sherri was anxious because of her biological clock and desire to have children.

After Sherri's best friend remarried, she had a series of discussions with the friend and her new spouse. Sherri decided to date only men she felt comfortable with, attracted to, and trusted. The man would have to put time and energy into their relationship and treat it as a first-class relationship.

Sherri met Charles while volunteering for a tutoring project. They were friends before they started to date. Once they became an emotional couple, intercourse followed 3 weeks later. The next month Sherri decided to be assertive and talk about what she wanted in their sexual relationship.

Initial sexual experiences were okay but not stimulating. Sherri told Charles that she liked and cared for him and wanted this to be a healthy relationship and the sex to be good for both of them. She told him that in the past 6 years she had been orgasmic irregularly. Sherri wanted to communicate and make requests so sex could be pleasurable, erotic, and orgasmic. Charles was receptive but a bit defensive. He, too, had been divorced, was tired of the dating scene, and was looking for a serious relationship. He wanted to be sensitive yet was afraid she would make sexual demands and view him as a "wimp." Sherri assured him she was looking for an intimate, sharing relationship in which she could make requests and engage in "give-and-take." She was not a demanding person, emotionally or sexually.

Charles and Sherri experimented with oral sex. Sherri was pleasantly surprised to find that within 3 weeks she was responding orgasmically. Sharing and communication increased emotional intimacy. Anxiety and anger are the major blocks to sexual response. Sherri and Charles dealt with difficult practical and emotional issues outside of the bedroom so these did not interfere with the development of their couple sexual style.

Charles enjoyed Sherri's orgasms. For the first time in her life Sherri was multiorgasmic, which was very arousing for Charles. Rather than pressuring herself to be orgasmic during intercourse, she gave herself permission to experiment and go with her feelings. What proved most effective in Sherri's learning to be orgasmic during intercourse was multiple stimulation. She thrust her pelvis as arousal built and stimulated herself while Charles was thrusting. Sherri preferred oral stimulation as an easier, more intense means of arousal and orgasm, but she also felt good about her style of sexual response and orgasm during intercourse.

Every woman has her own sexual style, so what Sherri enjoyed may or may not be good for you. What is important is to be aware of your sexual feelings and preferences, be responsible for your desire and orgasm, be open to sharing and experimenting, and establish a cooperative, give-and-take relationship.

You are a sexual person who deserves to experience sexual feelings, including orgasm. Each woman has her own sexual feelings, preferences, and scenarios. Do not be defensive about whether you have "right" or "wrong" orgasms. Find your unique sexual voice and orgasm pattern. Let arousal build to erotic flow and orgasm as the natural culmination of your sexual experience, preferences, and feelings.

EXERCISES

First Exercise: Sexual Responsibility

Be the initiator. Design a sexual scenario to promote your comfort, involvement, pleasure, arousal, and eroticism. You might begin with a relaxing bath or shower with your partner, hold hands and talk about romantic or erotic feelings, or receive a whole-body massage. Do what is best is for you; it is your sexual scenario.

If you are easily orgasmic with masturbation, you might stimulate yourself to orgasm with your partner present. Lie comfortably in his arms. If this is the first time you have stimulated yourself in front of him, he could close his eyes so you do not feel self-conscious. Utilize your "orgasm triggers" to carry arousal through to orgasm. This might include moving your pelvis rhythmically, tightening muscles, breathing faster, focusing on a highly charged fantasy, increasing the rhythm of clitoral stimulation, inserting two fingers in your vagina and firmly stimulating the anterior wall, making sounds. Let erotic flow build and allow it to proceed to climax. Most women find it is easier and more predictable to be orgasmic with masturbation. Being orgasmic with self-stimulation allows you to feel in control and can break down inhibitions about letting go with your partner.

If this exercise is not comfortable or you prefer not to be orgasmic with self-stimulation, begin with a partner exercise that emphasizes your responsibility for sexuality. Use a position in which you have freedom to be sexually expressive. You could lie on your side so he has easy access to your genitals, lie on your back with your legs bent so you can move your pelvis, or kneel over him so you can thrust your body toward his body and hands. Guide your partner, and let him know when you are ready for breast and vulva stimulation. Communicating what you want and setting the rhythm of erotic stimulation are crucial. Actively focus on feelings of arousal, enjoy your eroticism, and let go. Allow yourself to express your sexuality, make noises, breathe as loudly and rapidly as you like, move your body, ask for breast stimulation, put your hand over his and guide clitoral stimulation, have him put his finger in your vagina and specify how much pressure he should exert. Be an active, involved participant and share your pleasure and eroticism with your partner.

A sure way to kill arousal is for the man to ask, "Did you come?" Orgasm is not an isolated performance goal. You can share how aroused or erotic you feel and the sensations and stimulation you value. Request additional stimulation or suggest scenarios and positions to explore in subsequent exercises. If you experience orgasm, that's great. You can share this or discuss it the next day on a walk. If you do not, take what you have learned and continue to increase your pleasure, arousal, and erotic flow.

Second Exercise: Multiple Stimulation

There are two major strategies for building arousal/erotic flow to orgasm: (1) use multiple stimulation to heighten erotic flow; and (2) become comfortable with expressing yourself, letting go and using orgasm triggers. This exercise incorporates both strategies. While it still involves a temporary ban on intercourse, there is no prohibition on the variety and type of stimulation you can request and utilize.

Use the pleasuring positions in which you feel most expressive. Set the rhythm of pleasurable and erotic stimulation. Take your time. Allow yourself to be selfish, and set the pace that is best for you. Instead of second-guessing or worrying that your partner is bored or frustrated, realize he is learning that his best aphrodisiac is your being a receptive, responsive partner. Tell him when to begin genital stimulation (usually when your arousal is a 5 or 6 on a 10-point scale since insufficient arousal can be a self-conscious turn-off), and guide him to show how you like your genitals touched. Many women prefer beginning with light, teasing stroking of their breast; some prefer oral stimulation of the areola;

others choose rhythmic stroking of the vulva, with a focus on labial stimulation; others enjoy being touched from the mons to the clitoral shaft; still others prefer stimulation around the perineum and up to the labia. What is your preferred pattern? Share this with your partner.

Do you prefer to intermix nongenital and genital stimulation, or do you respond to focused erotic stimulation? Some women find oral breast stimulation and manual clitoral stimulation, coupled with erotic fantasy, a great combination. Or you might find that having your vulva orally stimulated and moving your pelvis in rhythm with your arousal while stroking his penis is the right combination. For others, a combination of clitoral shaft and manual stimulation of the anterior wall of the vagina while watching an erotic video is most arousing. Some women find that combining clitoral stimulation with anal stimulation while their partner verbalizes a sexually explicit fantasy allows them to let go and be orgasmic. Other women prefer one continuous focused stimulation rather than multiple stimulation. Each woman and each couple need to develop their unique style of sharing eroticism and coming to orgasm. Share arousal and orgasm "with" your partner rather than looking to him to "make" you have an orgasm. Do not try to will or force orgasm; it doesn't work.

What thoughts, actions, or sensations serve as your orgasm triggers? Some women let go with a specific fantasy, increase the rhythm of pelvic thrusting, touch themselves in special ways, focus on breathing, or verbalize that they are "going to come." Others increase stimulation of their partner, and as his arousal builds so does theirs. Are there orgasm triggers you have not shared because of embarrassment, lack of assertiveness, or the feeling that it's not proper? It is acceptable and healthy to share special turn-ons and orgasm triggers. This is the time to be assertive; share your erotic preferences and let go.

Some women know that if they touch themselves or use vibrator stimulation in addition to partner stimulation, they will be orgasmic. Yet they refrain from doing so because they think it is not "right" or are afraid their partner will be offended because it seems "out of control" or "kinky." Being orgasmic in front of your partner is a breakthrough. Instead of inhibiting yourself by saying "it's not the right way," give yourself permission to engage in erotic stimulation and utilize orgasm triggers. Most couples are pleasantly surprised to find that when the walls of inhibition and embarrassment fall, a host of alternatives for further experimentation and sharing open up.

The experience need not end at the point of orgasm (yours or his). You can pleasure your partner and help him be orgasmic. Whether either or both have been orgasmic, afterplay is an integral part of the sexual experience. Come down together, not with the burden of whether you succeeded or failed but sharing what you have enjoyed about multiple stimulation, orgasm triggers, special turn-ons, being expressive, and letting go. Tell him what you would like to experiment with next time as you discuss couple sexuality the next day on a walk or over a cup of coffee or glass of wine.

Third Exercise: Multiple Stimulation During Intercourse

Approximately 55 to 65% of women experience orgasm during intercourse. Does this mean 35 to 45% percent of women are dysfunctional? Not at all. Being orgasmic with erotic, nonintercourse sex is a normal, healthy expression of female sexuality. Many women prefer to be orgasmic during nonintercourse sex rather than during intercourse, while some prefer to be orgasmic during intercourse. Others—including those who can be orgasmic during intercourse—prefer to be orgasmic with manual, rubbing, or oral stimulation. There is no one "right" pattern.

Intercourse is a pleasurable, erotic, shared experience whether or not it results in orgasm. This exercise focuses on increasing involvement, pleasure, and arousal during intercourse. If it increases orgasmic response, so much the better; however, orgasm during intercourse is not the goal. The focus is on increasing involvement, eroticism, and multiple stimulation during intercourse.

Traditionally, women have viewed intercourse as the man's domain. In this exercise, you initiate intercourse and choose the position and intercourse scenario you find most pleasurable. A common pitfall is to establish a rhythm of arousal during pleasuring and then relinquish it when intercourse begins. Another common trap is the cessation of multiple stimulation with intercourse. In this exercise you set the coital rhythm and can engage in multiple stimulation throughout intercourse.

Do you want to initiate touching or would you like your partner to? Whoever initiates, it is you who determines when to transition to intercourse. Do not start intercourse at the first sign of arousal. Continue stimulation and allow arousal to build. Experiment with transitioning to intercourse at high levels of erotic flow (8 or 9 rather than at 5 or 6). Guide your partner's penis into you. After all, you are the world's expert on your vagina. Try intercourse in the woman-on-top or another position that gives you freedom of movement and expression. Variations of side, rear-entry, and sitting positions are commonly preferred alternatives. Be aware of multiple stimulation techniques that add to arousal and continue using them throughout intercourse.

Let your partner know what your favorite thrusting movement is. Set the speed and rhythm that facilitate your erotic flow. What additional stimulation do you enjoy during intercourse? Can he stroke your breasts or use his fingers to stimulate your anal area? Can you use your hands to massage your clitoris? Can you stroke his chest, kiss, verbalize erotic fantasies, use a vibrator for simultaneous clitoral stimulation, scratch his back? Clearly, directly, and assertively request what you want. Do not be embarrassed to utilize fantasies to increase arousal; erotic fantasies are the most common form of multiple stimulation. Do what increases involvement, arousal, and erotic flow during intercourse. If you like, you could interrupt intercourse, use manual or oral stimulation to heighten arousal, and then resume intercourse in a different position while continuing with multiple stimulation.

If you reach orgasm, how do you feel? Some women really enjoy the sensations, while others are disappointed because orgasm during intercourse is not as special or physiologically intense as they had hoped. If you are not orgasmic during intercourse, that's perfectly normal. Many, in fact most, women find it easier to be orgasmic during nonintercourse sex. Be aware of positions and techniques that allow you to be an involved, aroused intercourse partner.

Fourth Exercise: Being Responsible for Your Orgasm

You have experimented with pleasuring and intercourse positions, voicing your sexual preferences, using multiple stimulation, being active during pleasuring and intercourse, and making specific erotic requests.

This exercise asks you to develop your favorite erotic and orgasm scenario. As the expert on your sexuality, you are responsible for your comfort, desire, pleasure, eroticism, and orgasm. This responsibility cannot be assumed by your partner or determined by psychosexual skill exercises. Design your own sexual scenario for eroticism and orgasm. Start from the beginning: What are your conditions for sexual comfort and desire? Who initiates? When? Where? What is most important about your partner's attitudes, behavior, and feelings? What can he do to enhance your sexual receptiveness and responsiveness?

Once comfort is established, how can you increase pleasure? Do you like stimulation to be slow and tender, teasing and seductive, or erotic and genitally focused? Do you like romantic music, your partner verbalizing sexual feelings, use of pictures or videos, reading erotic material? Do you want to be pleasured (self-entrancement arousal), or do you prefer mutual stimulation (partner interaction arousal)? Do you like lying in bed, standing in front of a mirror, kneeling facing each other in front of the fireplace, being sexual in the shower? What are the special pleasuring positions and turn-ons that intensify arousal and erotic flow?

What initiatives or requests build arousal? Do you respond to special stimulation—a vibrator, touching yourself, simultaneous oral and anal simulation, breast and clitoral stimulation, clitoral and vaginal stimulation? Is your partner's arousal vital to your arousal? Feel free to request and guide. Are you most responsive to manual, oral, vibrator, rubbing, or intercourse stimulation? Focus on and enjoy your arousal, allowing it to build and flow.

What are your orgasm triggers and how expressive are you during orgasm? Do you make sounds and move or just allow your body to let go? Do you focus on a single form of stimulation, or do you prefer multiple stimulation? Do you actively move toward orgasm or let arousal build and sweep you to orgasm? Do you feel free to utilize orgasm triggers? Maximize your expressiveness and satisfaction by understanding what you need and guiding your partner to help you experience it.

CLOSING THOUGHTS

Orgasm is not the ultimate test of sexual satisfaction, nor is it a measure of femininity. It is a natural psychophysiological response to an involved, pleasure-oriented, erotic process that facilitates high levels of arousal and erotic flow that naturally culminate in pleasurable release. Each woman has her own style of being orgasmic. Enjoy orgasm as a way of sharing an intimate sexual experience that validates you as a sexual woman and enhances your couple relationship. Desire, pleasure, eroticism, and satisfaction are more important than orgasm. Be accepting of your arousal/orgasm pattern. Sexuality is ultimately about experiencing and sharing pleasure; it is not about having a G-spot orgasm, multiple orgasms, "vaginal" orgasm, extended orgasm, or whatever type of orgasm is currently the fad.

15

DEALING WITH FEMALE SEXUAL PAIN

While occasional discomfort or pain during sex is an almost universal experience for many women, chronic pain is neither normal nor acceptable. Sporadic pain is unlikely to undermine the positive cycle of sexual anticipation, pleasure-oriented sex, and a regular rhythm of sexual experiences, which is key to a satisfying and bonding couple sexuality. However, when sexual pain, most commonly pain during intercourse, becomes chronic and subverts the positive sexual cycle, it must be addressed as a couple issue.

The professional model of understanding, assessing, and treating sexual pain has undergone a dramatic change in the past decade. Traditionally, when a gynecologist did a pelvic examination and found no specific medical cause for pain, it was diagnosed as a psychosomatic sexual dysfunction, without a specific medical cause—"it's all in your head." In truth, sexual pain is a psychophysiological phenomenon with multiple causes, dimensions, and solutions. It is now viewed as a pain disorder, not a sexual dysfunction. As with other pain problems, the goal of the current biopsychosocial model for assessing and treating sexual pain is to help you manage the pain/discomfort so it does not stop you from engaging in valued intimate, erotic couple sexuality.

Biologically, the pain you're experiencing is real and is indeed in your vulva or vagina. The best person to consult is a gynecologist with a subspecialty in sexual pain. Contrary to common sense beliefs, most gynecologists are not well trained in dealing with sexual function issues, much less in assessing and treating sexual pain. Among the factors to examine with the gynecologist (or nurse-practitioner) is whether the pain is experienced during intromission, thrusting, or during deep penetration. Is it always present, or is it intermittent? Is pain present in other areas of your vulva or only within the vagina? Assessment includes an examination for physical tears, blockages, adhesions, infections, sexually transmitted infections, and hormonal levels—especially estrogen and testosterone.

It is important that the gynecologist be comfortable speaking with you about sexual issues generally and sexual pain specifically. Many women find it of great value to have their partner present during a consultation with a gynecologist. This reinforces the message that sexuality and sexual pain is a couple issue and that you need your partner as your intimate and sexual friend. Speaking with you as a couple can bring out the best in the gynecologist, especially if you make it clear to your physician that you are not asking for sex therapy but to be an aware, knowledgeable patient who wants to use all your physical and medical resources to enhance sexual comfort, confidence, and function.

In addition to the gynecologist, there is a new resource that can be very helpful—a female physical therapist with a subspecialty in pelvic floor musculature. In studies of women experiencing chronic pain during intercourse, treatment interventions with the physical therapist proved to be the most impactful. The role of the physical therapist is to help you understand and manage your pelvic muscles, increase awareness of both the anatomy and physiology of sexual response, use physical relaxation and mindfulness procedures, and help you feel in control of your body and sexuality. With increased awareness and practice, you can manage sexual pain. Psychologically, your goal is to enjoy the sexual experience, including intercourse, rather than be caught in the negative cycle of anticipatory anxiety, painful intercourse, and avoidance. The psychological challenge is to reestablish the cycle of positive anticipation, pleasure-oriented sex, and a regular rhythm of sexual connection. Whole-body relaxation, pelvic muscle relaxation, and mindfulness allow you to feel in control of your body and sexuality. Your goal is not to be totally pain free (although that is optimal) but to manage your discomfort/pain so that you can be an active, involved partner who values the sexual experience.

Relational and psychosexual skill factors are particularly important in dealing with sexual pain. That is why the third member of the treatment team, a couple therapist with expertise in managing sexual pain, is such a valuable resource. Like other sexual problems, sexual pain is best approached as a couple issue. You want your partner to be your intimate friend in confronting and managing sexual pain so his sexual needs are not met at your emotional or physical expense. Rather, he is your supportive ally in dealing with the pain problem. Coping rather than avoiding is your joint strategy. As a couple, you want to focus on sharing sexual pleasure rather than feeling pressure to complete intercourse, no matter how painful.

Whether trying this on your own or in consultation with a couple therapist, physical therapist, or gynecologist, you will need to use a variety of psychosexual strategies and skills. These include transitioning to intercourse at high levels of erotic flow, you guiding his penis into your vagina, using lubrication to enhance intromission and intercourse, using intercourse positions and types of thrusting that enhance arousal and minimize pain, and engaging in multiple stimulation during intercourse. If there is moderate to severe pain, you can transition to erotic, nonintercourse stimulation. Whether there is intercourse or not, you want to develop afterplay scenarios that increase bonding and satisfaction.

TONIA AND STEVE

When Tonia and Steve began their relationship 26 years ago, they were sure they'd be a special couple who would enjoy a vibrant sex life. This was a second marriage for both, and they took great pride in beating the odds and establishing a marital bond that was satisfying and stable. Tonia's daughter from her first marriage was already married and told Tonia that she and Steve had been a wonderful marital and sexual model for her.

Tonia was frustrated and embarrassed that at 54 she was experiencing painful intercourse, which caused her to avoid sex with Steve. Tonia experienced pain both on intromission and during thrusting. She was disappointed with Steve, feeling he blamed her for the sexual pain and discounted her sexual feelings. Tonia viewed Steve as her worst critic and sexual enemy, not her intimate friend. Steve felt betrayed because after many years of a mutually satisfying sexual relationship Tonia had set up a traditional male–female power struggle, with him as the "bad guy." Steve was trying to be a sensitive partner but felt like Tonia "demonized" him. Steve was emotionally offended because he saw himself as open to her feedback and thought of himself as a caring and sensitive lover. Steve felt that no matter what he did Tonia would complain and blame him, and he felt hopeless and helpless that after 26 years their sexual relationship had become so negative.

One of the hardest issues to cope with was that sex, which had been a strength and energizer throughout their marriage, was now a major problem and drain on their partnership. This was totally unexpected and felt unfair. Using the framework of the biopsychosocial model, the challenge for Tonia and Steve was to adapt to the aging process and their changing bodies. Tonia, like about one in four women, experienced chronic pain during intercourse caused in part by vaginal dryness and by less flexible vaginal walls. Although almost half of men experience some erectile anxiety by age 50, this was not true for Steve. This was a plus, but also a negative in that it made him less empathic to Tonia's sexual problems.

Sexual pain is best understood and approached as a couple challenge. The great advantage of sex with aging is that it requires the couple to be more of a sexual team. You need each other for sexuality to be comfortable, functional, and pleasurable. You need to use all your biological, psychological, relational, and psychosexual skills to enhance sexuality. Unfortunately, the opposite was happening with Tonia and Steve. They were caught in the blame–counterblame trap. Instead of turning to each other as intimate sexual friends, each felt alone and isolated. Tonia felt that her sexual days were over; desire, pleasure, and orgasm were overridden by fear of pain, which was occurring during more than 70% of their intercourse encounters. She felt sorry for Steve but also was angry at what she perceived as his insensitivity to her sexual pain. On his part, Steve felt that Tonia was negating his masculinity by withholding sex. Steve felt he tried to be sensitive and helpful, but she rejected his help.

Tonia had consulted two gynecologists, who minimized the pain problem by saying this was a normal part of menopause and that lubricants should help. As an advocate for her health, Tonia sought out a gynecologist with a subspecialty in pain. The gynecologist did an assessment the others had not, called a *provoked vulvodynia probe*, and found that Tonia was indeed suffering with vulvodynia, which is characterized by itching, burning, and stabbing pain in the area around the opening of the vagina. The gynecologist introduced the concept of a team treatment approach and made a referral to a couple sex therapist and a female physical therapist with a subspecialty in pelvic floor musculature. She also suggested that Tonia invite Steve to the next gynecological appointment.

Tonia felt hopeful about this new approach and scheduled a joint session with the couple therapist and an individual appointment with the physical therapist. In addition, Tonia signed information release forms so that the gynecologist, couple therapist, and physical therapist could communicate and work synergistically.

Tonia and Steve were not looking for a "miracle cure." They were aware that dealing with sexual pain would take time, focus, and effort. Perhaps the biggest change was Steve's positive involvement. For the first time since the pain problem had started 3 years ago, Tonia thought of Steve as her intimate ally.

Tonia found the physical therapy exercises to relax her pelvic muscles to be of great value as well as specific directions about how and when to guide intromission. Steve attended two of the physical therapy sessions and worked cooperatively with Tonia in practicing the recommended exercises. The major contribution of the couple therapist was the emphasis on rebuilding sexual desire and helping Tonia and Steve accept asynchronous sexual experiences and erotic, nonintercourse scenarios.

These interventions had an additive effect in rebuilding Tonia and Steve's comfort with couple sexuality generally and intercourse specifically. Managing sexual pain was still a challenge, but pain no longer controlled their couple sexuality.

YOUNG WOMEN AND SEXUAL PAIN

Although sexual pain is much more common among women after 45, it does occur in women in their 20s and 30s. This problem is even more disruptive and challenging for younger women and their partners because the pain is so unexpected. The good news is that the same multidimensional approach to pain management has proven successful for younger women. It is crucial to not blame or stigmatize the woman but to treat the sexual pain as a joint challenge. The trap to avoid is allowing yourself to feel defective or guilty and for him to feel negated sexually or that it is his responsibility to cure the pain (or cure you). You need to be intimate and sexual friends in managing the pain and rebuilding a couple sexual style focused on desire, pleasure, eroticism, and satisfaction.

EXERCISES

First Exercise: Managing Sexual Pain

Managing sexual pain is a challenge both for the woman and for the couple. This exercise has two phases. The first is to confront and banish self-defeating, catastrophic thoughts and attitudes. The second is to build positive, realistic expectations for pain management and healthy couple sexuality.

Each partner is asked to write from one to three of the most self-defeating attitudes and beliefs that influence them. Men, for example, often harbor two extreme cognitions: "If she loved me she wouldn't have pain" or "It's my responsibility to cure the pain." Other attitudes might include the following:

- "Sexual pain will become worse and stop us from having sex."
- "The pain problem is in my head and makes me a less desirable woman."
- "This pain problem will destroy our relationship."
- "Pain is God's punishment for my sexual past."

After you have individually written your self-defeating cognitions, together create positive, problem-solving attitudes and resolutions that effectively counter these defeatist beliefs. These could include, "We are intimate sexual friends who confront the pain issue together so we can enjoy both erotic sex and intercourse sex," and "The pain issue will not control our sexual desire and satisfaction." Be honest, specific, and personal. This is an opportunity to reestablish and solidify your relationship as intimate sexual friends.

For the second phase of this exercise, discuss your desires and values regarding couple sexuality. What do you value as a person and couple about intimacy, pleasure, and eroticism? What can each of you do to restore positive anticipation and pleasure to your relationship? What sensual, playful, and erotic scenarios do you find most inviting? Whether your sexual encounters are great, good, fair, or unsatisfying, how can you end them in a positive manner? Be clear, specific, positive, and realistic in creating healthy sexual scenarios.

Second Exercise: Pleasure, Eroticism, and Intercourse

A technique many couples find valuable is talking about pleasure on a 10-point scale, where 0 means neutral, 5 is beginning arousal, and 10 means orgasm. This allows you to communicate how subjectively aroused you feel. A very helpful guideline is not to transition to intercourse until your arousal is 7 or 8 and for you to guide intromission.

In this exercise you have three focuses:

1. Build your subjective arousal using the arousal style (partner interaction, self-entrancement, or role enactment) to which you are most responsive.
2. Use the hypoallergenic, water-based lubricant you prefer. You can decide whether you want to apply it before or during the encounter or have him apply the lubricant as part of the pleasuring process. Be sure there is sufficient lubricant both around your vulva and inside your vagina.
3. Guide intromission from the woman-on-top intercourse position and ask your partner to continue breast or clitoral stimulation before, during, and after intromission.

Be open to and enjoy the entire sexual process—pleasuring, eroticism, intercourse, and afterplay.

Third Exercise: Pleasure-Oriented Intercourse

Physically, you want to experience intercourse as comfortable. Psychologically, you want to rebuild your confidence with intercourse as a natural continuation of the pleasuring/eroticism process. Relationally, you want to turn to your partner as your intimate and erotic friend who cares about your sexual feelings and needs. In other words, use all your resources to promote a comfortable, pleasurable sexual experience.

In transitioning to intercourse, be sure you are well lubricated, your pelvic muscles are relaxed and receptive, you are in an erotic flow, your partner is involved and pleasuring you, and you guide intromission in a gradual, smooth manner. Many women prefer the woman-on-top intercourse position, but you can use your favorite position—whether sitting, kneeling, man on top, or side or rear entry. Once his penis is inside you, thrust in a slow, gentle, rhythmic manner so your vagina can acclimate to intercourse.

Most women enjoy receiving or giving multiple stimulation during intercourse. Engage in your preferred type of multiple stimulation. Or if your preference is a single focus on intercourse thrusting enjoy that. Remember, intercourse is a mutual experience of sharing pleasure/eroticism. Your sexual feelings and preferences matter. About half of all women find that indulging in erotic fantasies during intercourse enhances the sexual experience. If that is your preference, enjoy fantasies as a special form of multiple stimulation. Additional clitoral stimulation, with your fingers, his fingers, or a vibrator, is another technique for increasing erotic flow to orgasm. An orgasmic experience before, during, or after intercourse builds positive feelings and minimizes discomfort or pain. Some women find that giving stimulation during intercourse—testicle or buttock stimulation, kissing, scratching his back—facilitates involvement, which minimizes your pain or discomfort. Do whatever you prefer and feels right for you in order to enhance the entire sexual experience, including intercourse.

Afterplay is the most ignored aspect of healthy couple sexuality. Afterplay enhances feelings of satisfaction and bonding. Feel free to engage in your preferred afterplay scenario, whether it's lying in bed holding hands and talking, taking a bath together, having a glass of wine in bed and talking about a trip, sitting in the living room with a cup of tea and listening to music, or moving to the "spoon" position and going to sleep entwined. Don't forget to tell your partner how much you value his being your intimate ally.

Fourth Exercise: Alternative Sexual Scenarios

Sexual avoidance is self-defeating. It reinforces the cycle of anticipatory anxiety and tense, performance-oriented intercourse and results in heightened frustration and hypervigilance about sexual pain—which lead to further avoidance. So that you do not feel stuck between a rock and a hard place, we want you to be aware of positive sexual alternatives that you can utilize. Obviously, Plan A is a comfortable, pleasurable intercourse experience. Plan B is to slow down intercourse, switch positions or type of thrusting, or increase multiple stimulation and erotic flow. Plan C is to take a break from intercourse, engage in pleasuring/eroticism, use more lubricant, and engage in a slower, more inviting intromission in a comfortable position—with you controlling the type, depth, and speed of thrusting.

This exercise focuses on alternative sexual scenarios—either an erotic nonintercourse scenario or a sensual scenario. The erotic experience can be mutual (you are both aroused and orgasmic) or asynchronous (you pleasure your partner to orgasm or vice versa). The sensual encounter also can be synchronous or asynchronous (more pleasurable for one partner than the other).

The key concept is to have a feeling of choice which offers you a range of positive intercourse, erotic, or sensual scenarios. Choice allows you to reinforce the cycle of positive anticipation, pleasure-oriented intercourse and other sexual scenarios, and a regular rhythm of satisfying sexual encounters. Practice this exercise at least twice—using an erotic or sensual scenario—so both you and your partner are comfortable making this transition. We especially urge you to engage in afterplay to reinforce bonding and satisfaction. Whether the scenario is erotic, sensual, or intercourse you can end the encounter in a positive manner.

GUIDELINES FOR BUILDING SEXUAL COMFORT AND REDUCING PAINFUL INTERCOURSE

- Consultation with a competent, caring gynecologist can help you understand the pain problem and learn if there is a medical intervention or change in health habits that could facilitate your efforts at pain management.
- In cases of chronic and severe pain, an interdisciplinary treatment team includes a couple sex therapist, a gynecologist specializing in pain, and a female physical therapist with a specialty in pelvic musculature.
- It is important to view the problem as sexual pain, not sex dysfunction. You can learn to manage sexual pain and build sexual

comfort. You deserve to feel sexual desire, pleasure, eroticism, and satisfaction.

- Consistent use of a sexual lubricant (water-based and hypoallergenic) that feels and smells good can be helpful. Use the lubricant preventively, as part of foreplay/pleasuring. Waiting until you feel pain is likely to create distress and reduce your enjoyment of the sexual experience.

- Learn and utilize relaxation techniques, both cognitive and physical. Physical exercises can help you relax your whole body, including your pelvic muscles.

- During sexual activity, it is important that you feel comfortable and highly aroused before transitioning to intercourse. Guiding his penis into your vagina minimizes discomfort and increases your sense of control.

- Identify and make use of intercourse positions and types of thrusting that increase your comfort, pleasure, and eroticism.

- In situations when you are not aroused or you experience pain, you can suggest engaging in alternative sensual or sexual scenarios: erotic nonintercourse sex (manual, oral, rubbing, vibrator stimulation); a cuddly, sensual encounter; or asynchronous sex where you pleasure your partner to orgasm or he pleasures you to orgasm.

- You have a right to veto sexual activity that is painful, but you don't want to avoid sexual touching. Let your partner know that you value him and sensual and sexual touching but that you feel anxiety about sexual pain. Avoidance increases anxiety and—over time—intensifies the problem. Rebuild a sense of positive anticipation and confidence in your individual and couple coping techniques. Remember, you deserve pleasure through intimate touching.

- Be aware of the destructive sexual pain cycle: anticipatory anxiety leading to tense and painful intercourse, followed by avoidance. Keep your focus on the positive cycle of sexual anticipation, pleasure-oriented sexual encounters, and a regular rhythm of intimate and sexual experiences. With your partner, develop a variable, flexible sexual repertoire that includes, but is not limited to, intercourse.

- Many women who experience sexual pain create a dichotomy between intercourse and nonintercourse sex. They may enjoy manual, oral, rubbing, or vibrator stimulation but are afraid of intercourse and come to view it as strictly for the man's pleasure rather than their own. You and your partner can cooperate to make intercourse comfortable and functional for both of you.

- You deserve to feel comfortable with your body, with intercourse, and with nonintercourse scenarios and techniques. Use all your resources: relaxation, mindfulness, lubrication, touching, building eroticism, transitioning to intercourse at high arousal (erotic flow), and engaging in the types of thrusting that facilitate pleasurable intercourse.
- Your partner has an integral and positive role in helping you reduce pain and build sexual comfort. Think of him as your intimate, erotic friend and ally. Keep the focus on sharing pleasure, not on pressure or performance.
- Your sexual needs are as important as his. It is not healthy for you or your relationship to endure painful sex in an attempt to placate your partner.
- Remember, few women experience desire, arousal, and orgasm at each sexual encounter. A healthy approach emphasizes Good Enough Sex (GES). The GES criterion is that 85% of sexual experiences will be comfortable and enjoyable. A "perfect" performance goal of achieving 100% pain-free intercourse is self-defeating and subverts the positive change process.
- The prescription for GES involves intimacy, nondemand pleasuring, erotic scenarios, and positive, realistic expectations. Accept and enjoy the flexibility, variability, and complexity of healthy female and couple sexuality.

CLOSING THOUGHTS

Sexual pain is one of the most challenging sexual issues for you and your partner. Pain is multidimensional and has biological, psychological, relational, and psychosexual skill factors. The goal is to put positive anticipation, pleasure, and satisfaction back into your life and relationship. Of course, pain-free sex is optimal, but for most couples the pain management approach of using all your resources to enjoy your body, intimacy, touching, and eroticism is the right fit.

Sexual pleasure is an integral part of female and couple sexuality. Being intimate, sexual friends and approaching sexual pain as a couple challenge is optimal. The biopsychosocial model for building sexual comfort and reducing painful intercourse offers a comprehensive, multicausal, multidimensional approach for you to use as an intimate team to understand and reduce sexual pain and experience comfortable, functional, and satisfying couple sexuality.

16

AROUSAL AND ERECTION

Far too much of a man's self-esteem and sense of masculinity is tied to his penis. Fear of erectile dysfunction (commonly called *impotence* or *not getting it up*) is among the greatest of all male fears. A well-hidden fact of male sexuality is that 90% of men have experienced a problem either obtaining or maintaining an erection sufficient for intercourse on at least one occasion by the time they are 40 years old. Erectile dysfunction (ED) is, in fact, at least on occasion, an almost universal problem. Men are notorious liars and braggarts about sexual prowess. They adamantly deny sexual doubts or difficulties. Men are intimidated by the myth-based cultural expectation that a real man is able and willing to have sex with any woman, at any time, in any situation. This puts tremendous performance pressure on you and your penis.

The majority of ED for men under 50 is caused primarily by psychological or relational problems rather than physical or medical factors. Erection involves increased blood flow to your penis (vasocongestion), which fills the tissues and increases the size of your penis. As subjective arousal builds, rigidity (hardness) increases. These functions depend on a healthy physical body.

Your hormonal, vascular, and neurological systems must be functional for adequate erectile response. Common physical causes of ED include alcohol abuse, poorly controlled diabetes, prostate surgery, side effects from hypertensive or psychiatric medications, spinal cord injury, and chronic illness. As you age, your hormonal, vascular, and neurological systems function at lower levels of efficiency. Thus, you are more vulnerable to anticipatory and performance anxiety. A 50-year-old man is not the easy, automatic, autonomous sexual athlete he was at

20. As you age, your sexual response becomes less predictable and more variable. Psychological, relational, and psychosexual factors become more important with aging—although they are important for men of all ages. If you have questions about physical or medical aspects of your sexual functioning, the best person to consult is a urologist. Although not typically considered a male sex doctor, the urologist cares for men much the way a gynecologist does for women. Be sure the urologist is interested in doing a comprehensive assessment rather than in promoting Viagra, testosterone, penile injections, an external pump, or penile prosthesis surgery.

The major psychological factors contributing to ED are performance anxiety and distraction from erotic flow. You are so concerned with proving yourself or performing up to fantasy expectations that you become anxious. This interferes with sexual receptivity and responsivity. Anxiety is physiologically incompatible with feelings of pleasure. When you experience anticipatory or performance anxiety, worry, or tension, your erections are inhibited.

A crucial factor is the sexual transition that comes with aging. Young men learn that erections are easy, automatic, predictable, and autonomous (needing nothing from the woman). In your 30s and 40s, however, your hormonal, vascular, and neurologic systems change. Sexuality becomes a function of receptiveness and responsiveness to partner stimulation—a cooperative, interactive experience. As you enter your 50s, side effects of medications, stress, and health problems can affect your more vulnerable arousal system. Intimacy, pleasuring, and eroticism become more important in facilitating your arousal and erection.

Another cause of ED is negative reactions such as guilt, anger, depression, or ambivalence. If either partner feels negative emotions in regard to sexuality, this inhibits responsiveness and arousal—and therefore erections.

In order to increase pleasure and eroticism, no matter what the interfering factors, the couple needs to develop a cooperative, sharing, interactive sexual relationship. Lack of arousal and erection is not a problem for you alone; it is best addressed as a couple issue. Your partner's acceptance and enjoyment of her sexuality helps you regain comfort and confidence with arousal and erections. Her responsiveness is a friend to your sexual relationship, and extending the give-and-get pleasuring guideline facilitates erotic flow for both of you. A crucial step is to affirm the importance of working together to increase feelings of desire, pleasure, and eroticism. Sexuality becomes more of a "team sport"; you need each other as intimate and erotic friends.

THE SELF-DEFEATING CYCLE OF ERECTILE ANXIETY

You cannot produce an erection through self-pressure or partner pressure. The man who has difficulty getting or maintaining an erection concentrates on his penis and attempts to force an erection, which is self-defeating. The more you work at achieving an erection, the less success you will have. An erection is a natural result of involvement, receptivity to sensual and pleasurable stimulation, and enjoyment of your partner's subjective arousal. Erection is not something to be strived for. When you focus attention on the state of your penis, you take yourself out of the erotic flow and play the role of spectator. Rather than being an active, giving sexual person involved with your partner's feelings and response—which facilitates arousal and erection—you are a passive, anxious observer. Sex is not a spectator sport where your performance is judged. When sex and performance are linked, you are halfway to having ED. The positive association is between sex and pleasure, the give-and-take process of sharing arousal and eroticism.

ACTIVE INVOLVEMENT

The best way for the couple (not just the man) to feel comfortable and increase arousal is for both partners to be actively involved in giving and receiving pleasurable and erotic touch. Do not worry about your erection; instead, focus on pleasure. Break the vicious sex-as-performance cycle by focusing on receptivity and responsivity to pleasure; be aware of and build subjective arousal (feeling "turned on").

You can develop a giving, caring, sexually enhancing relationship. Positive anticipation, involvement, nondemand pleasuring, and erotic scenarios and techniques (especially multiple stimulation) counteract fears, anxieties, and distractions. Nongenital and genital pleasuring exercises involve sharing in a non-goal-oriented manner. Extend this to arousal, eroticism, and erection.

Your erection is a physical response that is the natural consequence of comfort, pleasure, genital stimulation, and erotic flow. Sexual arousal leading to erection is the natural outcome of positive emotions and being in touch with your own and your partner's sexual responsivity.

TERRY AND ROBIN

Terry and Robin were feeling very discouraged about Terry's ED. Previous attempts to find help had resulted in a runaround. After 9 months of increasing difficulty maintaining an erection, they consulted their minister, who referred them to an internist. He saw Terry alone and immediately prescribed Viagra. Terry was not given any sexual or relationship suggestions. He clung to the hope that Viagra would work as well for him as for the men in the TV ads, but it did not. The internist then referred Terry to an endocrinologist. The endocrinologist tested Terry for testosterone, which proved to be in the normal range. Nonetheless, the endocrinologist gave him a testosterone gel to see if it would help. It made Terry more sexually agitated and frustrated, and his irritability created more conflict with Robin. Terry was then referred to a urologist, who monitored Terry's erections for two nights in a sleep laboratory. He suggested penile injections, which resulted in firm erections. However, Terry disliked the injection process, and even though he became erect he felt little subjective arousal. Robin complained that his penis felt cold and mechanical inside her, which was a turn-off. In addition, intercourse was painful for Robin. The urologist determined Terry's problem to be chronic and recommended penile prosthesis surgery as the only lasting solution.

The medical process dragged out over a 16-month period. Meanwhile Terry's ED was becoming more severe. He had difficulty getting erections with Robin, although he had erections on waking and when he masturbated. Erection problems seldom remain at a plateau; if there is not a positive change, anticipatory and performance anxiety grow and erections shrink. Terry became increasingly discouraged, and Robin felt frustrated and unsure of her sexual desirability (the woman blaming herself is neither helpful nor valid). In retrospect, since Terry could get erections on waking, by masturbation, and during oral sex, it should have signaled that an extensive medical evaluation was not necessary. On the other hand, if you are unable to get an erection under any circumstances, a comprehensive medical evaluation is strongly recommended—especially to rule out possible cardiovascular or neurological disease.

A key element in regaining erectile confidence is to reestablish comfort with desire, sensual touch, pleasurable touch, and erotic touch. Both Robin and Terry had ceased to anticipate being sexual. For the past 3 years their sexual activity had been tension filled. They still valued their intimate bond and enjoyed sharing affection. However, as soon as there was nudity, genital touching, or incipient arousal, a curtain of anxiety came down.

The sex therapy strategy to reverse this self-defeating cycle began with a week of nongenital, nondemand touching in the nude, both inside and outside the bedroom. Robin was actively involved in dealing with and changing Terry's ED, a fact that relieved Terry and energized

Robin. She had not been invited to any of the medical appointments. In contrast, Robin was actively involved in the couple therapy sessions. If Terry became aroused by their mutual touching, he was to be aware of the sensations and enjoy them but not move toward intercourse. He and Robin were pleasantly surprised to find his erections returning. They would naturally wane, but with touching he would become erect again—a process called *waxing and waning of erection*.

Robin was told to refrain from penile stimulation until Terry was feeling aroused. She began with sensual stimulation, playfully and seductively stroking his inner thighs, scratching his pubic hair, and with one or two fingers lightly playing with his penis. Robin found genital touching pleasurable. Terry, however, could not let go and continued to be a spectator of his penis's performance. As soon as there was the beginning of an erection, he wanted to jump into action. Rather than castigating Terry, the exercise was modified. Terry was instructed to be active in touching and stroking Robin and to focus on sexual fantasies in order to counter his spectator reaction. Robin stimulated him until he had an erection and then ceased stimulation. Both became comfortable with the waxing-and-waning process.

As pleasure and eroticism increased, so did Terry's erections. The last stumbling block was for Terry to experience intercourse as a natural continuation of the pleasuring/eroticism process rather than a test of his sexual prowess. Reintroduction of intercourse was at Robin's initiative, and she guided Terry's penis into her. There were setbacks in this process, but it was clear they were over the hump. Both were looking forward to being sexual, not distracted by performance fears. When Terry's erection was not firm enough for intercourse, they made the transition to a sensual scenario or an erotic, nonintercourse scenario. Terry valued Robin as his intimate sexual friend rather than someone he had to perform for.

MEDICAL INTERVENTIONS AS AN ADDITIONAL RESOURCE

Viagra, introduced in 1998, is an excellent medication. It was the first user-friendly medical intervention for ED, much superior to an injection, external pump, or penile prosthesis. Many men find Cialis easier to integrate into their couple sexual style because it allows more freedom regarding when to be sexual. In the coming years more efficacious medical interventions will be available.

The issue is how to integrate pro-erection medications into your couple sexual style of intimacy and eroticism. The self-defeating aspect of these medications is that they are perceived as fulfilling the "need" of the man to revert back to his teens and 20s, when he had a totally predictable and autonomous erection and his partner had no role other than to be there. The guidelines of intimacy, pleasuring, and eroticism remain valid even when you're on a medication like Viagra or Cialis: sexuality involves the couple sharing pleasure, arousal, erection, erotic flow, and intercourse.

Viagra and other pro-erection medications are efficacious resources for combating self-consciousness and increasing erectile confidence. Rather than moving to intercourse as soon as you become erect, you have the freedom to enhance pleasure and eroticism and make the transition to intercourse at high levels of erotic flow.

Some men have major vascular or neurological impediments that make erectile function impossible without a medical intervention. For them, Viagra is a godsend and must be used at each sexual encounter. For the majority of men, however, pro-erection medications are used occasionally to promote erectile confidence and ensure against relapse.

EXERCISES

First Exercise: Waxing and Waning

Begin by sitting, holding hands, and discussing how you felt and what you learned in the nongenital and genital pleasuring exercises. What are the personal and couple sexual traps when it comes to erections? How can you avoid falling into them?

Proceed to a relaxing, sensuous shower. Wash each other, including genitals; rub and pat your partner dry. Use a comfortable pleasuring position. Let the woman be pleasure-giver, beginning with nongenital touching. Accept feelings of pleasure, and be receptive and responsive as she engages in playful, seductive touching of your inner thighs, scrotum, perineum, and perhaps, with a finger or two, the shaft or glans of your penis. When there is subjective arousal, she can move to stroking and caressing your penis while continuing a variety of additional pleasuring techniques. Direct penile stimulation is not pleasurable or erotic until there is at least a moderate amount of arousal.

To avoid being a passive, obsessive spectator, you are encouraged to touch your partner so you keep contact and are actively involved in the pleasuring process. When your erection grows, stop touching and lie together until your erection subsides. Be aware of feelings as your erection wanes. Do you feel anger, fright, anxiety, worry, tension, relief? When your erection has waned, she resumes nongenital pleasuring, then genital touching, combining pleasuring techniques that are enjoyable for her and to which you are receptive.

Instead of working to achieve an erection, just enjoy receiving. When your erection naturally occurs as a response to pleasurable, playful, and erotic stimulation, again cease activity until it is lost. If an erection does not occur, that is all right, too; simply proceed with pleasuring. Focus on accepting and enjoying touching. Enjoy sensations and feelings with no performance demand. An erection cannot be willed or forced; erection is a natural response to involved, pleasurable, playful, and erotic stimulation.

Now switch roles, with you as giver, focusing on her enjoyment. Be aware of giving pleasure and seeing her responsiveness. Often an erection will occur naturally. Partner response and arousal is a powerful aphrodisiac. A man with ED often falls into the trap of viewing the woman's arousal as a threat and performance demand. Instead, enjoy her arousal and allow these feelings to increase your pleasure and arousal.

Do this exercise, with whatever variations you want, until both of you are comfortable with achieving and losing an erection without feeling anxiety or pressure. Men are used to and prefer proceeding to intercourse on the first erection—the pattern they learned in initial sexual experiences. This is a positive, sexually inviting scenario, but you need to develop flexible, variable sexual scenarios so you do not feel dependent on your first erection and panic if you lose it. On average, your erection will become hard and then somewhat flaccid two to five times during a 45-minute pleasuring period. Couples dealing with ED rush to intercourse and become anxious or panicky if the man's erection subsides. Anxiety and distraction are what cause your penis to stay soft. Worry and pressure to regain erection inhibits responsiveness, thus blocking pleasure, arousal, and erectile response.

If you are troubled by recurrent worries about losing your erection, focus on a sexual fantasy such as making love to an exotic woman, being caressed by four pairs of hands, or having intercourse swinging from a bell tower—any fantasy that turns you on and gets you out of the spectator role. Fantasies are a bridge to arousal, used by three of four men during partner sex. Erotic fantasies or materials facilitate desire and arousal. They provide an erotic focus that displaces the distractions caused by anticipatory anxiety and performance anxiety.

After this exercise, share feelings you experienced as your erection became soft and hard again. Talk about the types of stimulation that you enjoy giving and to which you are responsive. Notice the difference: you are working together rather than making demands and feeling pressure. Be aware of the decrease in anxiety and worry as you accept the naturally occurring waxing and waning of your erection. Subjective arousal (feeling turned on) usually precedes objective arousal. You are regaining comfort and confidence with arousal, erection, and erotic feelings rather than being controlled by performance fears.

Second Exercise: Playing With Your Penis Around Her Vagina

Begin with mutual nondemand pleasuring. When you gain an erection, continue stimulation, but this time concentrate on trying to maintain the erection. You'll find that focusing on your erection almost invariably results in losing the erection. When you concentrate on your erection, your involvement and arousal decrease and you become distracted, which subverts the erotic flow; your erection dissipates and your penis stays soft. The way to maintain arousal is to focus on feelings and sensations, accept pleasure, stay involved psychologically and physically, and enjoy the erotic flow. Your focus on erotic sensations, faculties, and feelings counters being a distracted spectator of your penis.

To reinforce this point, shut your partner out and focus on working alone to regain your erection. Your penis will almost invariably remain flaccid, because psychologically and sexually you are not there. Notice the pressure and tension you put yourself under. You are no longer an involved partner who is giving and receiving pleasure, much less erotic stimulation. Instead you have become an isolated, distracted performer. Psychologically, you are alone in bed. You are shut off from the enjoyment and involvement of intimate contact, pleasuring, playful touch, give-and-take stimulation, and erotic flow.

The woman, meanwhile, is aware that sexuality has become a demanding, goal-oriented task to produce an erection as opposed to a mutual pleasuring and erotic experience. Notice how frustrated and worried she has become and how out of touch she is with you as you work alone. Her pleasure and arousal decrease. Touching and sexuality are no longer fun but a performance. Healthy sexuality is a positive feedback system of anticipation, comfort, pleasure, playfulness, arousal, and erotic flow. Instead it has become a negative feedback system of anticipatory anxiety, performance anxiety, self-conscious attempts to force erection, and avoidance of sex because it is stressful and results in frustration and embarrassment.

Be aware of these negative traps. Share feelings about the difference between being together in a nondemanding atmosphere, engaging in mutual pleasuring, and accepting naturally occurring responsiveness and arousal as opposed to working alone, worrying, feeling tense, being a spectator, trying to will an erection, being performance oriented, and ultimately ending up frustrated and embarrassed. One demonstration of the negative effects of focusing on sexual performance and erection is enough. Unlike other exercises, this one need not be repeated.

Return to pleasuring by using mutual nondemand touching. Be aware of the feelings and sensations of giving and receiving stimulation so each partner's comfort, pleasure, and arousal feed the other's. When you are feeling receptive and responsive, switch to the female-on-top intercourse position. You will not be engaging in intercourse, but it is important to experience comfort (low anxiety, no pressure to perform, enjoying what you are doing) with your penis near her vagina. Make yourselves at ease, perhaps with a pillow under your head. Your partner should have easy access to your genitals. Accept and enjoy her touch. If you are more responsive when touching and caressing, feel free to engage in a more active scenario. You can guide and make specific requests. Men with ED are shy about being sexually assertive; this is your time to break that pattern.

Your partner can massage your arms and chest, running her fingers over your face, highlighting your features. She can massage your genitals, beginning with your inner thighs, working up and over your penis and pubic hair, over your stomach, and back again in a rhythmic movement. When you develop an erection as a natural outcome of feeling pleasure and accepting erotic stimulation, she ceases activity until your erection becomes soft. This is a natural result of stopping touching; neither partner need feel worried or panicky. Your erection might wax and wane two to five times during a prolonged pleasuring experience. It is freeing to realize you can become comfortable and confident with the waning and waxing of erection. She returns to pleasuring, and you make requests and guide her. As receptivity and subjective arousal increase, erection will naturally occur.

She can take your penis in her hand, gently caressing and rubbing it around her vulva. Rub your penis on her mons, clitoral shaft, labia, and close to (but not into) her vagina. If at any point she notices you becoming tense or anxious, she should continue caressing but move back a step until both of you are feeling comfortable. Resume penile–vulval stimulation when you and your partner feel open and receptive. Repeat this sequence, with you regaining an erection with your penis around her vulva, then allowing your penis to become soft and remaining open to pleasurable and erotic stimulation so it can become hard again.

You might do this exercise just once or repeat it several times with variations of position and stimulation until both of you feel comfortable with your penis around her labia, clitoris, and vagina. Remember, in a typical pleasuring process your erection will not always remain "hard"; it is normal for your erection to wax and wane.

End the exercise either with the woman being the recipient or using mutual stimulation. It is important that she be involved in the pleasuring and erotic experience. She can feel the appreciation and caring in your gestures, words, and stimulation. There is a world of difference between "giving pleasure" and mechanically "doing" your partner as compensation for ED. Each of you can enjoy manual, oral, or rubbing stimulation to orgasm. Even after you have reintroduced intercourse, be open to both sensual scenarios and erotic, nonintercourse scenarios. A key to remaining sexual in your 60s, 70s, and 80s is to value variable, flexible couple sexuality.

Third Exercise: Going With the Erotic Flow

Enjoy mutual pleasuring and a sense of receptivity and responsivity. Then move to the female-on-top intercourse position. From this position she can use a variety of pleasuring techniques, and both partners can enjoy playing and teasing. She can rub your penis around her labia and clitoris, against her thigh, around her vagina. Be aware of her enjoyment and responsiveness, which includes, but is not limited to, your penis. Be aware of your arousal as well as hers. The natural result of pleasure and eroticism is subjective arousal and erection.

At her initiative, your penis is inserted into her vagina. You are not responsible for pushing or directing; the initiative and timing rests with her. If she notices tension increasing or your penis becoming soft, she can modify her stimulation until both of you are feeling receptive to intercourse.

She can guide insertion with her hand on your penis by leaning back at a 45-degree angle so it easily enters her vagina. If there is tension or a feeling of forced action, cease intromission and return to pleasuring. Intromission is part of the pleasuring/eroticism/erotic flow process. Be aware that a "rock-hard" erection is not necessary for intromission. Intercourse can be enjoyable with varying levels of arousal and firmness.

She can direct slow, rhythmic thrusting. The tendency is to force thrusting or make it rapid in order to maintain arousal. Slow, rhythmic thrusting facilitates arousal and erection because it allows you to focus on pleasurable movement and an awareness of vaginal warmth, wetness, and erotic sensations. Continue giving and receiving multiple stimulation during intercourse to heighten involvement and eroticism.

Feel free to continue intercourse to orgasm. Orgasm occurs as a natural consequence of sexual arousal and going with the erotic flow; it need not be strived for or forced. Sex need not abruptly end after orgasm. Orgasm is not the end of sexual feelings and responsiveness. Afterplay is as much an integral part of a sexual encounter as is pleasuring. This is true whether the scenario involves intercourse or erotic, nonintercourse sex.

You lose some of your erection shortly after ejaculation. This is part of the natural physiological resolution process. Some couples enjoy maintaining the intercourse position and continue caressing, holding, and talking. Others prefer to disengage and move to a different position to touch and share feelings. Examples of afterplay positions include sitting facing each other, lying side by side, you lying on your back and she laying her head on your shoulder, and the spoon position in which her back lies against your chest and your arms encompass her. Many couples prefer to wash the semen off; others would rather just lie there. Find what is most comfortable and sensual; share your preferences. Feel comfortable with afterplay, the natural culmination of your sexual encounter. You have shared an intense physical experience; now share coming down together. Afterplay facilitates bonding and satisfaction.

Fourth Exercise: Integrating Arousal and Intercourse

You have come a long way in sharing pleasure, feeling comfortable with sexual expression, and experiencing erection as a natural step in the process of receptivity, responsivity, arousal, and erotic flow. Experiment with scenarios and techniques to increase your comfort and confidence with erection.

Begin pleasuring in a position you both enjoy. When you are feeling receptive, she can rub your penis (whether flaccid, semierect, or erect) against her vulva and at the same time use your fingers to caress her clitoral shaft and labia. In the process of giving pleasure and attending to her feelings, you will naturally become subjectively aroused and develop an erection. The most common stimulus for your arousal is response to her arousal—an example of the give-and-get pleasure guideline. Be aware that she can respond to manual, oral, rubbing, and penile (whether flaccid, semierect, or erect) stimulation. An erect penis is not necessary for your partner's arousal and orgasm.

A man with erectile anxiety often avoids initiating sex because he is not sure he will be able to follow through and complete intercourse. Nor does he welcome her initiation because he views it as a demand for a sexual performance that he is not certain he can meet.

Both partners learn to accept that not every sexual experience needs to end in intercourse. Flexibility and variability enhance sexual desire. We urge you to embrace the Good Enough Sex (GES) model. Manual, oral, rubbing, and penile stimulation are all normal techniques for meeting your partner's sexual needs as well as your own. Some women feel they must have an orgasm during intercourse; this puts tremendous pressure on you and exacerbates erectile problems. In truth, the majority of women find it easier to be orgasmic with manual, oral, or rubbing stimulation. Orgasm achieved by erotic, non-intercourse stimulation is enjoyable and fulfilling for the great majority of women.

A full erection is not necessary for vaginal intromission. If you lie on your side and she lies on her back, leaning slightly toward and facing you, she can insert your penis. Do not force intromission or take the initiative; rather, relax, accept her initiative, and continue to be actively involved in pleasuring. She takes your penis with both hands and inserts it into her vagina, using pelvic movements to facilitate intromission. You can kiss, caress, and fondle while accepting her initiation. Frequently, after intromission or during thrusting, your arousal increases and your erection becomes firmer and more robust. If there are problems with intromission, she can be active in providing stimulation and facilitating intromission. Insertion can be tried from the woman-on-top position or another position she is comfortable with.

Do not panic or try to force your penis into her vagina. This results in your penis becoming flaccid, causing her discomfort and frustrating you as a couple. Performance anxiety causes people to react in self-defeating ways. If you feel anxious, you can verbalize that and request what you need to get out of the role of the anxious spectator and become actively involved in the sexual give and take. You might ask her to engage in fellatio right before intromission or to stroke your testicles while fondling your penis. You might suggest standing or kneeling and facing each other as you engage in mutual stimulation. You might stimulate her, since the arousal of each partner will build on the other's. Request what will increase your receptivity and responsivity. What neither you nor she should do is stop and avoid sexual contact. If anxiety persists, move to nondemand, sensual touching. You can end the encounter in this sensual manner. If one or both of you is desirous of erotic sex, you can utilize manual or oral stimulation to orgasm.

Experiment with other intercourse positions. Allow stimulation to be mutual and erotic. Remember the give-and-get pleasure guideline. Enjoy each other's pleasure and eroticism without being distracted by the state of your penis. Allow stimulation to be slow, tender, caring, rhythmic, and flowing. Do not try to hurry or force arousal. An involved, aroused partner is the best facilitator of your arousal and erection. Let intromission be a naturally occurring event rather than a major hurdle.

You can initiate and guide intromission. If you become anxious or try to force intercourse, move a step back. Intercourse is a continuation of the mutual pleasuring/eroticism process, not a goal to be achieved. Be aware of each other's feelings and continue to be caring, supportive, and giving during intercourse. Spend time in afterplay and share feelings of closeness and intimacy. Afterplay is integral to your sexual experience.

GUIDELINES FOR AROUSAL AND ERECTION PROBLEMS

- The majority of erectile problems (especially for men under 50) are caused primarily by psychological or relationship factors, not a medical or physiological dysfunction. To comprehensively evaluate medical factors, including side effects of medications, consult your internist or family practitioner.
- Erectile dysfunction can be caused by a wide variety of factors—including alcohol abuse, anxiety, depression, vascular or neurological deficits, distraction, anger, side effects of medications, frustration, hormonal deficiency, fatigue, not feeling sexual at a particular time or with a particular partner. As men age, their hormonal, vascular, and neurological systems become less efficient, making psychological, relational, and psychosexual skill factors more important.
- Medical interventions—especially oral medications like Viagra, Cialis, and Levitra—can be a valuable resource for facilitating erectile function, but they are not magic pills. You need to integrate the pro-erection medication (or other medical interventions) into your couple lovemaking style of intimacy, pleasuring, and eroticism.
- Do not believe the myth of the male machine, ready to have intercourse at any time, with any woman, in any situation; you and your penis are human.
- View the erectile difficulty as a situational problem. Do not overreact and label yourself "impotent" or put yourself down as a failure.
- A pervasive myth is that loss of your initial erection means you are sexually uninterested or turned off. It is a natural physiological process for erections to wax and wane during prolonged pleasuring. Almost all men prefer to transition to intercourse and orgasm on their first erection. But do not make this a performance demand.
- In a 45-minute pleasuring session, erections will wax and wane from two to five times. Subsequent erections, intercourse, and orgasm are quite satisfying.
- You do not need an erect penis to satisfy your partner. Orgasm can be achieved through manual, oral, or rubbing stimulation.

If you have difficulty getting or maintaining an erection, do not stop the sexual encounter. She finds it arousing to have your fingers, tongue, or penis (erect or flaccid) used for stimulation.

- Actively involve yourself in giving and receiving pleasurable and erotic touching. Erection is a natural result of pleasure, feeling turned on, and eroticism.
- You cannot will or force an erection. Do not be a "passive spectator" who is distracted by the state of your penis. Anticipatory anxiety and performance anxiety cause ED. Sex is not a spectator sport; it requires active involvement.
- Allow your partner to initiate intercourse and guide your penis into her vagina. This reduces performance pressure and, since she is the expert on her vagina, it is the most sexually inviting procedure.
- Feel comfortable saying, "I want sex to be pleasurable and playful. When I feel pressure to perform, I get uptight and sex is not good. We can make sexuality enjoyable by taking it at a comfortable pace, enjoying play and pleasuring, feeling turned on and erotic, and being an intimate team."
- Erectile problems do not affect your ability to ejaculate. You can ejaculate with a flaccid penis and most men can relearn ejaculation cued by an erect penis.
- One way to regain confidence is through masturbation. During masturbation you can practice gaining and losing erections, relearn ejaculation with an erection, and focus on fantasies and stimulation that are transferable to partner sex.
- Do not try to use a waking erection for quick intercourse. This erection is associated with rapid eye movement (REM) sleep and results from dreaming and being close to your partner. Men try vainly to have intercourse with their morning erection before losing it. Remember: arousal and erection are regainable. Morning is a good time to be sexual.
- When sleeping, you have an erection every 90 minutes—three to five erections a night. Sex is a natural physiological function. Do not block it by anticipatory anxiety, performance anxiety, distraction, or putting yourself down. Give yourself (and your partner) permission to enjoy the pleasure of sexuality.
- Make clear, direct, assertive requests (not demands) for stimulation you find pleasurable and erotic. Verbally and nonverbally guide your partner on how to pleasure and arouse you.
- Stimulating a flaccid penis is counterproductive. You become distracted and obsessed with the state of your penis. Engage in

sensuous, playful touching. Enjoy giving and receiving stimulation rather than trying to "will" an erection.

- Attitudes and self-thoughts affect arousal. The focus is "sex and pleasure," not "sex and performance."
- Realistically, 85% of encounters will flow to intercourse. When that does not happen, you can transition (without panicking or apologizing) to an erotic, nonintercourse scenario or a cuddly, sensual scenario.
- A sexual experience is best measured by pleasure and satisfaction, not whether you had an erection, how hard it was, or whether she was orgasmic. Some sexual experiences will be great for both partners, some better for one than the other, some mediocre, and others dissatisfying or dysfunctional. Do not put your sexual self-esteem on the line at each experience. The GES model of male and couple sexuality is much healthier than the perfect intercourse performance criterion.

CLOSING THOUGHTS

Be comfortable facilitating your own and your partner's receptivity and responsivity, which naturally lead to arousal and erection. Anticipatory anxiety, performance anxiety, being in the spectator role, feeling frustrated, and blaming need to be confronted and changed.

Does this mean you will never have an experience of not getting or losing an erection? Realistically, you will experience erectile difficulties from time to time. Most men do, especially after age 40. On occasions when you are fatigued, anxious about money or work, have little sexual desire, are interrupted, stressed, or feeling distracted, you will be less responsive. You might not get an erection or not have an erection firm enough for intercourse. That does not mean you have ED. What it means is that at this point, in this situation, you are not feeling sexually responsive or aroused enough for intercourse. You can decide not to have sex that day; use manual, oral, or rubbing stimulation to orgasm; relax and enjoy sensual pleasuring; give to your partner; or have your partner guide intromission with a semierection. Be aware you have alternatives for a positive sensual or erotic experience. There is no need to feel worried or panicky. As long as you do not fall into the traps of allowing performance anxiety to take over, acting the part of a distracted spectator, or trying to force intercourse, you will have a pleasurable, satisfying sexual relationship. You can continue to enjoy intimacy, with sensuality, pleasure, eroticism, and erection—with or without intercourse.

17

LEARNING EJACULATORY CONTROL

Myths about perfect male sex performance are among the most powerful negative influences on the man's and the couple's sexual desire and satisfaction. The old myth was that the more masculine you were, the faster you ejaculated. The new myth is that you prove your masculinity with intercourse that lasts for half an hour before ejaculating.

Premature (rapid) ejaculation (PE) is the most common male sexual problem. The majority of adolescent/young adult males begin as premature ejaculators, although most men, as they gain experience, do learn ejaculatory control. However, approximately 3 in 10 men, or 30%, have chronic difficulty with premature ejaculation. The average time for intercourse, from intromission to ejaculation, is between 2 and 7 minutes. The great majority of males ejaculate in less than 12 minutes no matter what you read on the Internet or hear from other men.

WHAT IS PREMATURE EJACULATION?

There is much confusion as to what PE is. Some people define it in terms of time (less than a minute after intromission), some in terms of activity (fewer than 10 strokes), and some in terms of whether the woman is orgasmic during intercourse (an extremely poor criterion). These definitions are arbitrary and performance oriented. A healthier approach is that if the couple is making good use of nongenital and genital pleasuring and the man's ejaculation is earlier than desired and interferes with pleasure, then there is a reason to work as a couple to improve ejaculatory control. The typical lovemaking experience ranges from 15 to 45 minutes, of which 2 to 7 minutes involves intercourse.

Many men could benefit from training in ejaculatory control. Instead of viewing PE as a major problem that makes you inadequate or causes the woman to feel her sexual needs are ignored, think of ejaculatory control as a skill the couple—not just the man—learns in order to enhance sexual pleasure and satisfaction.

HOW PE DEVELOPS

Men learn PE from a host of cultural and personal experiences as well as from a physiological predisposition to rapid neurological function. Adolescent masturbation is penis oriented and orgasm oriented, so rapid ejaculation is overlearned. Your first intercourse might take place in the back seat of a car in a hurried, unplanned way, on a couch in the woman's house with the fear that her parents might discover you, or with a prostitute who applies pressure to "hurry up and get it over with." These experiences have the common denominator of high sexual excitement mixed with anxiety and pressure to perform rapidly. You are more concerned with proving yourself than with enjoying your partner's pleasure or your pleasure with touching and sexual feelings. In learning ejaculatory control, you break the association between high anxiety and high arousal and learn to enjoy a range of sexual feelings and arousal techniques. You prolong arousal and associate awareness, comfort, and pleasure with ejaculation.

Some cultures believe ejaculating rapidly shows how masculine and sexually assured the man is. The man with this mind-set does not see intercourse as a mutual experience but as something he does to the woman; her needs and desires are unimportant.

There is evidence that for many men PE is caused by an overly efficient neurological system. These men often exhibit other behaviors that demonstrate a rapid neurological response. Premature ejaculation can involve psychological, biological, relational, and psychosexual factors. In addition, lack of sexual knowledge, masturbatory experiences that emphasize coming as fast as possible, neurological vulnerability, early experiences pairing sexual excitement with anxiety, a habitual pattern of PE, and not accepting sexuality as a mutual experience can lead to being a premature ejaculator.

LEARNING EJACULATORY CONTROL

Whatever the origin of PE, you can learn ejaculatory control. In the optimal situation, partners work cooperatively, for indeed the woman's role is highly important. Learning ejaculatory control is a couple task.

This is true whether or not medication is used as a resource to enhance ejaculatory control.

Ejaculatory exercises are built on the solid foundation of nongenital and genital pleasuring. You will be both giving and receiving pleasure as well as learning psychosexual skills. Ejaculatory control is not about you performing up to a standard or proving you can give your partner an orgasm during intercourse. It is about developing a mutually satisfying couple sexual style that includes pleasure-oriented intercourse.

TRAPS AND DISTRACTIONS

A man with a pattern of premature ejaculation frequently falls into psychological traps. You feel negative about ejaculation and apologize for yourself sexually. Rather than enjoying orgasm, you mentally kick yourself for coming too fast. This does not in any way help ejaculatory control. It can even cause you to avoid sex, which is counterproductive because the less regular the sexual interaction, the more likely that your ejaculation will be rapid.

Another trap involves distractions. Men try various distraction techniques in a vain effort to postpone ejaculation. You think of the bills you owe, a TV program, or your mother-in-law. You attempt physical distractions such as clenching a fist, biting a lip, or pinching yourself. Other men put anesthetizing cream on the glans of the penis or wear two condoms. These are all misguided, counterproductive techniques. In attempting to control orgasm, you distract yourself from touch, pleasure, and eroticism. You unwisely tune out sexual feelings. In the worst case, you turn yourself off, so you have difficulty maintaining your arousal and erection. Your partner feels neglected or rejected by your lack of involvement and excitement. This can lead to a decline in her arousal and negative feelings about your sexual relationship. Distracting strategies are based on the premise that it is solely your responsibility to control ejaculation and that the best way to do this is to avoid arousal and penile stimulation. That is false. Distracting strategies add to sexual and relationship problems. Treatment of ejaculatory control is counterintuitive. The emphasis is on increasing awareness, involvement, and sexual stimulation, not avoiding stimulation or trying to reduce arousal.

BERNIE AND CINDY

Bernie and Cindy had been married 8 years. Cindy had not raised the issue of premature ejaculation until 4 months before they sought therapy. Bernie became upset and defensive as well as obsessed with solving the problem. During the ensuing 4 months Bernie and Cindy's sexual experiences became a command performance in which the goal was for Cindy to reach orgasm first (during intercourse). It was a crucial test of manhood to "hold out" until she had an orgasm. Instead, Cindy stopped having orgasms of any kind, and Bernie was reaching orgasm shortly after intromission. This was not an intimate, sharing, erotic relationship. Theirs had become a dispirited sexual relationship sinking under the weight of performance pressure.

Rather than being relegated to a male performance issue, ejaculatory control needs to be gradually learned by a couple working in a cooperative manner. This typically requires intentional work by the couple over a 3- to 6-month period, including engaging in the ejaculatory control skill exercises.

Bernie was being his own worst enemy and turning Cindy off. The first priority was to return pleasure and intimacy to their sexual relationship. Bernie had misinterpreted Cindy's comments as meaning that he was a terrible lover. With therapeutic intervention, Bernie was able to understand that Cindy valued their marriage and saw him as a loving, attractive person. Her request was for Bernie to be a sensitive, slower lover. Cindy has a variable arousal and orgasmic pattern; she enjoys being orgasmic with manual and oral stimulation as well as intercourse. Intercourse would be enhanced by better ejaculatory control, but Cindy was not demanding a perfect performance. Bernie needed to realize that slower, longer intercourse would be of value for him. He was learning ejaculatory control for himself and their relationship, not to perform for Cindy. With this new attitude and couple commitment, learning ejaculatory control became easier.

Ejaculatory control psychosexual skill exercises can at times be tedious, but if you are cooperative and communicative you will find them enjoyable. Some women have voiced the complaint that the stop–start exercises are boring and make them feel like a marionette that stops on command. Cindy wanted to feel that she was an integral part of the sexual experience and that her feelings and needs were important. As a bonus of engaging in the interventions and exercises presented in this chapter, Cindy and Bernie expanded their repertoire of pleasuring and erotic techniques. Both learned to be sexually assertive, to express feelings, and to enjoy flexible, variable sexual scenarios.

SHARED RESPONSIBILITY

Learning ejaculatory control employs the one–two combination of the man increasing awareness and the couple working as an intimate team. The best way to learn ejaculatory control is through the couple's active participation and commitment. This strategy focuses on increasing comfort, building awareness of penile sensations, and learning ejaculatory control skills. This requires patience and persistence. You learn two key skills—to identify the point of ejaculatory inevitability and to increase the time from arousal to ejaculation.

Sexual arousal is a naturally occurring, voluntary response up to the point of ejaculatory inevitability. At this point, ejaculation becomes an involuntary response— that is, you will ejaculate even if you try to stop. When stimulation ceases before the point of ejaculatory inevitability, your urge to ejaculate is reduced. You gradually learn to maintain sexual arousal without going to the point of ejaculatory inevitability. When you are able to enjoy arousal during prolonged intercourse (2 to 12 minutes), you have learned ejaculatory control and can enjoy satisfying intercourse.

The traditional procedure was the "squeeze technique," which involves the woman squeezing the frenulum of the man's penis with her thumb and finger. Though effective, many people find it objectionable because it is too mechanical. We suggest you use the start–stop technique, which feels more natural for both partners.

GENERAL AND PELVIC MUSCLE RELAXATION

Physical and psychological relaxation is integral to learning ejaculatory control. Physical relaxation can be learned by systematically tensing and relaxing each body part in turn. Focus on relaxation sensations to enhance physical comfort. In addition, engage in slow, deep breathing with the self-instruction of "relax" as you breathe in and "calm" as you breathe out to promote psychological relaxation and mindfulness.

A specific exercise involves learning to relax your pelvic muscles, which you can identify by stopping urination midstream. You can strengthen the pelvic muscles by tightening them for 3 seconds and then relaxing them for 3 seconds. Repeat this exercise 10 times (1 minute). During sex, maintaining pelvic muscle relaxation increases conscious control of when you ejaculate.

MEDICATION AS A RESOURCE

There is a growing trend to use antidepressant medication, typically at a low dose on a daily basis, to treat ejaculatory control. Antidepressant medications do delay ejaculation for the majority of men. However, effectiveness requires continual use of the medication; if you stop, ejaculatory problems return—sometimes even more severely. Although men find taking a "magic pill" to solve the PE problem more inviting than working with their partner, we do not advocate medication as a stand-alone intervention.

If you choose to use medication, the preferred strategy is to use medication as an additional resource, in conjunction with the psychosexual skill ejaculatory control exercises. A major strategy is to slow down the entire sexual process, including intercourse. As comfort and confidence with ejaculatory control increase, most men gradually wean themselves off the medication.

EXERCISES

First Exercise: Stop–Start

Talk with your partner about positive feelings and experiences with nongenital and genital pleasuring. You can continue to learn to give and receive sexual pleasure and feedback.

Start with mutual pleasuring. Then arrange yourselves in a position where she leans back comfortably with her back supported by a pillow or cushion against the bed's headboard. Position your body between her spread legs, lying on your back facing her with your legs bent and lying outside her thighs. Vary positioning until you feel comfortable.

She begins massaging your chest, slowly and naturally, working down to your genitals. As responsiveness and arousal increase, you will naturally get an erection. A few moments after your erection begins, she stops penile stimulation.

After stimulation ceases, you lose both the urge to ejaculate and the rigidity of your erection—perhaps half of it. This happens because the cessation of genital stimulation interrupts erotic flow and the blood flow to your penis. Cease stimulation well before you experience the urge to ejaculate. This provides practice in using the stop–start technique.

After 30 to 60 seconds, she returns to sexual fondling and manual stimulation. She need not concentrate all her time on your penis. She can massage your stomach, teasingly play with your testicles, run her fingers along your inner thighs, and at the same time make the touching enjoyable and sensuous for herself. Responsiveness to sensual and sexual feelings allows your arousal to build. If you do not regain an erection, neither partner should worry; simply enjoy sensual feelings. For most couples, this is their first experience with the physiologically normal process of the waxing and waning of your erection. Men are conditioned to go to orgasm on their first erection.

Previously, you avoided focusing on penile sensations because you were afraid you would become too excited and ejaculate before you wanted to. In this exercise, focus on and accept arousing, erotic feelings. Awareness of sexual sensations allows you to become a better discriminator of your excitement, especially as you approach the point of ejaculatory inevitability. Identifying the sexual feelings that precede the point of inevitability is a crucial step in learning ejaculatory control.

This exercise enables you to develop a mutually agreed upon communication system to signal when to stop penile stimulation. Some common signals are you saying "now" or "stop," raising one hand, or tapping her hand. Signal *before* you reach the point of ejaculatory inevitability, and she stops penile stimulation immediately.

Use the stop–start technique for 10 minutes. There are usually at least three stops. For practice, she can stop early in the arousal cycle and again after you have an erection for a minute. If at any point you feel that you are approaching the point of inevitability, signal her *immediately* so she can stop. If you do ejaculate, neither partner need feel upset or guilty. Enjoy the ejaculation. Neglecting to signal your partner in time and ejaculating early is a normal part of the learning process.

When you feel comfortable with the concept of ejaculatory control and have utilized the stop–start technique at least three times, you have a solid base from which to proceed. You can request continued manual stimulation to ejaculation.

At this point, your partner deserves to be the recipient of pleasuring. She can guide you in the type of pleasuring she finds particularly sensual and sexually arousing. You are actively involved in giving pleasure and enjoying her responsiveness. Remember, the essence of healthy couple sexuality is giving and receiving pleasure-oriented touch.

Get dressed and over a drink or coffee share your feelings about the stop–start technique. Discuss what you enjoyed and valued. Then be honest in sharing negative feelings. Many couples state that stopping feels awkward or clinical. Some men report embarrassment at being the center of attention. Some women feel they are playing the role of sexual servant. Many couples feel funny about prohibiting intercourse and using manual sex to orgasm. If you have negative feelings, air them with your partner, who listens empathically and respectfully. You can consider alterations that will increase comfort but that do not cease the ejaculatory control focus. Be aware that learning ejaculatory control is a process that takes practice, feedback, and commitment.

Second Exercise: Building Skill and Confidence

Start with sensual, playful, nondemand pleasuring, and then change to the ejaculatory control position. Be sure you are comfortable, lying on your back with legs stretched out so that she has full access to your genitals.

She begins by massaging and caressing your penis in the most stimulating manner possible, bringing you close to the point of ejaculatory inevitability. She can stroke your penis with one hand and simultaneously touch your testicles in a teasing manner, caress your inner thighs, or run her fingers over your pubic hair. As you approach the point of inevitability, signal her to stop stimulation. During the 30- to 60-second break, you will lose the urge to ejaculate and most likely partially lose your erection.

Since you are learning to identify the point of ejaculatory inevitability, you will probably signal late at least once and will ejaculate. Do not worry; this is natural and important in the process of learning discrimination. If you are concurrently practicing ejaculatory control via masturbation exercises, realize you need practice to discriminate the point of ejaculatory inevitability. Gradually, you will increase confidence with prolonged genital stimulation. Enjoy ejaculation rather than being disappointed, frustrated, or angry. Your partner can accept this rather than feel she failed. Learning ejaculatory control takes practice and involves mistakes, feedback, cooperation, and persistence. After you ejaculate, proceed to female pleasuring. There is no reason for sex to end because you ejaculated. If you are interested and desire to, return to penile stimulation and the stop–start procedure after a 20- to 30-minute break.

Continue genital stimulation for at least 10 minutes. Do this even if you must stop 10 times. Wait 30 to 60 seconds and return to stimulation when you no longer feel the urge to ejaculate. Use a variety of stimulation techniques. Be aware of and enjoy your responsiveness. Reverse roles and allow the woman to enjoy and respond to pleasure, utilizing your personal style of pleasuring and enjoying her arousal to orgasm if she wishes. Both of you can be open to manual, oral, or rubbing stimulation to arousal and orgasm.

Repeat this exercise at least twice. In subsequent experiences, use a lubricant or a hypoallergenic lotion (e.g., abalone oil, baby oil, a body lotion from Crabtree and Evelyn) to lubricate your penis. The sensations are similar to those during intercourse when your penis is moving inside her lubricated vagina. An alternative is oral (fellatio) stimulation. The lubrication from licking and sucking and the high levels of arousal generated facilitate practice in ejaculatory control. Another stimulation technique is for the woman to use her breasts. She can begin by rubbing your penis around each breast in a gentle, sensuous manner and then proceed to rhythmic, erotic thrusting on her breast. She can place your penis in the crevice between her breasts. If she has large breasts, she can bring the breasts together and move them while encircling your penis, which simulates movement of the vagina during intercourse.

When you feel the urge to ejaculate, she immediately stops stimulation. Be sure that you can discriminate and identify the point of ejaculatory inevitability and use the stop–start technique to delay the urge to ejaculate. Focus on and allow yourself to enjoy feelings in your penis (and entire body) at high levels of arousal. Be sure you are comfortable and confident with these skills before moving to intravaginal exercises. When you are confident with the extravaginal ejaculatory control process, it is easier to generalize ejaculatory control to intercourse.

Third Exercise: Quiet Vagina

Now you can apply techniques of ejaculatory control during intercourse. The best intercourse position for practice is woman on top. This position is good for both ejaculatory control and for increasing female initiative, activity, and responsivity. Lie on your back with legs stretched out against the bed. She lies over you with her knees at your chest so her vulva is adjacent to your genitals. She rests her buttocks on your thighs. From this position she can manually stimulate your penis as well as rub it around her clitoris, labia, and vaginal introitus.

After utilizing the stop–start technique, restimulate your penis. When you are erect, she guides your penis with her hand, placing it inside her vagina at about a 45-degree angle and sliding back. After intromission, remain still; just allow your penis to acclimate to her vagina. This is called the quiet vagina exercise. Don't make any movement; simply enjoy the feelings of intravaginal containment. You can focus on the warm, sensual feelings of your penis being contained in her vagina. Some women find this arousing; others do not. Stay with and accept the pleasurable feelings; avoid thrusting. She can move slowly and nondemandingly; use only enough movement to ensure you maintain penile sensations.

If you feel yourself approaching the point of ejaculatory inevitability, signal her to stop movement. If that is not enough to reduce arousal, she can disengage from intercourse and lie next to you. Allow quiet vagina intercourse to proceed for 5 to 10 minutes. Feel free to use the stop–start technique as often as needed. Repeat the quiet vagina exercise at least once at a later time.

It is preferable to use the stop–start technique at least three times during intercourse. If you ejaculate (whether within the vagina or extravaginally), accept and enjoy it. You are learning to discriminate the point of ejaculatory inevitability as well as to elongate the time between arousal and ejaculation. This takes practice, supportive feedback, and refining ejaculatory control skills.

In the woman-on-top position, you have the advantage of mutual pleasuring. You can massage and touch her during intercourse. She can accept and enjoy feelings of pleasure and arousal. End the exercise by continuing intercourse to orgasm, using slow, rhythmic thrusting.

Repeat this exercise until you are comfortable and confident with ejaculatory control in the woman-on-top position. She can gradually increase coital thrusting and experiment with in–out, up–down, and circular thrusting using slower, longer movements. Most couples find rapid, in–out, short strokes the most difficult type of thrusting in which to maintain ejaculatory control. Talk about feelings of progress and pleasure as you continue to work together to enhance ejaculatory control and enjoy a pleasure-oriented sexual experience where touching, eroticism, and intercourse are integrated into your couple sexual style.

Fourth Exercise: Intercourse as a Pleasure/Erotic Process

This exercise involves the side-by-side position. She can gently stroke your face and chest, move to manual penile stimulation, and rub your penis around her clitoris, labia, and vagina. After intromission, she initiates gentle, slow, longer thrusting. When you feel an urge to ejaculate, signal her to stop the coital movement. After the urge to ejaculate decreases, she returns to slow, pleasurable thrusting. If you are having difficulty maintaining ejaculatory control, temporarily disengage from intercourse.

Many couples find intromission easier by beginning in the man- or woman-on-top position and then rolling into the side-by-side position. Allow the second intromission to be comfortable and gradual, with minimal thrusting. Then engage in thrusting controlled by her while you focus on arousal and penile sensations. As you approach the point of ejaculatory inevitability, signal her to stop stimulation, but maintain intercourse connection. As with other exercises, you are encouraged to repeat this process. Each repetition increases comfort and confidence. Remember, ejaculatory control is learned gradually and requires practice and feedback. As you become comfortable, slow or vary the rhythm of thrusting rather than totally stopping. Typically couples require 2 to

3 months to develop comfort and confidence with ejaculatory control during intercourse.

The next steps are as follows:

1. You initiate slow, nondemand thrusting.
2. She initiates more rapid, involving thrusting.
3. You initiate more rapid, involving thrusting.

In practicing each step, remember to use the stop–start technique as necessary. If premature ejaculation occurs, accept and enjoy your orgasmic experience. Remember, the sexual encounters need not end because you ejaculate.

At each step try for 2 to 7 minutes of intravaginal containment without ejaculation, even if you use the stop–start technique many times. Repeat each step at least twice and more if you want. As confidence builds, you will need to use the stop–start technique less. You can also use a variant of the stop–start technique: slowing rhythm of coital thrusting as you approach the point of ejaculatory inevitability. When the urge to ejaculate disappears, return to active thrusting.

When you have maintained ejaculatory control for 2 to 7 minutes, you can proceed to ejaculation. The decision to complete intercourse is a mutual one. Do not feel pressure to make each intercourse a perfect experience. Allow yourselves to enjoy intercourse and orgasm. Share the warm, intimate feelings of afterplay. Sex does not end with your ejaculation. Many women enjoy manual or rubbing stimulation after intercourse—either to achieve orgasm or to share physical closeness. Sharing feelings about your sexual experiences is important. Realize how far you have come, not only in learning ejaculatory control but also becoming an intimate, pleasure-oriented, sexual couple.

GUIDELINES FOR LEARNING EJACULATORY CONTROL

- "Do-it-yourself" techniques to reduce arousal (biting your lip, focusing on nonsexual thoughts like how much money you owe or your mother-in-law, using two condoms or a penile-desensitizing cream, masturbating right before couple sex) do not help you learn ejaculatory control and can cause erectile dysfunction or couple alienation.
- The keys to learning ejaculatory control are first to identify the point of ejaculatory inevitability (after which ejaculation is no longer a voluntary function) and then to build comfort and awareness at high levels of arousal without going to ejaculation.

- Ejaculatory control can be learned through self-stimulation as well as through partner stimulation. Practicing new psychosexual skills with self-stimulation develops awareness, comfort, and confidence. The major psychosexual skills involve whole-body relaxation, specific relaxation of the pelvic muscles, using self-entrancement arousal rather than partner interaction arousal, and slowing down the whole sexual process with a focus on pleasure.
- The strategy in learning ejaculatory control is counterintuitive. Increase comfort, awareness, and pleasure—do not decrease stimulation. Ejaculatory control during intercourse is complex and challenging.
- The most effective technique is stop–start. Signal your partner to stop stimulation as you approach the point of inevitability. Stimulation stops for 15 to 60 seconds until you no longer feel you are going to ejaculate and then resumes with a focus on relaxation and pleasure. This is superior to the traditional squeeze technique, which feels awkward and mechanical, especially for the woman.
- Stop–start is used first with manual stimulation, then oral stimulation, and before and during intercourse. Learning ejaculatory control is a gradual process requiring practice and feedback. It takes most couples 2 to 3 months to master ejaculatory control during intercourse.
- Realistic expectations and goals are crucial. The typical love-making session lasts for 15 to 45 minutes, 2 to 7 of which involve intercourse. Contrary to male bragging and media myths, intercourse seldom lasts more than 12 minutes.
- One in four women has the same response pattern as men, that is, a single orgasm during intercourse without additional stimulation. One in three women is seldom or never orgasmic during intercourse. The goal of improved ejaculatory control is to increase pleasure and eroticism for the man and couple—not to make the woman orgasm during intercourse. Allow intercourse to be an involving, pleasurable, erotic experience.
- Typically, couples begin ejaculatory control exercises for intercourse using the woman-on-top position with minimal movement (the quiet vagina exercise). She guides intromission and controls thrusting.
- The stop–start technique can be used before or during intercourse. He can either stop movement or withdraw. As com-

fort and confidence with ejaculatory control increases, the technique is to either slow thrusting or to use circular thrusting.

- With continued practice, other intercourse positions are added. Utilize longer, slower thrusting or circular thrusting. You can switch which partner controls the thrusting rhythm. Ejaculatory control is most difficult in the man-on-top position with short, rapid thrusting.
- The focus is maintaining ejaculatory control for 5 to 10 minutes with nonintercourse stimulation (manual or oral) and 2 to 7 minutes of intercourse stimulation.
- When you ejaculate, whether rapidly or voluntarily, enjoy the feelings and sensations, do not be upset or angry. "Beating up" on yourself or blaming your partner does not facilitate ejaculatory control.
- The feelings and sensations of orgasm begin at the point of ejaculatory inevitability and last 3 to 10 seconds.
- The woman's emotional and sexual feelings are integral in the learning process. Her role is as an intimate, involved partner. You can pleasure her to arousal and orgasm with manual, oral, rubbing, or vibrator stimulation, before or after ejaculatory control exercises.
- Some men use antidepressant medications at a low dose on a daily basis to promote ejaculatory control. New medications are being developed and are effective for the majority of men. However, success is dependent on remaining on the medication.
- The preferred strategy is to use medication as an additional resource. Integrate the medical intervention into your couple style of intimacy, pleasuring, and eroticism. Practice ejaculatory control exercises while taking medication and then gradually phase out the medication.
- Remember: do not try to reduce stimulation or arousal. You do not want to develop an erection problem. Focus on awareness, comfort, pleasure, and arousal without moving rapidly to ejaculation.
- The essence of sexuality is sharing pleasure, not putting on a perfect performance. Couple sex is inherently variable. The Good Enough Sex (GES) model is that 85% of the time you enjoy ejaculatory control during intercourse. Enjoy and share the entire sexual experience from pleasuring to afterplay.

CLOSING THOUGHTS

Learning ejaculatory control is like learning any skill. It is a gradual process requiring feedback and refining techniques. Practice the last set of exercises at least a couple of weeks before moving on to other intercourse positions. Man on top is the most difficult intercourse position for ejaculatory control. One of the best for ejaculatory control and mutual sexual responsiveness is side-by-side intercourse. You might use slower thrusting and stop–start techniques for a year or more. It is especially important to utilize these when you have intercourse after a break of a week or longer. Maintain open communication as you progress in feeling comfortable and confident (not worrying about performing to a perfect standard) with ejaculatory control. Integrate nongenital sensual touching, genital pleasuring, intercourse, and afterplay into your couple sexual style.

18

CONFRONTING EJACULATORY INHIBITION

The problem of women not reaching orgasm has been widely discussed by sex researchers, therapists, and the media, but scant attention has been paid to the equivalent problem for men. Many human sexuality books omit discussion of this particular sexual dysfunction, the man's inability (or great difficulty) to reach orgasm during partner sex even though he is physically aroused and erect. When it is mentioned, the terms used—*retarded ejaculation* or *ejaculatory incompetence*—have a derogatory connotation. We prefer the term *ejaculatory inhibition* (the term *delayed ejaculation* is also used) because it is a descriptive, nonpejorative term that describes the reality: the natural erotic flow leading to orgasm is inhibited.

Ejaculatory inhibition (EI) is the least recognized male sexual dysfunction and has been viewed as a rare and difficult to understand condition. Research on EI finds that in its most severe form, which involves the total inability to ejaculate, it is extremely rare. The inability to ejaculate intravaginally is more common, often coming to the clinician's attention because the couple wants to become pregnant. Approximately 1 to 2% of young men suffer from EI. The most common type is the inability to reach orgasm during intercourse or with partner stimulation, although the great majority of men with EI are able to be orgasmic during masturbation. EI is most common in its intermittent form, occurring in 1 to 2% of young males and with 8 to 15% of men over 50.

Men often mislabel the problem as erectile dysfunction because they lose their erection during intercourse. If intercourse lasts more than 2 minutes the real issue is probably EI; you lose your erection because you run out of sexual energy.

EI results when the man's psychological and sexual inhibitions interfere with the natural pattern of pleasure, arousal, and erotic flow leading to orgasm. Inability to ejaculate or difficulty ejaculating can be caused by a variety of inhibitions. These include beginning intercourse at low levels of arousal, inability to let go, not being emotionally involved, fear of pregnancy, inhibition about using multiple stimulation during intercourse, inability to communicate with and make requests of your partner. EI can lead to inhibited desire, sexual avoidance, a nonsexual relationship, and avoidance of all touch.

The most frequent pattern is intermittent EI, in which a man who has regularly ejaculated begins to have difficulty reaching orgasm, especially during intercourse. If not addressed and dealt with, EI becomes progressively more severe and chronic. The second most common pattern involves men who reach orgasm with a specific type of stimulation (rubbing against bed sheets or their partner's thigh, manual or oral stimulation, or a fetish arousal pattern) but not during intercourse.

Young males with primary EI are often mistakenly viewed as "studs" who can service and satisfy women and are admired by male peers who suffer from premature ejaculation. In truth, they are performing for the woman, not enjoying healthy male and couple sexuality.

EI is different from the normal aging physiological process, which entails a lessened need to ejaculate at each sexual encounter. With EI the man desires to ejaculate, but has great difficulty or is unable to do so. EI can affect males in their 20s but is most prevalent among men after 50. Ejaculation and orgasm are not the same phenomena, although the terms are used interchangeably. For example, most men develop retrograde ejaculation after prostate surgery—that is, they are orgasmic, but they ejaculate into the bladder rather than through the penis. If there are medical or physiological concerns (especially side effects of medication), consult a urologist with a subspeciality in assessment of sexual dysfunction.

Among the inhibitions that can cause intermittent EI are anger at your partner, lack of effective sexual stimulation, shutting yourself off from sexual involvement, beginning intercourse at low levels of subjective arousal, having performance anxiety or sexual guilt, being shy about requesting multiple stimulation, and servicing your partner's sexual needs at the expense of your sexual pleasure. Sex is a cooperative, sharing encounter between two people who are actively involved in giving and receiving pleasure. This process is blocked for the man with EI.

Sexual function includes desire, pleasure, eroticism, orgasm, and satisfaction. EI disrupts the natural cycle of anticipating sex and responding to stimulation with arousal that naturally culminates in orgasm. You (and your partner) push hard to reach orgasm. Even if you manage to "come," neither intercourse nor orgasm holds much pleasure for you. Rather than orgasm being the natural culmination of a pleasurable, erotic sexual experience, it becomes an anxiety-provoking goal you often fail to achieve. When you do reach orgasm, it is more a relief than a pleasure.

EJACULATORY INHIBITION AS A COUPLE PROBLEM

As with other sexual dysfunctions, EI is best thought of as a couple problem, not as "his" problem. The couple, not just the man, must learn to increase stimulation and allow arousal to naturally flow to orgasm. A comfortable, involved, sexually giving partner is essential. A particular trap is the belief that a "real man" does not need the woman's involvement and stimulation to reach orgasm. You mistakenly think you should be able to do it yourself without making requests of your partner. Don't believe the myth that suggests only "wimps" discuss sexual needs or feelings. As you begin the aging process in your 30s, you increasingly benefit from a sharing, intimate, and erotic relationship.

DEVELOPMENT OF EJACULATORY INHIBITION

There are three major forms of EI with myriad variations and individual differences. The first type involves men who have difficulty from the beginning of their sexual lives. While the great majority of men do ejaculate during masturbation, some develop an idiosyncratic arousal pattern or a fetish pattern that is not transferable to couple sex. Thus, the man finds it difficult or impossible to ejaculate with a partner. If this is the problem, we urge you to seek professional sex therapy. Although the psychosexual exercises offered here might be helpful, it is doubtful these alone will be sufficient to change this type of EI. Remember, EI is changeable for a motivated couple working with a competent sex therapist.

A second pattern emerges with men who experience orgasm with manual, oral, or rubbing stimulation but are unable to ejaculate during intercourse or have great difficulty doing so. Some men lose arousal during intercourse and then lose their erection; others maintain an erection for more than 20 minutes (and some for an hour or more) but are not able to let go and be orgasmic. The therapeutic strategy in these cases is to identify the man's inhibitions and fears and develop sexual scenarios and techniques to overcome them. The most common intervention is to utilize multiple stimulation during intercourse. Men with this type of EI feel embarrassed about requiring additional stimulation.

The third, and most common, form of EI involves men who have a history of orgasm during intercourse and then develop an intermittent problem. For some men this affects only orgasm, while for others it affects the entire spectrum of desire, arousal, and orgasm. This problem can remain intermittent but often becomes pervasive and chronic. Although sometimes only ejaculation is affected, it can cause erectile dysfunction, which leads to inhibited sexual desire and sexual avoidance.

In summary, EI is neither rare nor impossible to treat. It is prevalent, has many variations, and is a complex dysfunction. Most important, it is changeable. The couple can identify and overcome inhibitions, can increase comfort, pleasure, and eroticism, and can gain confidence that arousal and erotic flow will regularly culminate in orgasm.

LEO AND ALIX

Leo's experience is instructive. As a young man, the only times he had problems with ejaculation were the first one or two intercourse encounters with a new partner. After overcoming his initial anxiety, Leo had no difficulty reaching orgasm. Leo had begun masturbating at age 12 and masturbated once or twice a day. This pattern is well within the normal range for adolescent males, except that Leo experienced a strong mixture of arousal, shame, and anxiety during masturbation. His fantasies focused obsessively on the woman stroking his penis very hard, using a leather glove. Initially, he experimented with a number of fantasies, but since the age of 15 he had compulsively and exclusively employed the leather glove fantasy (this is an example of a fetish arousal).

Initially, Leo found couple sex exciting. He married Alix at 24, and sex went well for a year and a half. Then he began having occasional difficulties reaching orgasm. When Alix asked what the problem was or if there was any way she could help, he told her the problem was in her mind and to get over it.

When they came for therapy, Leo and Alix had been married for 18 years. Alix blamed their sexual problems on Leo's loss of erection during intercourse and his low sexual interest. Alix was frustrated, depressed, and at her "wit's end." Leo was an evasive, reluctant client. In careful questioning during the individual sexual history session, it became clear that Leo could function fine and had a high sex interest, as evidenced by daily masturbation to his glove fantasy. Leo was embarrassed by his fetish arousal pattern and wanted it to remain secret. He did not understand that much of Alix's frustration centered on her feeling that Leo did not communicate honestly, especially about sex issues.

With the therapist's help, Leo's "sexual secret" was disclosed. This allowed Leo and Alix to deal constructively with issues of desire, eroticism, and orgasm. Leo confronted the embarrassment, confusion, and guilt over his driven, yet inhibited, fetish pattern. The therapist helped Alix deal with her anger at being misled.

The sexual problem was redefined as EI, with the goal of increasing couple involvement, eroticism, and orgasm. Leo agreed to masturbate only when Alix was not at home or not interested in being sexual. Leo was strongly encouraged to expand his repertoire of sexual fantasies and to approach masturbation in a guilt-free, comfortable manner. He had to dramatically alter his fetish pattern if couple sex was to enhance desire, pleasure, eroticism, orgasm, and satisfaction. In couple experiences, Leo was not to retreat into the glove fantasy. He was to be an active, involved sexual participant.

Leo was receptive and responsive to Alix's manual stimulation. They did not proceed to intercourse until Leo was highly aroused. During intercourse he was assertive in making requests, especially for multiple stimulation. He increased the rhythm of coital thrusting, asked Alix to stimulate his testicles, and enjoyed stroking her breasts as he approached orgasm. Alix found Leo's involvement and multiple stimulation quite arousing, which in turn increased his arousal.

BUILDING SEXUAL INTIMACY

Leo and Alix illustrate the importance of working as an intimate team in treating EI. Verbal and physical intimacy breaks down the walls of inhibition and sexual isolation. Mutual involvement in the give-and-take of erotic sex is key in overcoming EI. Treatment can be conceptualized as a one–two–three combination: being an intimate sexual team, increasing comfort with nondemand pleasuring, and increasing erotic stimulation. The specific combination for EI is as follows:

1. Transition to intercourse at high levels of erotic flow rather than as soon as you are erect.
2. Engage in multiple stimulation during intercourse to facilitate erotic flow rather than relying solely on coital thrusting.
3. Use "orgasm triggers"—thoughts, movements, sensations that allow you to let go and be orgasmic—during intercourse to enhance erotic flow, which naturally results in orgasm.

Even more important than mastering sexual techniques are making changes in attitudes, being emotionally involved, letting go, and enjoying the orgasmic experience.

Shared intimacy and increasing sexual give-and-take is new for couples in which the man has a history of EI. He has been emotionally isolated and resents the lack of effective stimulation, although he is unable to request it. Meanwhile, the woman has fallen into a passive, frustrated, and ineffective sexual pattern, so increased intimacy, involvement, and eroticism are new for her also. Each partner takes personal responsibility for sexuality and is part of an intimate team committed to effecting change. Both need to learn to share sexual feelings, requests, turn-ons, and erotic scenarios and techniques.

EXERCISES

First Exercise: Sexual Involvement

Talk over a glass of wine or cup of tea and renew your commitment to work together to revitalize sexual expression, especially increasing involvement and eroticism. Focus on the present and future; put aside the anxiety, guilt, frustration, and embarrassment of the past.

Take a bath or shower and use that time to share feelings, increase contact, and use touch as play in this nondemanding situation. When you go into the bedroom, utilize the touching you have learned from nongenital and genital pleasuring exercises to enhance receptivity and responsivity. Be aware of touching and being touched; enjoy sharing pleasure.

Move to the position where you are lying on your back, perhaps with a pillow under your head, and your partner is sitting next to you with your legs over hers—a comfortable position for her to stroke your body, especially your genitals. This position enables you to maintain good eye contact and gives you easy access to her thighs and breasts. She can provide a range of stimulation to your penis, scrotum, inner thighs, perineum, and anal area. At the same time, she can touch your chest, stomach, neck, legs, and feet. Experiment with intermixing oral, manual, and rubbing stimulation. Allow touching to be slow, tender, rhythmic, caring, and flowing. You can experiment with keeping your eyes open or closed, being passive or stoking her as she touches you, being silent or talking. Break down emotional walls and inhibitions and really be there with each other. Become aware of what you need to feel sexually and emotionally involved. Does sharing sexual feelings and fantasies facilitate or inhibit arousal? During this exercise, keep a prohibition on orgasm so you can focus on feelings of involvement, pleasure, eroticism, and erotic flow.

End the exercise with mutual touching and caressing. Afterward, talk clearly and directly about what you can do to increase involvement, pleasure, and eroticism so sexuality is a shared experience.

Second Exercise: Requesting Multiple Stimulation

You can choose the position that is most involving for you and allows free expression of your sexual feelings. You might use a position from a previous exercise—for example, kneel over her so she can stroke you while you stimulate her and rub your penis against her breast, or stand in front of a mirror where visual stimulation adds an erotic dimension. As pleasuring proceeds, make at least two sexual requests to heighten arousal. The requests can be verbal or conveyed by guiding her with your hand, moving your body toward her so you get the stimulation you want, or moving her head or mouth. You have a perfect right to make sexual requests. Your request might be to stimulate her because your arousal is enhanced as her arousal grows. You could orally stimulate her breasts or vulva, rub your penis between her legs or breasts, stimulate her breast and anal area while she is giving you penile stimulation, or move your penis in rhythm with her pelvic movements. You might request that she verbalize feelings, share an erotic fantasy, or tell you how turned on she feels when you touch her. She is open to such requests but does not feel pressure to do something that is a turn-off for her. Remember these are requests, not demands. She is responsible for herself sexually, as are you.

You can lift the prohibition on orgasm. This does not mean creating a command performance to achieve orgasm. Feel your arousal and go with the erotic flow. Make requests for multiple stimulation, which can include touching, switching positions, being stimulated, utilizing a range of sensory modalities—movement, sight, smell, touch, and hearing. Use erotic fantasies to increase arousal. Most men employ erotic fantasies during partner sex. A few men share fantasies, but most find that fantasies work best in their imagination rather than when they are shared behaviorally. Fantasy and behavior are very different realms; fantasies should serve as a bridge to increase arousal, not as a wall to isolate you sexually. Be open to an orgasmic experience for you and your partner. Remember, orgasm is a natural result of increasing sexual involvement and arousal, not an isolated performance goal. The next day discuss the sexual requests and multiple stimulation techniques you enjoy and how to integrate these into your couple sexual style.

Third Exercise: Orgasm Triggers

Most men who experience EI have no trouble being orgasmic during masturbation. You are comfortable and confident that arousal will naturally flow to orgasm. Stimulation and arousal are under your control, and you are not self-conscious. Being orgasmic is expected; it is a habit. You know your orgasm triggers and are not inhibited in utilizing them.

In this exercise, share your orgasm triggers with your partner and utilize them during couple sex. When approaching orgasm, some men increase muscle tension by stretching their legs or curling their toes; others make sounds or breathe loudly and rapidly as they let go; some increase pelvic thrusting; others verbalize they are "going to come"; some imagine the culmination of their sexual fantasy as they experience orgasm in reality. What are your orgasm triggers? Share these with your partner before beginning this exercise. Verbalizing has a disinhibiting effect, making it easier to let go and use orgasm triggers during couple sex.

Allow arousal and turn-ons to build; enjoy the erotic flow. Sexual requests and multiple stimulation flow smoothly. Some men find it easier to be orgasmic with manual, oral, or rubbing stimulation, but others find intercourse easier and their preferred mode to share orgasm. Use the intercourse position where you are most sexually expressive. Most men prefer man-on-top or rear-entry positions, although woman-on-top and the side-by-side positions have gained popularity because they facilitate multiple stimulation. Multiple stimulation is not just for pleasuring; it is equally erotic during intercourse.

Do not rush sensual or sexual pleasuring. Too many men prematurely initiate intercourse just as they are becoming aroused or when they sense their partner is ready. Be selfish. Let arousal build. Delay intromission until you are feeling high levels of erotic flow. Be sure subjective arousal is as strong as your erection. Allow yourself to be involved throughout intercourse; use the type and rhythm of movement that is most arousing. Some men prefer slow rather than rapid thrusting, while others prefer circular movement to in–out or up–down thrusting. Request and engage in multiple stimulation during intercourse. Focus on your orgasm triggers and let go. Do not let anything inhibit or block your arousal, especially not self-consciousness or feeling it is "not right."

If it is easier to let go and use your orgasm triggers during erotic, nonintercourse sex, feel free to switch stimulation and position. Many men with EI have their first orgasmic experience during self-stimulation with their partner present. Your partner holding or caressing you during self-stimulation can enhance sexual feelings. Once you are comfortable and confident being orgasmic during manual, oral, or rubbing stimulation, you can practice being orgasmic with intercourse. Continue stimulation until you feel close to orgasm, and then initiate intercourse. Use thrusting and multiple stimulation to heighten arousal and facilitate letting go and ejaculating.

End this exercise in a manner that is pleasurable for both of you. You have focused on feelings of arousal and letting go; now feel the warmth and caring of being together in afterplay.

Fourth Exercise: Multiple Stimulation During Intercourse

Why should multiple stimulation cease when intercourse begins? People mistakenly believe a "real man" needs nothing more than thrusting into a wet vagina to reach orgasm. For some men, some of the time, that is true. Yet many men, especially as they age, want and need multiple stimulation.

The most common form of multiple stimulation is use of erotic fantasy. Approximately 75% of men utilize fantasy during intercourse. Fantasies serve as a bridge to heighten arousal and facilitate orgasm. Do not worry if your fantasies are "strange" and have nothing to do with your partner; that is the nature of erotic fantasies. Sexual fantasies are socially undesirable. Fantasies can involve being sexual with a "forbidden" partner who uses "kinky" techniques in bizarre positions or circumstances. This does not mean these are your true sexual desires. Fantasy and behavior are very different realms. The exotic "forbidden fruit" aspect of fantasies is what makes them erotic. Enjoy fantasies for what they are: a bridge to erotic flow and orgasm during partner sex. Fantasies are problematic only when the man becomes compulsive or uses them to isolate himself and block interaction with his partner.

Use the intercourse position that allows you the most expressiveness and eroticism. This could be a common position, or you might try a position where she sits on a chair or bed with pillows for back support and you kneel on pillows—both for comfort and so your penis is at equal height as her vulva. The kneeling–sitting position was developed for late-stage pregnancy (there is no pressure on her stomach) and adapted for treating EI because it facilitates use of multiple stimulation during intercourse and promotes freedom of movement. This position allows good eye contact and easy access to her neck, breasts, vulva, and clitoris. She can stroke your chest and stomach and has good access to your scrotum and testicles.

In this exercise you control coital thrusting and can utilize whatever type of intercourse movement you find most arousing. Having his partner initiate slow, extended coital thrusting might be arousing for one man, while another might prefer her to be passive while he moves in short, rapid strokes. Many men enjoy testicle stimulation during intercourse; others prefer kissing and stroking their partner or giving or receiving anal stimulation.

No matter which intercourse position you use, be active, involved partners in giving and receiving pleasure. You need to be aware of what stimulation, in what sequence, and with what timing is most arousing. You are free to make verbal and nonverbal requests. As arousal builds, focus on erotic feelings and sensations, be aware of orgasm triggers, let go, and allow your arousal to naturally culminate in orgasm.

Your sexual experience does not end with orgasm. Stay together to talk, stroke, and reaffirm your desire to share. Afterplay is the most ignored part of the sexual encounter but enhances emotional and sexual satisfaction for both partners. Acknowledge the changes that have occurred as you break down sexual inhibitions and become a giving, intimate couple who shares orgasm.

GUIDELINES FOR OVERCOMING EJACULATORY INHIBITION

- Men try to minimize or hide the problem of ejaculatory inhibition from their partner, feeling they can satisfy themselves later. In truth, your partner has a positive, integral role in helping you overcome EI and increase pleasure, eroticism, and satisfaction.
- The key issue in understanding EI is the difference between subjective and objective arousal. You may look fully aroused, with a firm erection and vigorous thrusts, but your body is "telling a lie." Your subjective arousal is really 4 to 5, even though your objective arousal appears to be 8 to 9 on the 10-point arousal scale.
- The key to changing EI is to enhance subjective arousal and involve the woman as your intimate, erotic friend. Delay the transition to intercourse until subjective arousal is at least 7 and preferably 8.
- The two key techniques to dealing with EI are to use multiple stimulation during intercourse and to identify and utilize your orgasm triggers.
- Cognitively, you can learn to associate sexuality with comfort, pleasure, and eroticism, with the woman as your intimate, erotic friend. Behaviorally, you need to integrate subjective and

objective arousal, enjoy interactive sexuality, request erotic and multiple stimulation, and feel comfortable using orgasm triggers. Emotionally, enjoy the pleasuring process, feel you have a right to sexual pleasure, and enjoy erotic flow that naturally culminates in orgasm. Value the Good Enough Sex (GES) model rather than feeling pressure to achieve perfect intercourse/orgasm performance.

- A number of factors can cause intermittent EI, including side effects of medication, not feeling sexually receptive or responsive, alcohol or drug abuse, lack of partner involvement, and fatigue. However, the most common cause is that you experience sex as routine and mechanical. As a young man you needed only intercourse thrusting, but now your subjective and objective arousal is muted so you need multiple stimulation during intercourse.

- To overcome EI, you need to turn to your partner for emotional encouragement and sexual stimulation. Approach your partner as your intimate, erotic friend and make requests for multiple stimulation during intercourse so orgasm/ejaculation is a natural continuation of the comfort/pleasure/arousal/erotic flow process.

- EI is different from the normal physiological transition of men over 60 who have a lessened need to orgasm at each sexual opportunity. With EI you want to let go and ejaculate, but you can't because your subjective arousal is low.

- You and your partner can experiment with a range of multiple stimulation scenarios and techniques to learn what is best for you. These can include rubbing your penis between her breasts and manually stimulating her clitoral area, standing while she orally stimulates you, or moving rapidly and rhythmically during intercourse. Erotic fantasies can accompany any of these scenarios. You can change intercourse positions two or three times; ask for testicular or anal stimulation; change intercourse movement from slow in–out thrusting to circular thrusting; transition from intercourse to manual stimulation and back to intercourse at high levels of erotic flow.

- Orgasm triggers are very individualistic. They allow you to move from 9 to 10 (orgasm/ejaculation). Use orgasm triggers when you are in high erotic flow (not when your subjective arousal is 5). Examples of orgasm triggers include tensing pelvic muscles and engaging in fast, rhythmic thrusting; focusing on an erotic fantasy and reaching orgasm both in fantasy and in reality; verbalizing "It feels so good; I'm going to come"; and feeling highly aroused by your partner's arousal and "piggy-backing" your orgasm onto hers.

- It is natural and healthy to use self-stimulation during partner sex to enhance your arousal, including to orgasm.
- Men and couples have different preferences for pleasuring and eroticism—manual, oral, rubbing, or intercourse. Some prefer taking turns, while others like mutual stimulation. Most prefer multiple stimulation, but others prefer single stimulation. Discover and enjoy your style of sexual pleasure, arousal, erotic flow, and orgasm.
- Remember: the essence of healthy couple sexuality is sharing desire, pleasure, eroticism, and satisfaction. Enjoy your sexuality; do not view orgasm as a pass–fail test. In the GES mode, 85% of experiences involve erotic flow, which naturally culminates in orgasm.

CLOSING THOUGHTS

Ejaculatory inhibition is a serious dysfunction that has been largely ignored. The challenge for the man is to break his silence and isolation and ask his partner for increased sharing, intimacy, multiple stimulation, and eroticism. Sexuality is best when it combines emotional intimacy, nondemand pleasuring, and erotic stimulation both before and during intercourse. You can learn to let go and experience the joys of orgasm during partner sex.

19

PREVENTING RELAPSE
Maintaining Resilient Couple Sexuality

Sexuality cannot be treated with benign neglect. We have been married for 45 years and continue to put time, energy, caring, and creativity into our sexual relationship. We want sexuality to continue energizing our bond and enhancing feelings of desire and desirability.

Three concepts have proved crucial to maintaining a vital, resilient couple sexuality:

- Adherence to the mantra of desire, pleasure, eroticism, and satisfaction
- Reinforcing the strengths of our chosen couple sexual style while carefully monitoring traps so that sexual desire and function remain resilient and vibrant
- Maintaining positive, realistic sexual expectations—specifically valuing Good Enough Sex (GES), enjoying both mutual and asynchronous sexual experiences, and accepting the reality of occasional sexual encounters that are disappointing or dysfunctional

THE NEW MANTRA FOR HEALTHY COUPLE SEXUALITY

Desire is the core component of healthy couple sexuality. We urge you to use all your psychological, biological, relational, and psychosexual skill resources to promote sexual desire and function. The truth is that positively anticipating experiences (anticipation is at the heart of sexual desire) in which you share touch, playfulness, and eroticism is much more meaningful than sexual performance. Ultimately, sexuality is a team sport, not an attempt to achieve your "personal best."

Perhaps the single most important sexual concept involves each partner valuing nondemand pleasuring. Affectionate touch is not sexual, but it is meaningful and anchors your intimate relationship. Sensual, playful, and erotic touch are valuable in themselves as well as serving as bridges to arousal and intercourse. An essential component in becoming an intimate team is to view intercourse as a natural extension of the pleasuring/eroticism process rather than a test of performance.

Erotic scenarios and techniques are the most contentious and value-laden concepts in this new sexual mantra. The message in most Internet posts, magazines, and books we read is to play out erotic fantasies, use porn videos and sex toys, perform for your partner so he or she is wowed by your eroticism, and have the longest, hardest intercourse you can, making sure the woman has 10 orgasms before the man comes. If that is who you are sexually and it fits your couple sexual style (especially the emotionally expressive sexual style using role enactment arousal), then go for it and enjoy. However, for the great majority of individuals and couples these erotic scenarios and techniques are intimidating, not empowering. They are more likely to make you feel awkward and self-conscious rather than erotic.

Erotic scenarios and techniques are integral to couple sexuality. Awareness, comfort, pleasure, arousal, erotic flow, intercourse, and orgasm are part of a natural, healthy process. The key to eroticism is sexual vitality, feeling turned on, creativity, mystery, and unpredictability. Eroticism involves a sexual intensity that is different from intimacy and pleasuring. For most couples, the major aphrodisiac is an involved, aroused partner (partner interaction arousal), while for others taking turns and going with the flow of pleasurable sensations (self-entrancement arousal) is the key. Find your "erotic voice" and the couple sexual style that fits your erotic preferences and feelings.

Satisfaction is so much more than orgasm (although we highly value female and male orgasm). Satisfaction is about accepting who you are as a sexual person and a sexual couple. Sexual satisfaction is facilitated by accepting GES, not about striving for perfect sexual performance. Satisfaction involves valuing a range of pleasuring experiences and the complexity of individual and couple sexuality and accepting the varied roles and meanings of intimacy and sexuality.

VALUING THE STRENGTHS OF YOUR
CHOSEN COUPLE SEXUAL STYLE

One of our favorite sayings is that sexually one size never fits all. A challenge for serious couples, whether married or unmarried, straight or gay, is to choose a couple sexual style and make it uniquely your own.

The strength of the complementary sexual style is that each partner is willing and able to initiate both intimate and erotic encounters. Complementary couples accept that sexuality can have different roles and meanings for each partner and at different times in your relationship. Having "her," his," and "our" bridges to sexual desire facilitates a strong, resilient couple sexuality.

The traditional couple sexual style offers clear guidelines for maintaining healthy sexuality without drama or conflict. The woman strives to reinforce intimacy and affection, and the man strives to maintain a regular rhythm of intercourse. Each values the partner's role. The partners value predictability and the shared loyalty of their stable relationship.

The soul mate sexual style emphasizes intimacy and mutuality. This secure bond reinforces valuing your relationship and feelings of caring, exemplified by knowing that your partner has your back. Being an intimate couple is much more important than intercourse frequency or technique. Personal and couple acceptance and trust are very high with soul mate couples.

The emotionally expressive couple sexual style is far and away the most fun and erotic style. Individuality, creativity, and unpredictability are your sexual fortes. You establish your own relational and sexual rules. The special emphasis on eroticism is a way to demonstrate resilience, both emotionally and sexually. This is the couple sexual style most likely to enjoy role enactment arousal scenarios, to emphasize sexual fun, and to bend the rules.

A crucial dimension of your couple sexual style is to be aware of potential vulnerabilities and avoid those traps. For the complementary sexual style, this involves making sure you don't take sexuality for granted. The recommended strategy is that every 6 months each partner initiates a new scenario—whether intimacy, pleasuring, eroticism, intercourse, or afterplay. This facilitates maintaining a vital couple sexuality. The strategy for traditional sexual couples is for the man to initiate an intimacy date at least every 6 months and for the woman to initiate an erotic date (which may or may not lead to intercourse) every 6 months. You can honor traditional sex roles while introducing some flexibility. For soul mate sexual couples the suggested strategy is to initiate a "selfish" or "playful" sexual date every 6 months to challenge the demand that every encounter must be mutual (the "tyranny of mutuality"). The strategy for emotionally expressive sexual couples is totally different. Each partner identifies "atomic bomb" issues and agrees that no matter how angry or hurt they commit to not "drop the bomb."

Value your chosen sexual style, embrace it, play to its strengths, and make sure you monitor and counter its built-in vulnerabilities.

MAINTAIN POSITIVE, REALISTIC SEXUAL EXPECTATIONS

Almost all couples place high value on mutual, synchronous sexual experiences, where both partners are desirous, aroused, orgasmic, and feel satisfied. We agree that this is optimal, but it is very important to be aware that this outcome occurs in less than 50% of the encounters among happily married, sexually satisfied couples. This does not mean that the sexual experience was negative or not worthwhile. In fact, 85 to 95% of sexual experiences are positive, even when not mutual or synchronous.

Strong, resilient sexual desire involves realizing that couple sexuality is variable and flexible. The GES approach embraces positive, realistic expectations. Often one partner is more desirous than the other. In younger couples this is more often the man, for whom arousal and orgasm are typically easier and more predictable. However, for couples in their 50s there is often a role reversal, and arousal and orgasm become easier for the woman. Sometimes the sexual experience is mutually satisfying and bonding, while at other times it is clearly better for one partner. Sometimes sex is primarily about tension reduction or fulfills the need for personal affirmation. Couples who embrace the multiple roles and meanings of sexuality will enjoy a vital, resilient sexual partnership.

A challenging issue is asynchronous sexual experiences. Examples of asynchronous sex include the following:

- Manually or orally pleasuring your partner to orgasm
- Holding your partner while he stimulates himself to orgasm
- You doing oral breast stimulation while she uses a vibrator to orgasm
- Playing out your partner's erotic fantasy even though it is not arousing for you
- The woman going along with intercourse at low levels of arousal
- The man continuing to stimulate you to multiple orgasms, although you are no longer aroused
- Accepting a warm, sensual encounter rather than the highly erotic intercourse you desired

These scenarios are just a few examples of asynchronous sexual experiences. Many couples find that enjoying asynchronous sexuality is of great value, while others (especially traditional and soul mate couples) have a strong preference for a mutual sexual experience. We are advocates of asynchronous sexuality, especially as you age. But as with other aspects of sexuality it is your feelings and preferences that matter.

It is crucial not to overreact to dissatisfying or dysfunctional sexual encounters. Remember, 5–15% of sexual experiences are disappointing or even "bombs." Don't let these define your couple sexuality or demoralize you. Sometimes a pattern of negative sexual encounters is a message that something is awry, but more often the message is nothing but normal sexual variability. Positive, realistic sexual expectations continually reinforce the cycle of desire, pleasure, eroticism, and satisfaction.

RYAN AND CINDI

Each phase of a person's and couple's sexual life has special rewards and special challenges. Cindi and Ryan met in their mid-20s, became a committed couple within seven months, and married 2 years, 2 months, and 2 days after their first date. Now in their mid-40s with children aged 14 and 10 they have a busy, somewhat chaotic life. They take pride in being among the 30% of couples who maintain a vital, resilient sexual relationship during the parenting years. Looking toward the future, Ryan and Cindi are committed to developing personally, relationally, and sexually so that when their last child leaves home in 8 or 9 years they will celebrate the "empty nest" life phase. In addition, they are committed to beating the odds and celebrating sexuality in their 60s, 70s, and 80s.

Ryan told Cindi that marrying her was the best thing he had done in his life and that he found her more sexually attractive now than when they were in their 20s. Cindi had great memories of their romantic love/passionate sex phase. She fondly remembers sex while trying to become pregnant and was grateful for their easy fertility—especially since her best friend struggled with infertility treatments for 4 years before adopting a child through an overseas agency. Cindi enjoyed each year of their life and the very different phases of parenting. She is particularly looking forward to the "couple again" phase. However, as Cindi tells her children, you need to take life one year at a time. What Cindi most values about couple sexuality now is taking advantage of "windows of opportunity" when the children are at an event, asleep, or away from the house.

Cindi especially looks forward to their monthly Thursday afternoon dates. She and Ryan organized their work schedules so that once a month on a Thursday they have a window from 11:30 to 2:30. They meet at home, and the running joke is whether they can get lunch, sex, a walk, and a nap in during that time. They seldom do all four, but it is a fun challenge.

One aspect of building anticipation for their Thursday date is that the sexual encounter is unpredictable. Sometimes it is an involved, creative hour of lovemaking, at other times a 2-minute "quickie," maybe being sexually playful to orgasm in the shower, or an asynchronous "blow job." This variability increases Cindi's desire. For Ryan, the sense of transgressive sex enhances his desire.

A favorite afterplay scenario is sharing dreams and plans for the future—whether a summer family trip, a fall weekend away without the children, making love in Paris after their son leaves for college, trying out a totally new erotic scenario for their fortieth wedding anniversary, at 75 going back to the place where they first met and making love. Cindi and Ryan value the present and look forward to maintaining a vital, satisfying couple sexuality in the future.

RELAPSE PREVENTION STRATEGIES AND GUIDELINES

- Set aside quality couple time and discuss what you need to do individually and as a couple to maintain a satisfying, stable sexual relationship.
- Every 6 months have a formal follow-up meeting either by yourselves or with a therapist to ensure that you do not slip back into unhealthy sexual attitudes, behaviors, or feelings. Set a new couple goal for the next 6 months.
- Every 4 to 8 weeks plan a sensual pleasuring date or a playful erotic date where you place a prohibition on intercourse. This allows you to experiment with new sensual stimuli (alternative pleasuring position, a different body lotion, or a new setting) or a playful, erotic scenario (being sexual in the shower, using a different oral sex position, or engaging in asynchronous sex rather than mutual sex). This reminds you of the value of sharing pleasure and maintaining a broad-based, flexible sexual relationship rather than focusing on intercourse performance.
- For couples, 5 to 15% of sexual experiences are dissatisfying or dysfunctional. That is normal, not a reason to panic or feel like a failure. Maintaining positive, realistic expectations about couple sexuality is a major resource.

- Accept occasional lapses, but do not allow a lapse to become a relapse. Treat a dysfunctional sexual experience as a normal variation, which sometimes provides an important lesson. Whether once every 10 times, once a month, or once a year, you will have a lapse and find sex dysfunctional or dissatisfying. Laugh or shrug off the experience and make a date in the next 1 to 3 days when you have the time and energy for an intimate, pleasurable, erotic experience. A relapse means giving up and reverting to the cycle of anticipatory anxiety, pass–fail intercourse performance, and frustration, embarrassment, and avoidance.
- The importance of setting aside quality couple time—especially intimacy dates and a weekend away without children—cannot be overemphasized. Couples report better sex on vacation, validating the importance of getting away, even if only for an afternoon.
- There is not "one right way" to be sexual. Each couple develops a unique style of initiation, pleasuring, eroticism, intercourse, and afterplay. Rather than treating your couple sexual style with benign neglect, be open to modifying or adding something new or special each year.
- GES has a range from disappointing to great. The single most important technique in relapse prevention is to accept and not overreact to experiences that are mediocre, dissatisfying, or dysfunctional. Take pride in your accepting and resilient couple sexual style.
- Develop a range of intimate, pleasurable, and erotic ways to connect, reconnect, and maintain connection. These include five gears (dimensions) of touch:
  - Affectionate touch (clothes on): kissing, hand-holding, hugging
  - Nongenital sensual touch (clothed, semiclothed, or nude): massage, cuddling, touching before going to sleep or on awakening
  - Playful touch (semiclothed or nude): mixing nongenital and genital touch
  - Erotic, nonintercourse touch: stimulation to high arousal or orgasm for one or both partners
  - Intercourse as a natural continuation of the pleasuring/eroticism process
- Keep your sexual relationship vital. Continue to make sexual requests and be open to exploring erotic scenarios. It is vital to maintain a flexible sexual relationship that energizes your bond and facilitates special feelings of desire and desirability. This happens when couples share intimacy, nondemand pleasuring, erotic scenarios and techniques, and planned as

well as spontaneous sexual encounters. The more ways in which you can maintain an intimate sexual connection, the easier it will be to avoid relapse.

Relapse prevention involves two exercises. Both are crucially important, and we strongly encourage you to engage in them. The first is designing a plan that facilitates maintaining a vital, resilient couple sexuality. The second is to implement a reliable prevention plan when your sexuality gets off track, which it inevitably will. What you can't allow is to treat a lapse of a week or a month with benign neglect, which can result in sexuality remaining off track for 6 months or 6 years.

EXERCISES

First Exercise: Commitment to Maintain a Strong, Resilient Couple Sexuality

Review the relapse prevention strategies and guidelines. Each partner chooses one or two that are particularly important. Commit to utilizing two to four of these guidelines for the next year.

Good intentions are important, but they need to be paired with a clear, specific implementation plan. We encourage you to write out a plan for each of your chosen prevention guidelines. Putting this plan in writing makes it personal and motivating and strengthens commitment. In addition, we suggest setting up a 30-minute couple meeting every 2 months to further motivate you to keep desire, pleasure, eroticism, and satisfaction on track.

This exercise is designed to keep you accountable and motivated. Value your couple sexual style and ensure that sexual desire and function remain strong and resilient.

Second Exercise: Preventing a Lapse From Becoming a Relapse

Remember: couple sexuality has a built-in variability, including that some sexual encounters are dissatisfying or dysfunctional. The challenge is to design a clear, specific plan to deal with sexual problems (lapses) so they do not turn into a relapse. The most demoralized couples are those who once experienced healthy sexuality and then relapse into the cycle of anticipatory anxiety, tense intercourse performance, and frustration, embarrassment, and avoidance. Don't allow that to happen to your sexual relationship.

The best strategy is a commitment to maintain the cycle of positive sexual anticipation, pleasure-oriented touching and intercourse, and a regular rhythm of affectionate, sensual, playful, erotic, and intercourse connection. The back-up strategy is that if you have three negative sexual encounters in a row, schedule a problem-solving couple talk. Try to determine what message these sexual problems are sending. Are they just a normal "blip," or do they emanate from increased self-consciousness, performance anxiety, frustration over relationship communication, an anger issue, a need for a booster session with a couple therapist, an undiagnosed medical problem, an individual problem that has not been shared with your partner, alcohol or drug abuse, regression to a secret sexual life of Internet porn or an affair, a return of feelings related to sexual trauma, or negative feelings about a specific sexual scenario?

In dealing with these issues, do not fall into the guilt–blame trap. Remember, the mantra is personal responsibility for sexuality and being an intimate, erotic team. If you are not able to change the pattern on your own, seek professional help. A decision to schedule a session with a therapist is a sign of good judgment, not weakness. What you cannot afford to do is neglect to deal with this sexual lapse. Sexuality does not continue in a static state. You either address the problem, or it becomes chronic and severe.

What you need to do personally and as a couple is to identify traps (psychological, biological, relational, or practical) and confront them. In coping with sexual problems, it is essential to focus on the GES approach to couple sexuality rather than expect perfect sexual desire and function.

The most common strategy couples use to get back on track sexually is to initiate a sensual or erotic date with a temporary prohibition on intercourse. The focus is to reduce the anxiety/avoidance pattern and reengage in pleasure-oriented touching. Another couple strategy is to have a cup of tea or glass of wine and talk about emotional or sexual issues. Make positive requests to try during a sexual encounter in the next day or two. A third strategy is for one partner to initiate his or her favorite pleasuring/eroticism scenario. These scenarios center on an anti-avoidance strategy and approaching the sexual problem as an intimate team.

FINAL THOUGHTS

Intimacy, pleasuring, eroticism, and satisfaction are important for you as individuals and for your relationship. You have devoted the time and energy to enhance your sexual awareness and develop your unique couple sexual style. It is hoped that the change process has been fun and worthwhile, but realistically it also has taken time and energy. Don't negate these new sexual attitudes, behaviors, and feelings by allowing yourself to relapse. You want intimacy and sexuality to continue to play a 15 to 20% role in energizing your relationship and reinforcing feelings of desire and desirability. Remember, sexuality is about sharing pleasure rather than putting on an intercourse performance. The GES model, which emphasizes variable, flexible couple sexuality, is more valuable than the individual performance approach.

We encourage you to reinforce and enhance your sexual awareness so you can enjoy couple sexuality now and continue to enjoy it in your 60s, 70s, and 80s.

APPENDIX A: CHOOSING A
COUPLE OR SEX THERAPIST

This is a self-help book, not a do-it-yourself therapy book. Individuals and couples are often reluctant to consult a therapist, feeling that to do so is a sign of craziness, a confession of inadequacy, or an admission that their life and relationship are in dire straits. In reality, seeking professional help means that you realize there is a problem. You have made a commitment to resolve the issues and promote individual, couple, and sexual growth.

The mental health field can be confusing. Couple therapy and sex therapy are clinical subspecialties. They are offered by several groups of professionals— including marital therapists, psychologists, psychiatrists, social workers, pastoral counselors, and liscensed professional counselors. The professional background of the practitioner is less important than his or her competence in dealing with your individual, couple, and sexual problems.

Many people have health insurance that provides coverage for mental health and thus can afford the services of a private practitioner. Those who do not have either the financial resources or insurance could consider a city or county mental health clinic, a university or medical school outpatient mental health clinic, or a family services center. Some clinics have a sliding fee scale based on your ability to pay.

When choosing a therapist, be direct in asking about credentials and areas of expertise. Ask the clinician what the focus of the therapy will be, how long therapy can be expected to last, and whether the emphasis will be specifically on sexual problems or more generally on individual, communication, or relationship issues. Be especially diligent in asking about credentials such as university degrees and licensing. Be aware of people who call themselves personal counselors, sex counselors, or personal coaches. There are poorly qualified persons—and some outright quacks—in any field.

One of the best ways to obtain a referral is to call or contact online a local professional organization such as a state psychological association, marriage and family therapy association, or mental health association. You can ask for a referral from a family physician, clergyperson, imam, rabbi, or trusted friend. If you live near a university or medical school, call to find out what specialized psychological and sexual health services may be available.

For a *sex therapy* referral, contact the American Association of Sex Educators, Counselors, and Therapists (AASECT) at www.aasect.org. Another resource is the Society for Sex Therapy and Research (SSTAR) at www.sstarnet.org.

For a *marital therapist*, check the Internet site of the American Association for Marriage and Family Therapy (AAMFT) at www.therapistlocator.net or the Association for Behavioral and Cognitive Therapies (ABCT) at www.abct.org. Another good resource is the National Registry of Marriage Friendly Therapists, whose members are dedicated to helping relationships succeed www.marriagefriendlytherapists.com.

If you are looking for a psychologist who can provide individual therapy for anxiety, depression, sexual compulsivity, behavioral health, or other issues, we suggest the National Registry of Health Service Providers in Psychology: www.findapsychologist.org.

Feel free to talk with two or three therapists before deciding with whom to work. Be aware of your level of comfort with the therapist, degree of rapport, whether the therapist has special skill working with couples, and whether the therapist's assessment of the problem and approach to treatment make sense to you. Once you begin, give therapy a chance to be helpful. There are few miracle cures. Change requires commitment and is a gradual and often difficult process. Although some people benefit from short-term therapy (fewer than 10 sessions), most find the therapeutic process will require 4 months or longer. The role of the therapist is that of a consultant rather than a decision maker. Therapy requires effort on your part, both during the session and at home. Therapy helps to change attitudes, feelings, and behavior. Although it takes courage to seek professional assistance, therapy can be a tremendous help in assessing and ameliorating individual, relational, and sexual problems.

APPENDIX B: RESOURCES—BOOKS, VIDEOS, AND TRUSTED WEBSITES

SUGGESTED READING ON COUPLE SEXUALITY

McCarthy, B., & McCarthy, E. (2009). *Discovering your couple sexual style*. New York: Routledge.

Metz, M.E., & McCarthy, B. (2010). *Enduring desire*. New York: Routledge.

Perel, E. (2006). *Mating in captivity*. New York: HarperCollins.

SUGGESTED READING ON MALE SEXUALITY

McCarthy, B.W., & Metz, M.E. (2008). *Men's sexual health*. New York: Routledge.

Metz, M.E., & McCarthy, B.W. (2003). *Coping with premature ejaculation*. Oakland, CA: New Harbinger.

Metz, M.E., & McCarthy, B.W. (2004). *Coping with erectile dysfunction*. Oakland, CA: New Harbinger Publications.

Zilbergeld, B. (1999). *The new male sexuality*. New York: Bantam Books.

SUGGESTED READING ON FEMALE SEXUALITY

Foley, S., Kope, S., & Sugrue, D. (2012). *Sex matters for women* (2nd ed.). New York: Guilford.

Heiman, J., & LoPiccolo, J. (1988). *Becoming orgasmic*. New York: Prentice-Hall.

Boston Women's Health Book Collective. (2005). *Our bodies, ourselves* (4th ed.). New York: Touchstone.

OTHER NOTABLE SEXUALITY READINGS

Joannides, P. (2009). *The guide to getting it on.* West Hollywood, CA: Goofy Foot Press.

Maltz, W. (2001). *The sexual healing journey.* New York: HarperCollins

McCarthy, B., & McCarthy E. (2003). *Rekindling desire.* New York: Brunner/ Routledge.

Michael, R., Gagnon, J., Laumann, E., & Kolata, G. (1994). *Sex in America.* New York: Little, Brown.

Snyder, D., Baucom, D., & Gordon, K. (2007). *Getting past the affair.* New York: Guilford Press.

SUGGESTED READING ON RELATIONSHIP SATISFACTION

Doherty, W. (2001). *Take back your marriage.* New York: Guilford.

Enright, R.D. (2007). *Forgiveness is a choice.* Washington, DC: American Psychological Association.

Gottman, J., & Silver, N. (1999). *The seven principles for making marriage work.* New York: Crown Publishing.

Johnson, S. (2008). *Hold me tight.* Boston: Little-Brown.

Love, P., & Stosny, S. (2008). *How to improve your marriage without talking about it.* New York: Three Rivers Press.

Markman, H., Stanley, S., & Blumberg, S.L. (2001). *Fighting for your marriage.* San Francisco: Jossey-Bass.

McCarthy, B., & McCarthy, E. (2004). *Getting it right the first time.* New York: Brunner/Routledge.

McCarthy, B., & McCarthy, E. (2006). *Getting it right this time.* New York: Routledge.

INTERNET SITES: MENTAL HEALTH

Obsessive Compulsive Foundation: www.ocfoundation.org/

National Institute of Mental Health (NIMH) home page: www.nimh.nih.gov/

NIMH, Anxiety: www.nimh.nih.gov/anxiety/anxietymenu.cfm

NIMH, Depression: www.nimh.nih.gov/publicat/depressionmenu.cfm

INTERNET SITES: HEALTH

National Institutes of Health (NIH): www.nih.gov

National Institute on Alcohol Abuse and Alcoholism: www.niaaa.nih.gov

WebMD—information on many illnesses, including diabetes, cancer, and heart disease: www.webmd.com

PROFESSIONAL ASSOCIATIONS

American Association for Marriage and Family Therapy (AAMFT): 112 South Alfred Street, Alexandria, VA 22314-3061. Phone (703) 838-9808, Fax (703) 838-9805. www.therapistlocator.net

American Association of Sex Educators, Counselors, and Therapists (AASECT): 1444 I Street, NW, Suite 700, Washington, DC 20005. Phone (202) 449-1099. www.aasect.org

Association for Behavioral & Cognitive Therapies (ABCT): 305 Seventh Avenue, New York, NY 10001-6008. Phone (212) 647-1890. www.abct.org

Sex Information and Education Council of the United States (SIECUS): 130 West 42nd Street, Suite 350, New York, NY 10036. Phone (212) 819-7990. www.seicus.org

Smart Marriages—the coalition for Marriage, Family, and Couple Education. www.smartmarriages.com

Society for Sex Therapy and Research (SSTAR): 6311 W. Gross Point Road, Niles, IL 60714. Phone (847) 647-8832. www.sstarnet.org

SEX BOOKS, VIDEOS, AND TOYS

Good Vibrations: 938 Howard Street, Suite 101, San Francisco, CA 94110. Phone (800) 289-8423. Fax (415) 974-8990. www.goodvibes.com

The Sinclair Institute: P.O. Box 8865, Chapel Hill, NC 27515. Phone (800) 955-0888. www.sinclairinstitute.com

Sex Smart Films: Promoting Sexual Literacy. www.sex.smartfilms.com